3wk-E   D8

Transmedia Storytelling and the New Era of Media Convergence in Higher Education

Transmedia Storytelling and the New Era of Media Convergence in Higher Education

Stavroula Kalogeras

Business College of Athens, Greece
Tiffin University, USA
Queens University of Charlotte, USA

First published 2014 by
PALGRAVE MACMILLAN

Palgrave Macmillan in the UK is an imprint of Macmillan Publishers Limited,
registered in England, company number 785998, of Houndmills, Basingstoke,
Hampshire RG21 6XS.

Palgrave Macmillan in the US is a division of St Martin's Press LLC,
175 Fifth Avenue, New York, NY 10010.

Palgrave Macmillan is the global academic imprint of the above companies
and has companies and representatives throughout the world.

Palgrave® and Macmillan® are registered trademarks in the United States,
the United Kingdom, Europe and other countries

ISBN: 978–1–137–38836–0

This book is printed on paper suitable for recycling and made from fully
managed and sustained forest sources. Logging, pulping and manufacturing
processes are expected to conform to the environmental regulations of the
country of origin.

A catalogue record for this book is available from the British Library.

A catalog record for this book is available from the Library of Congress.

In loving memory of my dear father, Nikolao.
I dedicate this book to him.

To my mom, Evangelia. Thank you for believing in me
and for giving me opportunities that you never had.

With gratitude and affection to my grandmother
and guardian angel; yiayia, Sophia.

Thank you for sharing your life stories.

Contents

List of Figures

Foreword

I first encountered the ideas presented in this book in 2010. I was tutoring on a module in the MEd in eLearning at the University of Hull. Stavroula Kalogeras was taking part as a student and was the first student to bring a storytelling pedagogy to the module. I have to admit that this approach challenged some of my own thinking, and that is a good thing. I have always enjoyed working on the course, as it has brought me so much learning. The class of 2010 was notable because of Stavroula's participation.

The Internet is still very young. Younger still are the World Wide Web and social media, where users have become producers, not just consumers. As the Internet develops, people's behavior is changing. The task of understanding this continuous change and the opportunities it brings for education seems almost impossible. This book helps.

We all have stories. Here is one of mine. This book reminded me of my daughter's curiosity when Greek mythology was covered in her primary school (kindergarten) class in the 1990s, at the dawn of the World Wide Web. She was excited about the Lernaean Hydra. Quizzing the teacher about what this creature looked like, the class was still unable to form a mental image. At home, we were able to search the Internet for a picture, which we printed, and then my daughter took it to school the following day. The teacher shared the picture with the class. The children were thrilled to see it, and the discussion continued. Storytelling and the use of multiple media (spoken word, image) and multiple channels (teacher, dad, Internet, other students) to support storytelling really worked for this group of pupils. It is now 2014, and I wonder just how far we have moved on from my early experience.

This is an important book. It is the first to address multiplatform education via narrative discourse. It provides a useful vantage point from which to view the challenges and fantastic possibilities of transmedia storytelling in education. Relevant current literature is explored comprehensively. The book shows a number of areas where the general classification and understanding of transmedia education is lacking and offers useful suggestions for improving or extending current theory.

Not only are educators challenged to rethink their own pedagogy, the entertainment industry and educational institutions are challenged to come together to build compelling edutainment offerings. Considering such a collaboration opens up immense critical and creative learning possibilities consistent with the behaviors of today's learners.

As an educator, this book made me question a number of things about current practice. The arguments for change are compelling. It may take more than one read to fully appreciate all the possibilities. I am sure that this book will be a really useful reference for me and other educators on many occasions in the future.

Patrick Lynch
eLearning Coordinator,
University of Hull, UK
Module leader for eResourcing and
eLearning Technologies modules

Preface

Today we live in a world of digital communication in which every person has the potential to be their own media company, creating and distributing digital artifacts. This democratization of the production process has been made possible by desktop publishing. However, despite this shift, education remains locked in tradition, giving little, and sometimes no, consideration to the change taking place all around us. In this new era of media convergence, transmedia (cross-media/cross-platform/multiplatform) storytelling is catering to users who are interacting with their most-wanted entertainment content.

Although education may have shifted to the digital sphere with e-learning, it remains rooted in outdated practices and needs to become multidirectional, matching who we are with what we do and how we learn. This can be accomplished through storytelling. The capacity to tell and respond to stories is innate in all humans. Simply put, we tell stories, receive stories, and learn through stories. In the education setting, the persuasive power of, and our emotional engagement with, stories can lead to ground-breaking pedagogies in today's media-rich environments. Marshall McLuhan wrote, 'Anyone who tries to make a distinction between education and entertainment doesn't know the first thing about either', and I would have to agree with him.

This book focuses on *transmedia storytelling edutainment* as a pedagogical practice in higher e-education. Story is at the forefront of my investigation because it is the basis for developing entertainment media franchises that can be incorporated into pedagogical practice. My analysis includes practice-based research via narrative inquiry. A transmedia storytelling framework is introduced that both assists in screenplay creation and, as importantly, establishes a basis for evaluating a screenplay's appropriateness for educational use. My screenplay *The Goddess Within* is evaluated as a screentext (textbook) in higher e-education, because it is believed that the more visual the input, the more likely it is to be memorized and recalled.

The Goddess Within screenplay can be found on the Palgrave Macmillan website (http://www.palgrave.com/products/title.aspx?pid=716647). It won the Orson Welles Award at the California Film Awards in 2010, the highest level of recognition. It was also runner-up at the

2013 Los Angeles Greek Film Festival and has been a semi-finalist in other prestigious screenplay contests. *The Goddess Within* is a romantic 'dramedy' with elements of fantasy. The story is about a modern-day Greek Goddess who is destined to relive a myth when she moves to Greece to win back her ex-boyfriend. But first she must uncover the secret behind an ancient artifact known as the Apple of Discord.

The Goddess Within is a diasporic narrative about the search for identity; it links two worlds: the real and the imaginative. I like to call it an 'autobiographical myth' because the narrative structure intersects fantasy and autobiography. Above all, the hero of the story seeks her self through encounters with her other self. Mythology may help us come closer to the truth of our being, and surrendering to our consciousness may bring us closer to enlightenment. I suggest that you read the screenplay after you have read the book in order to enjoy both the theoretical and creative components of this transmedia project. It is my hope that you will become emotionally engaged with both stories.

Acknowledgments

Thank you to my devoted husband Ioanni, who believed in this project and encouraged me to embark on it. His vision, strength of character and persistence cannot be expressed in words. To my beloved son Faidona, for his deep understanding, which goes far beyond his years. Thank you so very much for allowing me a bit of your playtime.

I wish to thank the real 'goddess of wisdom', Dr. Athina Karatzogianni, for her patience, support, and understanding, for without her knowledge, this work would not have been possible. A special thanks to Patrick Lynch who was most supportive during my exploration of the concepts set forth in this book (and has graciously provided the Foreword). My sincere gratitude to the transmedia experts Laura Fleming, Henry Jenkins, Jeff Gomez, and Aaron Smith for their generous feedback and insight, and to the students of Hull University who participated in the e-module case study. Thank you all for your feedback and support.

And thank you to my mentors, whom I come to appreciate more and more each day: Jim Riley (sales- and revenue-generating executive), best known for being savvy and remarkably innovative; Steve Rockabrand (distribution, marketing, and production executive), best known for being an intelligent and incredible leader; and Henry Winkler (actor, director, producer, and author), best known for his role as Fonzie in the 1970s American sitcom *Happy Days*. Thank you for your continued generosity and kind support, which I feel even though we live nearly five thousand miles apart. As Henry so graciously says, 'If you will it, it will come', to which I would like to add 'An act of kindness lives in the heart for eternity'. Thank you all for embracing me with your kindheartedness.

1
Introduction, Theory, and the Media–Education Landscape

1.1 Introduction

It is time to imagine an education system that, rather than hindering, nurtures and encourages creativity. The research outlined in this book acknowledges the limitations of knowledge and the opportunities for different perspectives and approaches. More importantly, it 'recognizes that not-knowing is a fundamental starting point for creativity' (Seel 2012: 835). In the end, knowledge has to be about choices, and therefore about innovation, imagination, and possibilities (Wallerstein 2004: 56).

This book started out as a media-oriented investigation into transmedia storytelling that was to build on my prior experience in the field of media. However, it turned into something far richer. While reading the literature about transmedia, I discovered that professionals in the field believed there was an educational space for transmedia storytelling, although there was no research or literature directly related to this topic. This was not surprising, as transmedia storytelling is a relatively new discipline. In fact, it was only when I enrolled in an e-module called 'The Foundations of Online Learning' while conducting this research that the idea of merging the two disciplines (media and education) came to me, setting the stage for a convergence perspective.

Before we move ahead, it is important to take a brief look at my backstory. Throughout my formal education, I was challenged by the educational system. Not only did it generally fail to engage me, but on those few occasions when it did engage, it failed to create any long-term retention. Looking back on this experience motivated me to move forward with great vigor on this current research. I had suffered under the traditional model of education because my learning style, which was visual, and then kinesthetic and auditory, was not accounted for.

Proponents of the concept of learning styles believe that individual learning styles should be assessed and classroom methods should be adapted to the individual needs of learners. My learning style has never been assessed in any classroom situation. As a result, I was intrigued to formulate a new model of education in a new environment. A sense of self-investigation and an innovative spirit, along with a deep interest in storytelling, media, and education, became the underlying drivers for this work. This book is a creative and critical inquiry.

The inquiry set forth in these pages was to discover how transmedia storytelling could be used as a learning strategy in e-learning environments. However, these strategies can also be used in traditional settings. During my literature review, I discovered there was no theoretical framework for writing a screenplay that could then be used as part of a transmedia pedagogy; therefore, it was crucial initially to first develop a framework that could be used during story development. I also considered educational parameters that could assist with the creation of the components of what I term 'Transmedia Storytelling Edutainment' (TmSE). While enrolled in 'The Foundations of Online Learning', I was exposed to e-education, and thus was able to determine the differences between online and offline learning environments. This was also where I discovered that excellent module design and content aggregation, as well as strong tutor performance, were needed to sustain a successful learning environment. Simply put, good performance creates a good educational experience. Performance takes into account the way the module flows, as well as the online interaction and collaboration. In addition, while going through the module and interacting with the hypermediated environment, which is engrained into e-learning environments, the idea of adding hyperlinks to the screenplay under investigation came to mind.

I came to understand that the screen was the central focus as well as the mediating factor between the teacher and the learner. The screen has certain affordances that the classroom does not, and it was crucial to acknowledge these differences and create material that would play to them. The notion of manipulating the conventional textbook into a form that was far more appropriate for the screen, along with the idea of using instructional stories, coalesced in the form of a screenplay (termed a 'screentext' for e-learning purposes). The thought of using fewer words in the reading material that could create images in the mind was appealing because fewer words on a computer screen would be ideal for human–computer interaction. Also, the use of a combination of image and text seemed to benefit different learning styles, as text and image could reinforce one another and perhaps create retention.

After developing the screentext, I went on to develop the multimodal edutainment (a portmanteau word combining 'entertainment' and 'education') module, which was based on the knowledge I had gained thus far about transmedia storytelling and online learning (it is important to note that I had prior experience with teaching media modules in higher education). The e-module that I developed, entitled 'The Practice of Digital HIStorytelling: Exploring the Trojan War', focused on the use of narrative technique to teach digital storytelling. The theme of the course material was history/mythology. In this case, students learned about story creation and about ancient Greece; however, the overall premise is that stories can teach any subject, whether they are narrative history or not.

The theory that broadly informs my book is Jenkins's (2006) Media Convergence Theory, from which I have made my observations. However, various theories, models, and frameworks underlie my theoretical perspective and practice-based work. The practice-based research methods include the development of a screenplay and the design and execution of an e-module. The applicable theories are listed in Section 1.2 (The overview of the route to discovery) and described briefly in each chapter.

This work is important because of the rise of reformative social movements that will demand alternative practices and models of education. The present book is structured into eight chapters with narrative at the core, and it draws on empirical research from a diverse set of disciplines. This chapter outlines the methodology, introduces media convergence, and provides an overview of the media landscape. Chapter 2 discusses the impact of media convergence on storytelling. Chapters 3 and 4 outline the impact of media convergence on education. Chapter 5 brings together pedagogy and fiction: the screenplay *The Goddess Within* (written specifically for this research for application in e-learning and to develop a transmedia storytelling framework) is discussed, and the transmedia storytelling framework is introduced. In addition, narrative theory and reflective practice are applied to test various theories for use in the digital classroom. Chapter 6 reflects on and analyzes the e-module and includes student feedback. In Chapter 7 the respondents to my research questionnaire provide their thoughts on the research questions. The chapter also summarizes the interviews and discussions with these professionals. Chapter 8 concludes the study. Goffman (1959) believed it was important to understand the relationships between *narrative, experience,* and *meaning.* This book attempts to put these relationships into a more contemporary perspective, and to compensate for media convergence experienced on an unprecedented scale.

The mode of inquiry set forth in this book, which is outlined in this chapter, links traditional qualitative methods of study with alternative forms of qualitative research. With the emergence of creative disciplines and cross-disciplinary modes of study, it is necessary to recognize alternative forms of reporting. Although the majority of the work presented is theoretical, the alternative form of research included is practice-based. Gray (1996) has defined practice-based research as that which 'is initiated in practice, where questions, problems, challenges are identified and formed by the needs of practice and practitioners; and ... the research strategy is carried out through practice, using predominantly methodologies and specific methods familiar to us as practitioners' (p. 3). The next section provides an overview of the route to discovery, and the individual chapters that discuss the practice include an explicit introductory methodology. The reason for providing the methodology and application together in a single chapter is to eliminate repetition and aid recall.

1.2   Overview of the route to discovery

The multi-method research approach employed for this work was designed to build on the synergy between traditional and artistic qualitative research methods, as well as case-based practices. The research process was not one of gathering materials but one of gaining knowledge, and as more knowledge was gained, more questions arose. I gained knowledge by reading scholarly literature on diverse topics: the Internet, education, entertainment, media, media literacy, technology, narrative, screenwriting, digital storytelling, transmedia storytelling, psychology, sociology, learning through play, multimodal learning, neuroscience, and the biology of learning, to name just a few. I then applied those theories that corresponded with my beliefs to develop the course and the screenplay (screentext). The research questions that came out of this process were designed to generate further knowledge to support the use of fictional stories and multimedia/multimodal delivery methods in education.

The practice-based research was viewed from the wide-ranging perspective of Media Convergence Theory (Jenkins 2006) and can be broken down into three components. First, a Hollywood-style screenplay was created in order to develop a transmedia framework. The transmedia framework is employed as a guideline for developing a screenplay that can later be used in e-learning environments as part of a transmedia edutainment approach. Second, the screenplay was transformed into a screentext, hyperlinks were added to some of the text, in order to be used in the e-module as part of the TmSE pedagogic strategy. Third, the case study in teaching tested the use of the screentext and the multimedia/ multimodal edutainment approach. Student feedback was gathered on the e-module. Feedback was also obtained via a questionnaire on the transmedia storytelling method that was sent to a sample of transmedia professionals.

Heisenberg (1972) reveals that there are different models of inquiry, which in turn yield different forms of knowledge. The mode of study here was to combine narrative practice, a relatively new form of qualitative method, with traditional forms of qualitative research to see how one can inform the other. Before moving into the practice, however, it is important to introduce the narrative point of view.

1.2.1 Narrative theory and perspective

The narrative theory examined here has been applied by a variety of modern writers. It is perhaps best known from its application by George Lucas to the *Star Wars* stories, and Lucas acknowledges a debt to its originator, Joseph Campbell. Campbell's theory of 'the hero's journey', which was extracted from his 1949 book *The Hero with a Thousand Faces*, has particular relevance to the analysis of myth. The theory states that all stories consist of a common model, or structure, found universally in myths (and in movies), and that all the world's heroes, both old and new, share the same path. (Academics refer to this as the 'classic paradigm', which fails to give credit where it is due.) Another proponent of 'the hero's journey' is Christopher Vogler, who used Campbell's work in Hollywood. Vogler wrote a now-legendary company memo for screenwriters entitled 'A Practical Guide to *The Hero with a Thousand Faces*', which he distributed to Disney executives in the mid-1980s (Vogler 2006). The memo later developed into his 2007 book *The Writer's Journey: Mythic Structure for Writers*. This narrative methodology will be introduced in more detail in Chapter 5, where it will also be applied to the screenplay.

1.2.2 Screenplay

The empirical research centers on a screenplay entitled *The Goddess Within*, which I wrote as part of the practice-based research. *The Goddess Within* is a story that encompasses themes from Homer's *Iliad* the story of the Trojan War and the Judgment of Paris (a contest among the Greek goddesses Hera, Athena, and Aphrodite as to who should receive the

Golden Apple with the inscription 'To the fairest'). My aim in writing a screenplay was to inquire from within, and from observation of, the creative process. One drawback of practice-based research is objectivity, however, the intimate connection of artists to what they do can provide further understanding (McNiff 2009). Conversely, detached observation neglects involvement and runs the risk of reducing the phenomenon to what we already know (Levine 2004).

The Goddess Within is fictional. And as Carmi says, 'fiction is the language of vision – why shouldn't it also constitute research? If we truly want to create new realities, we have to imagine them before we can move into them' (see Sameshima 2008: 54). The writing of a Hollywood-formatted screenplay was undertaken in order to develop a transmedia framework. The framework is a guide that can be used in developing transmedia-oriented stories and in evaluating existing stories for educational purposes. The process of creating the screenplay was a socio-cultural one, conducted through online peer collaboration. This kind of cross-cultural collaboration exemplifies sociocultural convergence in a media-saturated sphere. The screenplay, or more accurately, the 'screenplay-to-understanding' (a term coined for this book), is intended to offer practice in understanding a fictional story within a non-fiction context, or, simply put, a *displaced* story. 'Displaced' refers to the author dealing with some of the same themes present within the story, but in a different time and place; here, it can also refer to using a fictional story as an educational tool within an e-learning environment. One benefit of fiction is that it exposes students to experiences that they might one day encounter; in this way, it prepares them to deal with these experiences (their feelings) in advance through story.

The educational theory employed in developing the screenplay was Bruner's Constructivist Theory (1960), which asserts that learning is a process in which learners construct new ideas or concepts based on their current and past knowledge. This follows the principles of story development, where an author builds on events that are eventually resolved at the ending of the story.

1.2.3   E-module

The e-module, entitled 'The Practice of Digital HIStorytelling: Exploring the Trojan War', is a cross-mediated, story-based approach to e-learning that uses an entertainment component to entice and engage learners. Designing the course required the consideration of several educational theories, the most appropriate of which were selected to support the e-module. The e-module centered on the following theories, models, and frameworks, which I consider important when developing story-based curricula: Cognitivism (Bruner 1960; Schank 1975), Constructivism (Bruner 1960; Vygotsky 1978), Cognitive Theory of Multimedia Learning (Mayer 2009), Multiple Intelligence Theory (Gardner 1993), Communities of Practice (Lave and Wenger 1991), Social Development (Vygotsky 1978), Instructional Scaffolding (Sawyer 2006), Laurillard's Conversational Framework (1993), Kolb's Learning Cycle (1984), and the Cone of Emotion (Zull 2002). The teaching–learning approach implemented was Salmon's Five Stage Model (2000).

1.2.4 Questionnaire

A questionnaire was developed and administered to a non-random, theoretical sample of transmedia professionals. Their areas of expertise included transmedia storytelling, higher education, and the business of film production. Currently, the field has a limited number of experts, and therefore the sample size was small. However, the inputs of these professionals are immensely significant. According to Deacon and Pickering (2007), with regard to theoretical sampling, 'the researcher seeks respondents who are most likely to aid theoretical development' and 'seeks people who are most likely to extend and even confound emerging hypotheses' (p. 54). This was exactly the intention with the sample chosen. Asking questions of the topmost professionals in the field was the preferred method of inquiry. Transmedia storytelling professionals are a rare breed, and therefore feedback from the innovators themselves was required.

1.2.5 Framing the research question

There are two approaches to practice-led research. One approach is to formulate questions and then design experiments and situations that will further understanding (McNiff 2009). The second approach states that

> Framing a research puzzle is part of the process of thinking narratively. Each narrative inquiry is composed around a particular wonder and, rather than thinking about framing a research question with a precise definition or expectation of an answer, narrative inquirers frame a research puzzle that carries with it 'a sense of a search, a "research," a search again', 'a sense of continual reformulation'. (Clandinin and Connelly 2000: 124)

This is not to say that narrative practice involves working aimlessly; rather, it involves working with an aim that is open to new insights and new questions. The problem or puzzle under investigation here is storytelling in the context of transmedia practice, and bringing the educational benefits associated with this practice into higher education. On this road to discovery, questions have been formulated (to adapt McNiff 2009), and a practice of continual reformulation was applied (to adapt Clandinin and Connelly 2000).

1.2.6   Gathering information

One of the data-gathering methods used was Inquiry Circles, which derives from practice-led research. This method involves planning, acting, and observing the process and consequences of change and 'reflecting on these processes and consequences, and then replanning, acting and observing, reflecting and so on' (Kemmis and McTaggart 2003: 381). The Inquiry Circles methodology is not documented in this book because it was used as a planning method; however, the final chapters reflect on the process of developing the screenplay and the e-module.

There is limited research on and direct inquiry into the educational aspects of transmedia storytelling, and no instructions on how to incorporate transmedia edutainment into e-learning are currently available. Therefore, one outcome of this study is progress toward developing a transmedia storytelling pedagogic strategy for higher education. The process of study was designed to draw on my past experiences in the media industry and to gain new experiences through theory, case studies, and practice. Research methods can benefit from flexibility, accommodating the time and place of the investigator. I worked within an intercultural framework (the United States, Greece, the United Kingdom – and even worldwide through an online participatory culture), and it is important to note that these factors, which open up possibilities for insightful and useful knowledge creation, have been taken into account in this study. It is also worth noting that at the time the research was conducted there was no transmedia framework that could determine whether a core narrative would make for a good TmSE project.

My work merges various elements of popular culture and entertainment-initiated content with education – the authoring of truth through fiction, where fiction is not totally fictitious; the application of media tools in culture; and, finally, the art of knowing in transmedia ecologies. Beveridge (1950) believes that original knowledge is generated when ideas are placed in new relationships to one another, a process that requires crossing the boundaries of separated domains, such as those constructed between art and science. Thus, research does not have to follow an established methodology and can have an imaginative dimension. My approach was to bind together an established method and an imaginative dimension, and there was a constant tension between the two. Levine (2004) states, on the Lesley University website:

> This conception of thought as antagonistic to the imagination goes back at least as far as Plato. What is interesting, however, is that in the Platonic dialogues themselves, the tension between image and word, imagination and thought, is maintained, not eliminated. ... We must have faith that the imagination can inform us, that art is not non-cognitive but that it binds together both feeling and form in a way that can reveal truth.

If allowed, the imagination can inform and produce new understanding and open up new research areas. Moreover, 'narrative methods can be considered "real world measures" that are appropriate when "real life problems" are investigated' (Leiblich et al. 1998: 5). This book addresses popular culture in a real world and provides insight into the opportunities afforded by the use of narratives in education. Storytelling is a narrative of events, and whether it is real or imagined, it conveys meaning.

To summarize, the transmedia storytelling framework came out of the practice-based research around the screenplay, which is a vehicle for determining whether a story can be categorized as cross-media. The screenplay was then used as a textbook in the digital classroom. The screenplay, the e-module, and the feedback from the both students and professionals will be discussed in more detail in Chapters 5–7.

1.3 Media–education convergence theory

Media Convergence Theory can be used as a paradigm for understanding educational change. Jenkins explained media convergence in his 2006 book *Convergence Culture: Where Old and New Media Collide*: 'by convergence, I mean the flow of content across multiple media platforms, the cooperation between multiple media industries, and the migratory behavior of media audiences who will go almost anywhere in search of the kinds of entertainment experiences they want' (p. 2). Jenkins is referring to cross-platform experiences with media products and narratives, which have shifted from the traditional model of the singular, linear story to broader contexts, and which now bleed into the physical space of the consumer. Through the social and technological space that is shared by the consumer and the producer comes the concept of transmedia world-building: the creating and interweaving of stories that stem from a fictional universe driven by the entertainment industry. Using Jenkins' theory of convergence culture as an instrument, this book examines how entertainment can emerge as a learning resource and as a practice within education, and how it can facilitate student-centered learning-by-doing in the age of media convergence. The concept of combining education and entertainment is not only an argument but an ideology of contributing to society in a worthwhile manner.

Media convergence is an old theory taking on new meaning, since convergence is not unique to new media. According to Standage (1998), it is as old as the telegraph, which generated the same concerns in the mid-19th century that the Internet generated at the end of the 20th century. The hype and skepticism associated with the Internet about new forms of communication and business practices mirror the expectations and worries stirred up by the telegraph.

Media convergence has been influenced by several developments, and, according to Jenkins (2001), media convergence encourages transmedia storytelling through five processes: the digitization of all media content, which allows content to flow across multiple platforms (technological); the horizontal integration of the entertainment industry (economic); the multitasking of consumers (social); the rise of a participatory culture, which is supported by desktop software tools, and the need to recreate and recirculate content (cultural); the crossbreeding of culture that results from the wide circulation of content (global). To Jenkins' five processes I add a sixth: the distance-learning paradigm, which is influencing and changing the traditional methods of education, leading to the formation of virtual universities and the transformation of learning for the masses (educational and informational); it is this process that I emphasize in this book. The transformation of technology, the economic integration of the entertainment industry, the social multitasking of consumers, the rise of a new participatory culture, and the crossbreeding of culture have all inspired interest in convergence as it relates to education.

The Internet, the technology that ended media dictatorship by offering choice in entertainment, is the same technology that will end educational inequalities. In the past the media was controlled by a few, and these few controlled a mass audience. According to Frankel (2000) and Baran (2010), and documented by many other communication historians and professionals, the first mass medium was print, which was the general public's primary source of information until the early 1900s. Technology continued to evolve, but the model did not change much throughout the first half of the century – One message to the masses. Radio offered the same news in a more immediate form, and the arrival of television at mid-century caused little variation in terms of information provision: the overall principle stayed the same. However, the advent of satellite technology allowed the same information to flow further. Broadcasting in the United States could now reach an entire nation, and there was one source of information, which was disseminated to local stations.

By this time, according to Frankel (2000), the media industry had began to consolidate, and by the 1960s three national networks (ABC, CBS, and NBC) were in existence. These networks purchased broadcast rights in some territories and made affiliate agreements with others; however, it was all pretty much the same content that was distributed. Millions of individuals were watching the same program at the same time. Although the term 'mass media' was coined in the 1920s, it became more prominent as the media grew more powerful as a result of their ability to aggregate a mega audience. When cable television arrived, it managed to offer an alternative through original programming. According to Frankel (2000: 20), what spurred the change was '*Saturday Night Live*'s comic representation of *Wayne's World*, a recurring bit about two post-adolescent dopes who broadcasted their public access show from their basement'. Suddenly, cable companies were flooded with requests for public-access broadcast time. This was an early example of the public wanting to participate in cultural production, or as Frankel argues, a 'point at which *mass media* becomes *media for the masses*' (ibid.). Then the Internet arrived and disrupted all the years of cable and satellite television niche programming and specialized formats. As Frankel (2000: 21) states, 'for the first time in history, the masses have choice'. The Internet brought not only choice but connectivity and interactivity. It also offered a sense of empowerment. However, with this empowerment, a new form of consumerism arose, that of media consumption.

Mass media and mass education appear to be running on parallel lines, and as media for the masses arrived, so too education for the masses emerged. Mass media delivered one message to the masses, while mass education provided standardization to ensure all the children of a society had basic skills and knowledge. Both media and education are influenced by technology, and now they are integrated, for the first time in history, on the Internet. Multiple forms of convergence are leading higher education toward a period of transition and transformation. The mass education period in higher education, which was one of control, is giving way to a new order. In education, convergence is a response to pressures arising from a complex set of social, cultural, economic, and technologically advanced systems. The result is cross-national similarities in education – similarities that are supported by an integration of networks, whether technological or organizational, such as the United Nations Educational, Scientific and Cultural Organization (UNESCO) – through which standards and practices are shared.

At the same time, the distance-learning paradigm is influencing and changing the traditional methods of teaching and learning with the formation of virtual universities – or alternative education for the masses. Today, students in higher education have more choices, including the choice between online, blended, free, open, and traditional classroom instruction. These new forms reflect the experience of being students of the 'global village', a term closely associated with McLuhan and popularized in his books *The Gutenberg Galaxy: The Making of Typographic Man* (1962), and *Understanding Media* (1964). Online education was once used to replicate traditional education; now, however, it is extending to a much broader context that is more social and collaborative. E-learning is no longer a simple substitute for physically attending university, because it has its own delivery style, made possible by technology. The plethora of media found on the Internet, as well as the practices of Internet users, differentiate it from the learning environments of the past. This differentiation, along with the evolution of e-learning programs and storytelling initiatives, makes edutainment a viable student-centered approach to learning, and this is the focus of the present book.

Massy and Zemsky (1995) predict that technology will open up the education market to entrepreneurs who feel they can meet the needs of learners by adopting both media and technological advances that higher education institutions have avoided. At the moment, higher education holds the students as well as the product. The challenge for institutions is to use this advantage by incorporating technology to reach out to learners and prospective learners in new ways. Jenkins (2006) notes that the experience of convergence is uneven between the overdeveloped and the developing world. He states: 'audiences outside "developed" economies often have access only to the films and in some cases, only to pirated copies that have scenes missing' (p. 114). These audiences may not have access to fan-based activities or even multiplatform components, such as games or comics. However, the disparities between the United States and less economically developed countries may be more extreme than Jenkins acknowledges. There are inequalities in terms of technology and participation in media consumption in underdeveloped countries, which have resulted in the positioning of the consumer as a passive spectator rather than an active participator in media consumption.

Convergence culture is a new form of media culture, as Jenkins (2006) argues, and it marks a shift in power from media producer to media consumer, but for others it marks a shift toward more inequality (Castells 1998; Canclini 1997). As Canclini (1997) argues, 'the sense that we can be near to others without being concerned about understanding them is hidden beneath the appearance of a friendly reconciliation of cultures' (p. 29). Further, there are certain portions of society that cannot avoid exclusion, and there are other portions that cannot escape a mediated culture, and those who create media must bear this in mind. At the present time, media-rich environments may provide richer experiences, but these experiences are not distributed equally.

The ideal model for edutainment pedagogy is to blend the best practices of each culture. A fusion of two is better than one on its own. The hierarchical situations in which one culture dominates another or in which there is inequality of media consumption create uneven experiences; nonetheless, educational convergence is dramatically and fundamentally transforming education for the first time in history, and transmedia storytelling offers the potential to reach a broader audience.

1.4 Media–education landscape

This section further explores how the Internet challenged the media industry's value chain. It explains the importance of the narrative, the concept of transmedia storytelling in education, and the benefits of interactivity and choice brought by the Internet age. It discusses how and why edutainment failed in the past, and how a student-centered approach to edutainment is necessary for effective learning. The intention of edutainment is for students to be emotionally and cognitively engaged in learning and not entertained, amused, or diverted (which is a common misconception). However, enjoying the learning process is advantageous as well.

Initially, the media industry was slow to understand the impact of the Internet. Before the expansion of the Internet, content producers were connected to the public by distributors of entertainment content, who acted as gatekeepers. Since the 1980s, the gatekeepers have become increasingly concentrated as a result of mergers, such as that of AOL and Time Warner. The Internet is a place of expansion and is horizontally integrated. American media conglomerates are buying up digital real estate for their brands. For example, Viacom owns Paramount Motion Pictures Group, MTV Networks, VH1, BET, Nickelodeon, Comedy Central, and more; Time Warner has interests in television, film, and print; and Warner Brothers has several subsidiary companies in industries such as interactive entertainment, cinema, records, television, animation, and even comics (Free press 2011).

Moreover, entertainment conglomerates have expanded their businesses online with company and content-specific websites. Corporate media have expanded the scope of their business models in order to profit from a global audience. This is clarified by Fisher, who identifies an overall paradigm shift where television executives now view themselves as content producers. He quotes Jeff Zucker, former CEO at NBC Universal, who argues: 'What it really means is producers can no longer just come in with a TV show. ... It has to have an online component, a sell-through component and a wireless component. It's the way we're trying to do business on the content side, giving the consumer ways to watch their show however they want to watch it' (Fisher 13 March 2006).

The Internet has opened up the production process, allowing direct access to the public. Previous media models are no longer relevant in this environment, in which the metrics for success have shifted from viewership to usership. McClelland and Markel (2009) acknowledge two things that seem clear in the new media value chain: '1) innovations around delivery of media will continue to proliferate, and 2) the only valuable links in today's media value chain are those that foster or facilitate an emotional connection with audiences by delivering a unique, consistent point of view' (p. 2). They believe the new media value chain will no longer depend solely on maintaining a physical connection with the audience; rather, it will require an emotional one. It will no longer be an emotionally connected individual but an emotionally connected network. This is a key point, and the emotional aspects of learning are discussed in Chapter 3, which looks at educational convergence.

The web has some characteristics of a mass medium, but it also has characteristics that differentiate it from other mass media. Often, the Internet is compared to television, because it enters the home, is viewed on a screen, and provides access to information and entertainment. Web users surf from page to page using a mouse, much like television viewers channel-surf using a remote control. The Internet may also have similarities to traditional mass communication, but it is a very different animal, largely due to its interactivity and the freedom to engage with content at any time. (This is in contrast to television, where viewers are required to meet at a scheduled time to watch their favorite programs, although digital video recorders are changing consumer behavior.) McLuhan (1964) believed that any new medium contains all prior media within it. The Internet is a prime example of this where while different technologies underlie radio, film, and television, in digital formats they are one and the same. It is customary that new media tend to be viewed and understood in terms of the older media that precede them; however, at the base of this inquiry is the uniqueness of the Internet and other social networking digital media and how they are changing the notions of teaching and of learning. McLuhan's (1964) concept of media ecology provides a theoretical approach to this. He argues that it is the shaping of communication tools that in turn shape people's perceptions, experiences, and behavior. McLuhan (1964) states: 'The "medium is the message". This is merely to say that the personal and social consequences of any medium – that is, of any extension of ourselves – result from the new scale that is introduced into our affairs by each extension of ourselves, or by any new technology' (p. 7). I would add that an 'extension of self' is not evenly weighted and that people of power may represent 'self' much larger, broader, and stronger. Therefore, edutainment must be developed to respect and represent minorities and different cultures.

At first glance, the 'medium is the message' suggests that the channel surpasses the content in terms of significance; however, McLuhan appears to be telling us to look beyond the obvious. He wants people to notice the effects of a new medium before it becomes pervasive. He explains that the content of any medium can be deceiving, blinding us to its actual character. Media effects can take years to evolve; however, by considering some of the consequences in advance, we might be able to influence a medium's development in a way that diffuses any negative impact and perhaps instills positive growth. When commerce is the focal point, however, the moral message or good is not the first consideration for industry content creators or even educational institutions that are interested in profits. Beck (2004) elaborates: 'In the United States, the entertainment industry is a business driven by bottom-line considerations and an artistic medium protected by law' (p. 213). Entertainment and education are businesses, which like any other business need to make a profit to exist; however, their tremendous influence on society requires that they also provide a media/education balance. Media balance refers to offering content that is socially responsible, that reflects societies in terms of culture, gender, and race. Educational balance refers to offering students what they actually need, when they need it, in the manner they need it.

Although there has been some discussion around transmedia education, that discussion has not been contextualized or documented in a comprehensive manner. This work is the first attempt toward meaning-making through transmedia storytelling education in the age of media convergence.

Transmedia storytelling edutainment involves the use of stories to create learning content around a discipline. These may or may not be popular stories; however, it appears that the more popular stories – distributed across multiple platforms – may provide a better hook to capture the attention of learners. That is, recognizable stories from popular entertainment, and their extensions, may create greater anticipation and have broader appeal and an established atmosphere for engagement.

Today, a feature film moves across media platforms and can consist of several parts, including a book, a game, and online and TV components. I contend that these self-contained story extensions, along with traditional learning tools, can be utilized as teaching aids when the context of the material supports the subject matter. Since transmedia storytelling is already engrained into people's daily lives, it can be considered a holistic teaching method that is student-centered rather than technologically oriented. Within the story domain there are already professionally produced stories and student-produced narratives that take the form of web-based stories and 'mashups' (videos that combine and modify existing digital media works to create a derivative work).

Transmedia storytelling edutainment includes the use of media tools and storytelling practices in e-education, but it is not limited to online, and may consist of components that do not include moving images, such as story-centered curriculum (fiction or non-fiction) that include scenario-based case studies and activities. According to Schank (2011), people must be taught to deal with 'real-life issues that arise in any situation they are preparing to work in. The magic word is *scenario*. Scenarios are like plays. Things happen and you have to deal with them' (p. 72). Schank describes a scenario as a fictional circumstance that focuses on a situation that could arise on the job. A distinction should be made here between story education (SE), which covers this use of narrative to educate via case studies and scenarios, and TmSE, which uses stories to educate via the journey of a protagonist. Best practice for story-based curricula would include a combination of SE and TmSE whereby the learner engages in both popular and non-popular stories. TmSE includes narrative curricula, or simply the use of transmedia storytelling, as a tool to teach about a specific topic. Furthermore, with TmSE, learners have the option to synthesize a new narrative via a digital story rather than write a term paper. This is a fundamental skill for the 21st century.

The importance of narratives in education is manifested by the evolution of new media-rich environments, by the democratization of the storytelling production process, and by the advent of global models in e-education. So, much like the Internet challenged the media's industry value chain so too will the Internet challenge higher education's long standing value change. The media industry and higher education have much more in common than they actual realize. The commonality between the two is they both offer intangible products (information). According to Mierzejewska (2011), 'the underlying economic characteristics of information products differ from those of other types of tangible goods in critical ways. These fundamental economic characteristics are related to crucial differences in demand, production, market, and distribution conditions...' Most important, media products have extremely high social externality value because of the central role information and media content plays in economic, political, and social processes' (pp. 13–14). In the next chapter, the focus turns to storytelling in the age of media convergence. Media Convergence Theory is a paradigm for understanding converging narratives and educational convergence. The sociocultural logic of media convergence is also impacting the creation of stories, which can be user-generated, collaborative, minority-driven, and fandom-oriented.

2
Media Convergence's Impact on Storytelling, Marketing, and Production

The chapter examines the practice of transmedia storytelling for its implementation in higher education. Digital storytelling, which has made its way into higher education, is explored both singularly and collectively as a pedagogical tool that can expand transmedia practice. The chapter also sheds light on the Internet as a source of information, entertainment, and education; it integrates media and content, audience and advertising, and reconsiders the meaning of the brand as behaviors and a source of production. Transmedia storytelling is also viewed from a theoretical perspective. Established media are eroding, and this chapter shows how this is providing opportunities for both media and education. It explains what educational institutions are doing to stay abreast of digital practices.

Whether you look at media convergence from a media or an educational perspective, it is clear that convergence is ever-present in the digital space. Converging narratives are self-reflective, intertextual, social, collaborative, user-generated, cross-mediated, educational, informational, promotional, branded and non-branded, and can be told via any combination of approaches or processes. My empirical research *The Goddess Within* is a prime example of a converging narrative, and it is discussed in detail in Chapter 4.

2.1 Narratives and folk culture

Storytelling is the most ancient form of teaching. Humans are capable of communicating abstract concepts in the form of story. Before reading and writing became widespread, oral storytelling was the way humans passed down their history, knowledge, and wisdom from generation to generation. According to Linda Stender, 'folk tales are as significant to the study of literature as the number system is essential to the study of mathematics' (quoted in Kuyvenhoven 2009: 104). Ancient storytellers often recited tales that the community would reenact in the form of religious rituals. Miller (2008) believes that 'these ancient reenactments of myth were a form of participatory drama' (p. 6). It is possible that interactive narrative was first seen around campfires, as ancient storytellers would adjust the story according to the reactions of the audience, and therefore interaction with the story world is not unique to the digital age. Today's narratives, though, are produced many-to-many for a range of platforms; this is in contrast to polysemic narratives, which were directed to several different audiences via one channel. Thomas Schatz (1993), an expert on American cinema, in particular the Hollywood films and filmmaking in the 1940s, notes the Disney films of the 1970s as examples of polysemic narratives. These were made to appeal to very young preschool-aged children as well as to their adult parents via the inclusion of grown-up references that children could not understand. This is still true of many children's films; however, today multiplatform stories allow people to interact with stories in multiple ways. These new story forms are the modern equivalent of myths, and they come in many shapes and sizes, such as books, film, television, the Internet, religion, themed festivals, and even standup comedy.

Mattingly (1991) recommends using the term 'narrative inquiry' for those who do not consider the term storytelling to be formal enough. She singles out Aristotle's use of narrative as the natural framework for representing the world of action. Mattingly also points out that narratives not only give meaningful form to experiences we have already lived through but also 'provide us a forward glance, helping us to anticipate situations even before we encounter them, allowing us to envision alternative futures' (cited in Schön 1991: 237). According to Hesse-Biber and Leavy (2008), any examination of narrative today should consider a broader picture, one which examines not only the internal structure of stories but also 'the social organization of the storying process as meaning-making activity in its own right' (p. 261).

The term 'storytelling' warrants a brief explanation. The National Council of Teachers of English (NCTE) defines storytelling as 'relating a tale to one or more listeners through voice and gesture' (NCTE 14 August 2008). Most dictionaries define 'story' as a narrative account of a real or imagined event(s). Polkinghorne (1988) and Sarbin (1986) contend that narratives organize episodes and actions, and stress the organizational logic of a story, which is expressed in the plot and theme, and also the product – the story, tale, or poem – as a unit.

Lodge (1990) comments, 'Narrative is one of the fundamental sense-making operations of the mind, and would appear to be both peculiar to and universal among human beings' (p. 4). A key aspect of storytelling is the use of emotion to draw the audience into the story world. McDrury and Alterio (2003) state that 'our ability to communicate not just our own experiences but the experiences of others enables us to transcend personal frameworks and take on wider perspectives. This attribute, together with its international, transhistorical, and transcultural usage, makes storytelling a powerful learning tool. It is therefore not surprising that it has endured' (p. 7). Parents and teachers tell stories to children all the time. Stories teach lessons, entertain, and engender cultural pride and unity. The way people reflect upon history is influenced by story-tellers. Koralek explains:

> Historians say there are several reasons why storytelling has been a part of so many cultures. They believe storytelling was used to: teach history; settle arguments; make sense of the world; satisfy a need for play and entertainment; honor supernatural forces; communicate experiences to other humans; and record the actions and character-istics of ancestors for future generations. (Reading is Fundamental Organization n.d.)

Storytelling has reemerged in this century enhanced, with more technol-ogies delivering these fables across borders. Far more stories are available to humans than ever before, in various forms of converging narratives. Fulford (2001) highlights that 'the rise of industrialized narrative – story-telling that's engineered for mass reproduction and distribution – has emerged as the most striking cultural fact of the 20th century and the most far-reaching development in the history of narrative' (p. 149). In his keynote address delivered at the Siggraph 97 Conference, entitled 'Storytelling: The World's Oldest Profession', Ferren talked about the future of the Internet:

> Every time a technology has been introduced that allows one or more people to do better or more compelling storytelling, like language or writing … or what the computer will be, it has changed the course of our society. It has become a permanent part of our

lives, and it has had a startling impact in establishing the kind of step functions that are characteristic of how our society runs. The power of the Internet to reach out and connect people as a story-telling conduit or new storytelling media is going to make it the most important technological invention since the printing press. (Ferren 1997)

This research provides a global perspective, in terms of the internet; however, the focus is on US-generated media since they are a major force behind the production of transmedia storytelling content, and the United States is where advancements in technology and business surround the World Wide Web. The practice of transmedia storytelling has a significant place on the Internet, where converging narratives and online learning co-exist.

2.2 Transmedia storytelling

Transmedia storytelling is also referred to by industry professionals as cross-platform, cross-media, multiplatform, and integrated media. Cross-media storytelling, according to Davidson et al. (2010), 'refers to integrated experiences across multiple media, including the Internet, video and film, broadcast and Cable TV, mobile devices, DVD, print and radio' (p. 7). In addition, 'the new media aspect of the "cross media experience" typically involves some high level of audience interactivity' (ibid.). In digital media, interactivity most commonly occurs when a user performs an action in one platform that causes an action to occur in another platform, as when a video-game player controls an on-screen character's action. That being said, transmedia storytelling conveys storylines over multiple platforms. For example, on one platform you can follow the main story, on another a minor character, but the overall theme remains the same.

According to Giovagnoli (2011), the terms 'cross media' and 'trans-media' identify narratives that develop across multimedia platforms. The difference between the two lies in the way the stories are told. Giovagnoli explains that there are narrative forms that do not change when released on multiple platforms, and there are narrative forms that do change depending on the platform. The second type, he argues, is more effective and is called cross-media in Europe and transmedia by the Hollywood film industry. However, he points out, academic definition such as cross-media tend to be superseded by professional practice, and today, the terms 'cross-media' and 'transmedia' are used interchangeably, though the latter is generally preferred (ibid.). Similarly, I use the terms 'story' and 'narrative' interchangeably in this book. Nichol distinguishes between the two with an analogy:

> Narrative is the structure of events – the architecture of the story, comparable to the design of a building. Story is the sequence of events, the order in which the narrative occurs – the tour through the building. Plot is the sum of the events, told not necessarily in sequential order, but generally consistent with the story and often considered synonymous with the narrative – the building itself. (n.d.)

The Producers Guild of America (PGA) provides this definition of transmedia storytelling:

> A Transmedia Narrative project or franchise [must consist] of three (or more) narrative storylines existing within the same fictional universe on any of the following platforms: Film, Television, Short Film, Broadband, Publishing, Comics, Animation, Mobile, Special Venues, DVD/Blu-ray/CD-ROM, Narrative Commercial and Marketing rollouts, and other technologies that may or may not currently exist. These narrative extensions are NOT the same as repurposing material from one platform to be cut or repurposed to different platforms. (Producers Guild of America 2010)

Although the PGA does not include video games in its definition, they are considered transmedia, and game producers do receive credit for their work.

The requirement for three or more narrative storylines is easily attainable for a Hollywood franchise; however, this may be difficult for an independent film producer to achieve. Nevertheless, a certain amount of story presence is essential for the audience to *trans-engage* with the story world. The term 'trans-engage' ('trans' from transmedia and 'engage' from engagement means to transcend) describes the user's connection with the multiple media platforms. Moreover, transmedia storytelling is not an isolated practice. Dena argues (2009), 'Indeed, the nature (to some extent) and breadth (to a greater degree) of transmedia practice has been obscured because investigations have been specific to certain industries, artistic sectors and forms' (p. 3). The changed media landscape and the producer's role in the new mediums have recently been recognized by the PGA, which has decided to expand its Code of Credits to include one for Transmedia Producer. President Marshall Herskovitz explains:

> As technology evolves, it's no longer adequate to think of a project as simply a television show or a movie; we now understand that the audience will want to experience that content across several platforms – online, mobile, VOD, Blu-Ray, and now iPad – often with different or additional material. It's the producer who oversees the complex and creative process that allows that to happen. (Herskovitz 6 April 2010)

In transmedia storytelling, the producer is responsible for building and extending the story world across multiple platforms. Crawford, in a blog post entitled 'The Upside Down of New Media', recaps Jeff Gomez's thoughts about transmedia. Gomez, co-founder and CEO of Starlight Runner Entertainment and an expert in transmedia storytelling, contends that most people shift from one medium to another, adapting to it easily and naturally; however, most content does not. Instead, content is 'repurposed and repeated' and does not build on the story world. Gomez elaborates:

> With transmedia, each part of story is unique and plays to the strengths of the medium. The result is a new kind of narrative where story flows across each platform forming a rich narrative tapestry that manifests in an array of products and multiple revenue streams. (quoted in Crawford 2009)

Playing to the strength of the medium is a key aspect of transmedia storytelling to acknowledge (as is the fact that the power of the Internet platform has yet to be fully discovered and exploited in education). The Producers Guild of America New Media Council (PGA NMC) highlights what Gomez identifies on the *PGA NMC Blog* as the eight defining characteristics of transmedia production:

1) Content is originated by one or a very few visionaries
2) Cross-media rollout is planned early in the life of the franchise
3) Content is distributed to three or more media platforms
4) Content is unique, adheres to platform-specific strengths, and is not repurposed from one platform to the next
5) Content is based on a single vision for the story world
6) Concerted effort is made to avoid fractures and schisms
7) Effort is vertical across company, third parties and licensees

8) Rollout features audience participatory elements, including:
 – Web portal
 – Social networking
 – Story-guided user-generated content (Gomez 2007)

Miller (2008) and Davidson et al. (2010) believe that interactivity should be added to this list. Moreover, Davidson et al. (2010) define the cross-media genres as entertainment and art, education and training, activism and public relations, and marketing and advertising. For the purposes of this book, I combine entertainment and education to create a new genre.

The transmedia approach takes the narrative of a story and, as seamlessly as possible, extends it to different platforms. Audience members are encouraged to participate by commenting, interacting, or creatively contributing to the medium. Transmedia storytelling is not, however, about adapting a story in its entirety to a new medium, something many theorists consider redundant. Dena (2009: 148) elaborates:

> The premise of this adaptations-are-redundant argument is that any repeating of a story adds no value to the experience or meaning-making process. While I certainly agree that any expansion or addition or continuation of a fictional world across distinct media is a significant phenomenon, what I wish to challenge here is the rationale behind these arguments: that adaptations are automatically redundant.

Dena is referring to Jenkins' theory (2006) of transmedia storytelling. Jenkins argues that a 'story unfolds across multiple media platforms with each new text making a distinct and valuable contribution to the whole' (pp. 95–96). Jenkins further contents that the 'current licensing system typically generates works that are redundant' which does not allow for 'new character background or plot development'. Therefore, for the work to be considered transmedia it should 'offer new insights and new experiences' and not be redundant (p. 105).

Dena also refers to transmedia theorist Long's argument:

> Retelling a story in a different media type is *adaptation*, while using multiple media types to craft a single story is *transmediation*. For example, Peter Jackson's film versions of *The Lord of the Rings* are adaptations of J.R.R. Tolkein's *The Lord of the Rings* novels. While this shares some of the same benefits as transmedia storytelling, primarily the creation of 'access points' to a narrative world through alternative media types, it differs from transmedia storytelling due to the

lack of one of the key components in Jenkins' definition: distinction. (quoted in Dena 2009: 148)

Dena provides an example of adaptation that is not automatically considered redundant, citing Nava's music remixes, which involve 'a reinterpretation of a pre-existing song' (2009: 149). Her view is useful because 'reinterpretation' offers the 'new level of insight and experience' Jenkins argues for. Dena (2009) challenged Jenkins' original adaptation theory as it relates to transmedia by showing that adaptations to some degree add to meaning-making, and therefore, Jenkins' view of adaptation evolved:

> To translate *Harry Potter* from a book to a movie series means thinking through much more deeply what Hogwarts looks like and thus the art director/production designer has significantly expanded and extended the story in the process. It might be better to think of adaptation and extension as part of a continuum in which both poles are only theoretical possibilities and most of the action takes place somewhere in the middle. (Jenkins 2011)

With the theorists in mind, I put theory into practice by writing *The Goddess Within* screenplay, which consists of adaptation, extension, and distinction. That being said, the portion of the story that was adapted is by no means strictly a reproduction that can be considered redundant, which leads me back to Dena (2009) who states adaptations should not be considered automatically redundant.

It is important to clarify the meaning of 'adaptation' as it is used in film studies because the term 'film adaptation' is ambiguous. According to Aragay (2005), adaption studies views the adaptation process as 'appropriating or recreating past texts in/for different contexts' (p. 230). Nonetheless, nuances of the word have influenced the study of film adaptation and this is exhibited in the 'criterion of fidelity', which has been the benchmark for evaluating film adaptations. McFarlane's *Novel to Film: An Introduction to the Theory of Adaptation* (1996) points out that 'fidelity criticism depends on a notion of the text as having and rendering up to the (intelligent) reader a single, correct meaning which the film-maker has either adhered to or in some sense violated or tampered with' (p. 7). He suggests that critics must first try to figure out what type of adaptation the filmmaker was attempting before they can begin to judge whether or not the adaptation was successful.

Most criticism of film adaptations of books focuses on how closely the film resembles the book. It is evident that many filmmakers try to be faithful to their original sources, and in these cases, fidelity criticism can help judge whether or not the filmmaker succeeded. Other filmmakers, however, take great liberties with their sources, and these films cannot be judged strictly by fidelity criticism. Leitch (2003) argues that fidelity criticism is deeply rooted in misconceptions, because it values literature over film, pretends that the predecessor's text is original, and ignores the fact that all texts are essentially intertexts. Film adaptation editor Naremore emphasizes the need for adaption studies to move away from formalistic concerns and to study adaptations in light of intertextual and contextual factors, such as economic, commercial, cultural, political, or industrial and educational factors (quoted in Stam 2000: 10–12). This view aligns with *The Goddess Within* because it was influenced by some of the above listed intertextual and contextual factors. From an 'economic' perspective, as it relates to the production process, it privileges a joint venture between Greece and the United States. It was written within a 'commercial' context because it uses a narrative formula that Hollywood follows. It also combines two 'cultures' and periods in time, and as a screentext (a form of online textbook) it provides an educational perspective. It is a converging narrative in every respect.

Furthermore, similar to Naremore, Cattrysse (1992a) places adaptation studies in an intertextual framework, asserting that 'film adaptation had better be studied as a set of discursive (or communicational, or semiotic) practices, the production of which has been determined by various previous discursive practices and by its general historical context' (p. 62). Kristeva aligns with other poststructuralist theorists in stating that every 'text is an amalgam of others' and part of 'a larger fabric of cultural discourse' (1980: 64–91). Barthes (1977) writes, 'A text is a multidimensional space in which a variety of writings, none of them original, blend and clash' (p. 146), and theoretician Stam elaborates, 'The text feeds on and is fed into an infinitely permutating intertext, which is seen through ever shifting grids of interpretation' (2000: 57). Stam employs Bakhtin's (1981) concept of dialogism and proposes viewing adaptation as *intertextual* dialogism, where film adaptations 'are caught up in the ongoing whirl of intertextual reference and transformation, of texts generating other texts in an endless process of recycling, transformation, and transmutation, with no clear point of origin' (2000: 66).

In general, there are three categories of adaptations: those that are (1) faithful to the original work, (2) faithful to the original work with modifications, or (3) new creations inspired by the original work. It is in this latter respect that *The Goddess Within* can be considered an adaptation because it uses the 'The Judgment of Paris' myth to create something entirely new. According to the theorists (Dena 2009; Jenkins 2006; Long 2007), adaptations that add something new can also be considered transmedia. *The Goddess Within* represents an intertextual dialogism because it is shaped by two Greek myths, 'The Judgment of Paris' and 'The Trojan War'. Intertextual studies illustrate that all stories are derived from other stories. Even the ancient Greek playwrights based their plays on stories that had already been told. Booker, a British scholar, published research in which he showed that most stories of the world can thematically and structurally be reduced to seven basic plots: overcoming the monster, rags to riches, quest, voyage and return, comedy, tragedy, and rebirth. (Booker 2006).

Stam, in 'The Dialogic of Adaptation' (2000), suggests that we should consider a film adaptation to be a new work of art that has a dialogic relationship with its original source, in which the film becomes one of many possible readings of the source, and not an attempt to convey the original, or the one true, meaning of the source. It is important to note that while *The Goddess Within* can be considered an 'intertextual dialogism', it does not try to provide 'one of many readings' of its original source – because it is an entirely new plot and story. The term 'intertextuality' refers to the shaping of text by another text. Texts are basically interrelated, or they influence one another. *The Goddess Within* is related to the 'The Judgment of Paris' and to the Trojan War myths as narrated by Homer. A transmedia storytelling project employs interrelated texts from various forms (movie, video, website, etc.). Moreover, TV shows which reference other TV shows, or parodies which provide greater insight into the meaning of the original work being mocked, are also intertextual. It is important to reiterate that transmedia storytelling is not considered a strict adaptation of one media format to another.

Narrative has the capacity to evolve into a pedagogical practice with multimodal delivery capabilities. Gomez believes that 'narrative will become one of the most effective tools to educate people on an array of subjects' and elaborates 'after all, if we are growing up to be perfectly comfortable with an array of media channels, why not put them to use teaching us what we need to know in a carefully designed and fully interactive way?' (quoted in Thompson 2009). Jenkins (2007) states, 'Transmedia storytelling practices may expand the potential market for a property by creating different points of entry for different audience segments.' By entering a story franchise at different points, a user is able to experience the story in different ways, and subsequent visits enrich the experience. For example, a user may first engage with a television show and then go online to connect with the characters via their fictional blogs. Multiple entry points are providing diverse experiences and opportunities in e-learning environments as well. Just as storytelling has grown from being an oral tradition around the campfire to print, radio, television, film, and the Internet, the experience of storytelling for listeners and readers (consumers) has gone from being a passive one-to-one in which consumers are creating stories as user-producers (or 'produsers', a word coined by Brunes in 2008 combining the 'media producer' and 'consumer' of Internet content).

Steinem adds, 'humans have been storytelling for 100,000 years around the campfire; the media is now our campfire' (quoted in Margolis 2009: 25). This 'media-infused campfire' is extending throughout the world, impacting consumers and learners alike. In an interview with Dinehart, Gomez said:

> The technology inherent in transmedia implementation grants storytellers the ability to 'read faces' again. The internet provides us with thousands of voices, sometimes many times that amount. This creates an instant feedback that brings us full circle, placing us all back around that primal campfire. Our storytellers can gauge our response, hear our voices, and the narrative can respond. Transmedia is bringing back the shaman, only this time the story is being told to the world. (quoted in Dinehart 2009)

Transmedia storytelling, which is now supported by the Internet and other digital platforms, has brought back a 'communal' environment in the form of interactivity and participation by users that extend across many different cultures.

Digital storytelling, or the creation of video content, is gaining recognition in higher education. Education is no longer always top-down and teacher centered. It is becoming more student centered and activity based, creating situations in which students 'learn by doing' rather than 'learn from lecturing'. Digital storytelling is an excellent form of learning-by-doing that uses new media and technology that transmediate narratives around the interests of students.

2.3   Digital storytelling

Technology advancements have created new forms for stories; however their purpose – communication and learning – remains unchanged, and online environments are already using them. Digital storytelling can make e-learning engaging by deepening the learning experience. A digital story is a short form of a digital production narrative. Digital stories combine moving images with voice, music, sound, text, and graphics; they can be educational, instructional and informational. Raines (2010) quotes Sharad who contends that 'digital storytelling is the art of telling stories with digital multimedia to share a reflective narrative. Through effective use of perspective, drama, emotion, context and sound, digital storytelling helps people to connect, explore and understand'.

In recent years, digital storytelling has surfaced as an alternate means of knowledge construction in higher education, and instructors are creating assignments that employ stories and multimedia production to engage students in creative and critical practices. According to Oppermann and Coventry (n.d.), communicating in the 'new language' of multimedia brings to students greater awareness of the components of traditional writing. The feeling is that having students author multimedia projects not only engages them but also enriches the writing experience. 'Digital stories have proven to be a powerful medium for students to represent a theoretically informed understanding of texts and contexts in a form other than "traditional" writing' (ibid.). According to Kadle, 'Digital storytelling creates an environment where learners can associate with the characters and learn while the story unfolds. This brings about an effective transfer of knowledge to the learner and leads to its usage in the work environment' (Kadle 2010).

The terms digital stories and web-based stories are used interchangeably in this book. On the Internet, all stories are in digital format, therefore, the term 'digital storytelling'; however, digital formats are not limited to the Internet. Web-based storytelling is a better term because it is specific to the Internet; however, the term web-based storytelling is not as widely used. Moreover, user created content has exploded onto the Internet only in recent years. Audiences are now creating their own digital stories which can take the form of original work, or the combination of original with pre-existing sources to create a derivative work (mashups). Mashups tend to blur the lines between the original creation and the consumer. Mashups can be derived from pre-existing content such as popular entertainment and they can be produced for fun, or they can be produced to increase knowledge in educational settings. A digital story which is produced to meet learning objectives can consist of pre-existing sources or it can be an original piece of work. It is the content that distinguishes whether the story is informative or fun, however, many of the same skills are used to create either original or derivative stories. The principles of good storytelling that are exercised by master storytellers are applied to developing digital stories. Oppermann and Coventry contend:

> Digital storytelling works at the intersection of the emotional and the epistemological aspects of learning, bridging story and theory, intellect and affect. For many students an emotional engagement with the topic – or a problem in the most generative sense of the word – is the point of departure that allows them to connect their stories to the relevant theories. As emotions are reclaimed cognitively, they enable students to write themselves into existing discourses and to contribute personal perspectives to an academic community. (n.d.)

Digital storytelling has materialized, and through the process of storying one can develop meaningful communication, as well as synthesize and analyze information. The story process also accommodates diverse learning styles, which is necessary for reaching a broad range of students. According to the Educause Learning Initiative (ELI, a community of higher education professionals committed to advancing learning through technology innovation), 'The oral tradition of knowledge transfer and exchange has served as the basis for education since humans began teaching one another, and digital stories build on this model by incorporating rich, dynamic media' (Educause 2007). In a TmSE context, digital storytelling is extending the story world into the academic setting for the purpose of conveying knowledge.

A number of educators believe that storytelling, as an instructive technique, can be used with virtually any subject (see in particular Schank 2007; Bareiss and Singh 2006). Kendall Haven in his book *Story Proof* (2007) provides examples of the use of story in different subject matters. David Crenshaw, a high school science educator teaches Introduction to Biology and comes dressed in a period costume to present his Darwin lesson in 'first-person story form'. The result, his students tested better, on average, by the story delivered material. Seth Kahan, a corporate knowledge management lecturer incorporates a story poem at the beginning of his presentation. He then passes around the room a 'Native American talking stick', which allows the person holding the stick the opportunity to share their feelings about the poem. His technique allows participants to share more openly and more truthfully and this 'induces them to listen' more cognitively and emotionally. The result, 'it makes each participant relevant to others and creates a new level of context through which they can work with each other.' Dan Fossler, a high school music educator created a story of the Italian composer Vivaldi and told it to his 'student orchestra [...] before assigning them a Vivaldi piece to learn. He was amazed how quickly his students mastered the difficult music'. The result, 'ten students had gone to the library to check out additional reading material on Vivaldi. This 'made Vivaldi real, meaningful, accessible, and interesting in a way that the music alone never had'. Moreover, 'constructing a narrative in the form of a story and communicating it effectively requires the storyteller to think carefully about the topic and consider the audience's perspective' (Educause 2007). These transferable skills are thought to be highly valuable to learners who will one day join the workforce. Working with different media forms challenges students to develop new skills and literacies. Educators tend to agree that digital storytelling develops their skills in the following areas: research, interviewing, organization, writing, presentation, problem-solving, and assessment as well as their technological and interpersonal skills. Also, digital storytelling can provide improved opportunities for assessment that challenge the older and more familiar ones. According to Jenkins and Gravestock, students become accustomed to and internalize processes for coping with traditional assessment, whereas different media forms, such as visual communication, challenge students to work outside of their comfort zones, and this presents opportunities for assessment (quoted in Jenkins 2009).

Oppermann and Coventry view digital storytelling as a social pedagogy; and student engagement as its important benefit. They believe that 'digital storytelling allows students to work on authentic assignments, develop their personal and academic voice, represent knowledge to a community of learners and receive situated feedback from their peers' (n.d.). Oppermann and Coventry contend that students working with narratives and media seem to be more engaged with assignments and with the subject matter. The use of new media and technology will not by itself make learning better; however, the way these tools are used will have significance.

According to Barrett, 'digital Storytelling facilitates the convergence of four student-centered learning strategies: student engagement, reflection for deep learning, project-based learning, and the effective integration of technology into instruction' (2006: 1). I strongly agree with Barrett's argument that 'the ancient art of storytelling can be a powerful tool for deep learning and reflection. Add today's multimedia technology and you have a highly motivating project-based learning activity as well as a powerful artefact' (2008: 1). Digital storytelling, as a nexus for student-centered learning, supports the argument for incorporating narrative in education.

Moreover, creating a story is a strong stimulus for reflective practice and reflection (see Boud et al. 1993; McDrury and Alterio 2003; Dewey 2005; Sanders 2009) that encourages 'students to sidestep habitual approaches to reflection and engage in a more intuitive and creative way' (Sanders 2009: 15). Kolb's experiential learning cycle (1984) brings the stages of reflection into relief. Kolb emphasizes the importance of experience (concrete experience), which, through reflection (reflective observation), can be related to theory (abstract conceptualization), and then applied to other situations (active experimentation). In other words, for learning to take place, a student needs to experience, reflect, generalize, and then apply. Fundamentally, then, reflective practice helps learners to look at an event, understand it, and, more importantly, learn from it. In the process of constructing a story and communicating it to others, the storyteller shifts from actor to observer, in a process that is consistent with the stages of Kolb's experiential learning cycle. For example, let's imagine that you are going to create a story. Some people may choose to begin by reflection, watching other stories to learn. Another person might prefer to start abstractly, by reading and analyzing story instruction books. Yet another person may experiment and begin creating a story immediately. The practice of storytelling follows Kolb's experiential learning cycle and students can enter the cycle at any point. In story creation, students move from watchers to doers and from doers to watchers. Wells states:

> Constructing stories in the mind – or storying as it has been called – is one of the most fundamental means of making meaning, as such, it is an activity that pervades all aspects of learning. When storying becomes overt and is given expression in word, the resulting stories are one of the most effective ways of making one's own interpretation of events and ideas available to others. (1986: 194)

Creating and sharing stories encourages students to reflect on their own experiences. Dewey contends, 'We do not learn from experience. We learn from reflecting on experience' (1933: 78). I would add that we learn from reflecting on converging narratives as well.

In Pagano's view, 'when we teach, we tell stories about the world. Some stories are scientific, some historical, some philosophical and so on' (1991: 197). There appears to be a strong connection between storytelling and knowledge construction. Further, McDrury and Alterio

(2003: 36) believe that 'the ability to accommodate multiple perspectives, along with ongoing transcultural usage, suggests that storytelling is a learning tool which can transcend cultural differences'. This is an important factor when working in an online learning environment that reflects diverse cultures.

The use of storytelling as a pedagogical method is firmly established in many universities, and more are also adopting digital storytelling. Technology-enhanced education is challenging prior institutional norms by offering new forms to engage learners and instill reflective practice. Transmedia and digital storytelling provide an emotional connection needed to engage, foster learning, and instill reflective practice.

2.3.1 Transmedia and digital storytelling in collaboration

There is no question that transmedia and digital storytelling will continue to evolve and merge with education, and Hollywood is uniquely positioned to participate in the educational mission. Transmedia has a lot to offer educational institutions if the gatekeepers of the those institutions will allow TmSE to penetrate. The barriers to rolling out transmedia are significant for higher education. Gomez contends, 'I'm also looking forward to seeing these techniques adopted more for higher learning, but the barriers to this are formidable, ranging from the cost of production for implementations that are going to be engaging and respectable to older students, to the rarity of good designers of such experiences' (e-mail to author, 13 March 2011).

The transmedia phenomenon cannot be studied by isolating it into one category or by studying one discipline, one industry, one media, and one artistic vision. The area of study is complex because of the many fields that enrich the practice. Therefore, media theorists on the topic have each contributed a different viewpoint, and this is the process which unfolds in this book. The idea set forth here is to discuss film in a new era, and to introduce an educational perspective to transmedia in order to begin to theorize it. Media theorists have documented media's impact for years but when media work together there is no single way to express it. Transmedia theorist Christy Dena (2009) refers to the transmedia practice as a 'unity in diversity'. She states, 'Just as a transmedia project cannot be created with one medium, the phenomenon cannot be understood through the lens of one research field' (p. 331). The 'unity of diversity' or the 'unit of focus' has been introduced here as TmSE and is explored more in the section on educational convergence.

Although it is too early to develop a theory around transmedia, because it is relatively new as an area of research, a general overview as it relates to film is important to investigate. Moreover, since this work supports the use of moving image in education, it is important to contextualize converging narratives in their current environment.

2.4 Theorizing transmedia storytelling from a film perspective

The theory of transmedia is contextualized from a film perspective because films are key components of transmedia productions and because the practice-based, empirical research is a screenplay. That being said, a political economy view of film focuses on the factors of film production and the economics of the film industry versus aesthetics. A political economy view examines the reason particular films get produced and sees the aesthetic view as answerable to economic and institutional constraints. It is associated with media ownership, control, distribution, modes of production, representation, and identity. Therefore, understanding these factors and implications is crucial for TmSE. It all begins with the film's blueprint – the screenplay, or script.

In mainstream Hollywood, a 'spec script', that is, one that does not include camera direction, may get green-lighted by a studio but the process of selection is not a justifiable one. The entertainment business is a relationship business, and who you know provides an extra level of security. Studios fear getting sued by authors who send in unsolicited scripts for review and then claim their ideas were stolen. Moreover, scripts are often purchased based on similarities and are benchmarked against other success factors in order to warrant future box office success. There are also economic and marketing concerns to be considered. Such bureaucracy limits creativity. Script selection is a highly subjective process, and very few scripts make it past the first reading. No one really knows which story will be the next blockbuster, and many stories that get purchased by the studio never get made into movies. Scripts are read by either readers (who may be assistants, interns, recent film grads, inspiring screenwriters, for example) or by professional script analysts, whose job is to prepare coverage for producers, agents and executives. Typically, coverage includes a detailed synopsis of the plot and characters and a rating, typically, 'recommend', 'consider', or 'pass'. Most scripts that get read (about 100,000 screenplays are speculated as being written each year) are poor and receive a pass. Readers tend to be extremely cautious in evaluating projects, recommending scripts that get made into films that do poorly at the box office can cost them their jobs.

With any script, the biggest challenge is getting a Hollywood insider, such as an executive, director, producer, or actor, to support the work. *The*

Goddess script, for example, does not fit the typical Hollywood formula, that is, it is not a low-budget comedy aimed at young males. However, based on the success that the story has achieved in screenplay contests, along with the right support, it could easily be considered a profitable film for Hollywood. *The Goddess Within* is not considered a traditional epic story in the likes of other Greek-themed films such as *Troy* (2004), *Alexander* (2004) and *Clash of the Titans* (2010). Alternatively, *The Goddess Within* does not fall into the category of films such as *My Big Fat Greek Wedding* (2002) or *My Life in Ruins* (2009). The uniqueness of *The Goddess Within* is that it does not follow a strict genre. *The Goddess Within* is a 'dramedy' with fantasy elements. It is a converging narrative that falls somewhere in the middle of an epic film and a romantic comedy, and films that cross genres tend to be considered a risk for Hollywood, which prefers to play it safe. Likewise, the protagonist is a woman which is not the target market for Hollywood. Therefore, *The Goddess Within* is a screenplay that needs the right relationships for the story to *come to life*. The good news is that audiences definitely want to see more women on the screen, women of all shapes and sizes who are interesting and engaging. In light of Cate Blanchett's recent Oscar win for playing a dominant female role in Woody Allen's *Blue Jasmine*, this may become a reality. *The Goddess Within* anyone?

Throughout its history, cinema has proved itself to be resilient. It survived the deregulation of national broadcasting, the arrival of multiplex cinema, the introduction of niche content, the spread of satellite and cable networks, the proliferation of digital communication technologies, and most recently, the social aspect of production where the consumer is also a producer. During the studio era, studios controlled all film development and production. Then the studio system broke down, opening up new avenues of production, including independent film production, and most recently, online collaboration.

Once a film has been produced, 'exhibition windows' are the opportunities to watch movies in a number of distribution outlets. The distribution cycle begins with a theatrical release, home video, pay-per-view, pay TV and video on demand (VOD), and finally, free-to-air TV. The internet release is new to the film distribution platform, as well as simultaneous releases, when a movie is available on many media at the same time or with a slight variation. Among simultaneous release projects are *Bubble* (2005) by Academy Award-winning director Steven Soderbergh. Moreover, the theatrical performance of a film in the United States is considered to be critical to its success because how well a film does in US theatrical exhibition determines its value in other markets. The key factors around theatrical exhibition are large marketing budgets, word of mouth, publicity, and box office performance. According to Hawkins

(1995), 'Disney's *The Lion King* released in 1994 earned North American box revenues of $250 million, approximately a third of its total worldwide box office. Within 2 years, more than 50 million videos were sold and retail merchandise sales exceeded $1.5 billion. *The Lion King* "isn't a movie. It's an industry"'.

Hollywood dominates the global movie market, although some studios have foreign investors, and many top actors and directors come from outside the United States. America is also influenced by other cultures because it has a diverse culture within. Despite that, the global dominance of Hollywood's film industry is largely based on economic factors: because movies are costly to produce, they need a huge audience to make a profit. Moreover, the English language and the overall political dominance of the United States in the world system support movie production. European producers have failed to achieve the same kind of large-scale success in the global market because they must first serve domestic demand, and their budgets are not as large as their US counterparts. Nevertheless, as the foreign market expands, more films will be produced abroad. This is appealing to some moviegoers who think Hollywood films are too formulaic, though films made in foreign countries can be just as prescriptive. Likewise, there are several American filmmakers whose films do not fall into the formulaic category, such as directors Tim Burton, Quentin Tarantino, and the Cohen brothers, just to name a few.

According to Klein (2004), in the late 1940s American filmmakers began shooting films outside the country because it was cheaper; these productions (known as 'runaway productions') increased during the 1990s, which meant job losses for American film workers. Klein reports that Canada was Hollywood's foreign location of choice; in the late 1990s, it was home to more than 80% of all runaway productions. The Canadian government was offering film production companies tax rebates to shoot there, which together with the favorable exchange rate, could reduce a film's costs by approximately 25%. Today, however, Canada must compete with countries offering more generous tax breaks and even lower labor costs for foreign crews, for example Australia, the Czech Republic, Brazil, Romania, and Hungary are also vying to host Hollywood productions.

The film industry has moved from Canada to other locations and corporate collaborations, again for economic reasons. Some foreign countries are now investing more in Hollywood films; however, Hollywood's reinvestment within these countries may overlook local film production. The industry is focusing its attention on distribution and on setting up operations around the world, in effect creating branch offices. Thus, it is likely that mainstream films will continue to be produced for a global audience, ignoring local cultures. At the same time, some countries are already prominent in film production around the world, and India is one of them.

2.4.1 The Hollywood System Abroad: Hollywood to Bollywood

US films still dominate the global film market, but America is no longer the number one filmmaking nation. India is the number one film-producing country in the world.

And the Dubai Government is one of the most forward thinking governments in the world. It has worked consistently towards the development and strengthening of new industries and commercial enterprises to replace the wealth generated from oil. Although India produces a lot of movies it has yet to acquire high regard on a large scale. According to Indiaonestop.com (n.d.), today, technology has progressed in India, and it is perhaps the best among all developing countries in terms of filmmaking; however, the films themselves remain mostly repetitive in storyline. This may be due to the inequality of compensation with screenwriters, earning far less, in comparison to the salaries of stars.

According to Ramanathan (2008: 8), '150 Hollywood films (English/sub-titled/dubbed) are released in India every year since 1998. Despite Hollywood's market penetration, only the film "Titanic" has ever made it to India's top five list'. This is a strong indication that local cinema is desired and needed. Ramanathan states that in 2007 five Indian films made it to the top five list in both the United States and the United Kingdom. Indian film screenings in America and Great Britain are likewise increasing. Nonetheless, Indian cinema tends toward Westernization and promotes lifestyles in which local cultural nuances are often lost. 'The new trend of commercial films fashioned in culturally alien settings aims to reach "global" urban audiences and the diaspora' (Ramanathan 2008: 22). So, while the growth of film in India and other countries offers opportunities for new types of converging narratives, a lot of the content offerings outside the United States mirror Hollywood and are made with a global audience in mind. Below are examples of some of the stories that were repurposed from Hollywood productions, or more specifically, 'Bollywoodnized'. India's film industry is centered in Mumbai, formerly known as 'Bombay', hence 'Bollywood' (Bombay + Hollywood), the name given to India's film capital (Ramanathan 2008). Earthwit provides a list of the top ten Bollywood movies copied from Hollywood. As an example, three out of the ten listed on the Topyaps website are listed here:

1. *Kyon Ki* (One Flew Over the Cuckoo's Nest): This was a brilliant script that had brilliant direction and so-so acting but it was all

stolen from the Oscar winning *One Flew Over the Cuckoo's Nest*, starring Jack Nicholson.

2. *Koi Mil Gaya* (E.T. the Extra-Terrestrial): With this film Indians jumped into the sci-fi era of movie-making and director Rakesh Roshan was appreciated for making such a great copy. ...

3. *Agneepath* (Scarface): In this film there was a strong attempt from actor Amitabh Bachchan to copy Al Pacino. (Earthwit 2011)

Based on this list, one might argue that repurpose and remix cinema is nothing new. The difference today is that technology is making it easier than ever to repurpose content and has taken such production into the mainstream; however, it is still the corporate collaborations that are leading the way at home and overseas.

In 2009, DreamWorks co-founder Steven Spielberg was looking for capital; it was a time the financial crisis had made it difficult for American studios to find financing (Voice of America 2009). DreamWorks Studios struck a partnership deal with Reliance Big Entertainment, India's largest entertainment conglomerate, to develop new projects. Reliance Big Entertainment was to finance the production of five or six films a year by DreamWorks. It is no surprise that this deal followed the 2008 Oscar-winning film *Slum Dog Millionaire* (Internet Movie Database, 'Slum Dog,' [n.d.]). The deal between Reliance and DreamWorks may be a harbinger of the future of film production. For now, it helps Bollywood to be taken more seriously by Hollywood.

According to UniJapan (2009), after hitting a peak in the 1960s, Japan's film industry has been in decline. Back then, five major film companies (Shochiku, Toho, Toei, Daiei Motion Picture, and Nikkatsu) controlled the Japanese film business. In the 1970s, production was separated from the rest of the filming process to reduce costs, and outsourced. In the 1980s, Japan entered its financial bubble, and Japanese companies from various industries began to invest in films; however, the companies investing in film at the time were doing so to spread their risk, rather than to complement each other's strengths. Thus, the Japanese film industry came to be dominated by a group of companies that were financially driven. The production committee, which consists of film companies, publishers, and network television, used their own resources for a synergetic effect. The theatrical release of a film would be made by the film company, the video release by the video company, the advertising would be created and publicized by broadcast and in print. In the process, outlined above, the 'production committee is the copyright holder of the film and sales are divided among its members according to their investment ratio' (UniJapan 2009). An advantage of this production process is that companies come together to multiply their resources.

As medium- to low-budget Hollywood films production began suffering following the financial crisis, US entertainment conglomerates based in Japan went 'local'; that is, they began entering the local production market and making Japanese films (UniJapan 2009). Currently, these majors include Twentieth Century Fox, Warner Bros., Sony Pictures, Paramount Pictures, and Walt Disney Studios Motion Pictures. Moreover, Dreamworks' live-action films are distributed by Walt Disney Studios Motion Pictures, Japan, and Dreamworks' animated films are distributed by Paramount pictures (ibid.: 33–36). It is evident that these conglomerates have a strong influence on the film business worldwide. What form future encounters between Asia, India, Europe, and the West will take is hard to predict; however, it will likely remain true that the more international the production, the more ambiguous the nationality of the film. Today, there are a plethora of strategic partnerships and alliances with companies based in other countries and this has led political economists to focus on the transnational economy. Moreover, political economists from diverse regions are now working collaboratively on common projects (Calabrese and Sparks 2004; Murdock and Wasko 2007) much in the way films are being produced. According to Mosco and Schiller (2001), there is an emphasis on the amalgamation of states, classes, and corporations across national and regional areas, creating what Chakravartty and Zhao (2008) view as a 'transcultural political economy'. Similarly, the transcultural political economy can integrate, support, and collaborate in the area of transmedia education. Mosco elaborates, 'Where once, corporations, including those in the communication industry, were based in one country and moved through the world as an external force, today they are increasingly integrated into the fabric of societies to the point where it is often difficult to determine their national origin' (2008: 48).

The markets for film and video products were once national; now there is a global market, and media, which are marketable commodities in a capitalist society, have expanded to become digital. As a result, there is more commercialism and media concentration, with rich nations dominating the global economy. According to Mosco (2008), the growth of communication not only serves capitalism but also disrupts it, in three ways. First, technologies are challenging traditional ideas of production and consumption; for example, the ability to download music and video and to share and copy all kinds of material challenges the ability of capitalism to police its property. Second, social networking and social movements can enable people to disrupt the system, and disruptive software allows hackers to penetrate secure systems, where they can create problems for free enterprise. For example hackers go after organizations and corporations whose practices conflict their own ideas of justice and social responsibility, as in the taking down of CIA's website or Sony PlayStation. Third, knowledge workers are less likely to give up control of their ideas to management, making top-down control and discipline more difficult (Mosco 2008). The amount of disruption possible in transnational cinema, which includes both world cinema as well as global film production, remains to be seen.

2.4.2 Transnational cinema

With global economic instability it is hard to imagine the shape of the film industry in the future or to provide a clear definition of transnational cinema. According to Higson (2009), cinema is not a strict reflection of a national culture or identity although it certainly privileges and reproduces a limited view. He believes it can be viewed as being actively involved in trying to construct subjectivity. Transnational practices in film production, combined with the local and global community, thus provide an argument for a transnational perspective. Moreover, transnational cinema transcends national borders to generate its own cultural products and representations.

Babel, a 2006 film about border crossing directed by the Mexican film director Iñárritu, was a co-production of five corporations in different countries, and presented four stories in four languages (English, Arabic, Japanese, and Spanish). The film is an example of global sociocultural convergence, both in front of the camera and behind the scenes. According to Kerr (2010), *Babel* illustrates a structure of mechanisms based on collaboration and human relationships. He believes the social relations of production characterize a global film (*Babel* was an international co-production among companies based in the US, Mexico, and France). Williams describes *Babel* 'as the homology between the mode of production and the mode of (film) practice by looking in detail at the case: as a co-production, as a film *both about and based on* border crossing, and as a vehicle for both an ensemble cast of unknown and three major international stars' (cited in Kerr 2010: 43).

The mode of production on Babel included the talent and their representation, festivals, and international distributors. Castells (2006) talks about a technological network society in which social arrangements are structured around electronic information networks. *Babel* portrays this 'digital divide' between the characters who have access to technology and the characters who do not. *Babel* brings to light the realities of a network society.

According to Wang and Yeh, since the 1990s there has been a huge demand for 'the localization of global products and the globalization of local products' (2005: 177). Wang and Yeh use the term 'delocalization' to describe how cultural products are made less objectionable to foreign audiences:

> Through a process of deculturalization, all of the elements that are culture specific, including those that are ethnic, historical or religious, that create barriers to intercultural reception or are deemed unfit for a new presentation style, may be contained in a familiar narrative pattern that not only plays down cultural differences, but also guarantees comprehension across viewer groups. (2005: 178)

The result is a new kind of *non-cultural* content, which could be devastating to culture and cultural representation. However, the process of deculturalization does not include all narratives, although there are familiar narrative patterns in many stories. For example, the screenplay *The Goddess Within* is based on a Greek myth, and the screenwriting process was more of a co-culturalization rather than a deculturalization because it converges two worlds: The ancient myth; the Judgment of Paris with the current Judgment of Peter; ancient Greece with modern-day Greece; New York City with Athens; American culture and the Greek culture, and so on. The plot is shaped by a cross-cultural perspective and represents the cultural values and norms of the author. Likewise, the time and place of the story are most relevant as it explores the inner needs and questions that were present in me at the time. Moreover, *The Goddess Within* is derived by my experience in an era of globalization. This story was not simply inspiration from experience or a fictionalized autobiography, it is a 'structural homology' and follows Kerr (2010) in that both the social relations and the mode of production come together in the 21st century. The idea of making *The Goddess Within* came to me from my awareness and need to connect with my roots, while at the same time, I felt like a fish out of water. The diasporic narrative is discussed in more detail in Chapter 5. All the same, *The Goddess Within* as a produced film could have similarities to *Babel* as Kerr argues:

> *Babel* is an internationally packaged art film, produced by a global network of companies, staffed on short, casualized contracts by a team of workers many of whom are as deracinated as Iñárritu himself,

and the resulting film exhibits precisely the acculturalized content and international form accommodated by such a mode and such relations of production. (2010: 48–49)

The Goddess Within could potentially have similar intercultural elements and the global feel of the internationally packaged film *Babel*.

Huaiting Wu and Joseph Man Chan suggest that 'The major agent of transculturation is the media organization, the character of which has immense influence on both the production process and consumption' (Wu and Chan 2007: 198). They argue that 'for world cinema to cross national borders and overcome the international audience's socialization by Hollywood films, national cinemas need to enable Western audiences to cross what they call the "cultural psychic distance"' (ibid.). The hybrid story *The Goddess Within* is an example that closes the 'cultural psychic distance' between Hollywood and Europe, and according to Wu and Chan's theories, stories that feature the 'incorporation of globalized norms and concepts in the production of local cultural products' are evolving (ibid.).

Furthermore, it seems quite difficult to attribute national identities to heterogeneous created works; however, as a concept, national cinema still remains. According to Hagerman (2006) Iñárritu describes himself as 'a director in exile' (p. 18). The idea for *Babel* grew out of his acute sense of being an immigrant (ibid.). Films engage audiences on an emotional level, which is a universal and a key element of all good films, and bridges cultural divides. The tag line for *Babel* on the cover of the DVD is 'Pain is universal – but so is hope'. This is most certainly the language of emotion.

2.4.3   The disdain for popular entertainment

Several decades ago, the entertainment media were viewed and even subject to a condescending judgment by the upper classes. Elites believed that it 'was mindless, worthless, and even sinful' (Gans 1975: 3 cited in Singhal and Brown 1996). Mendelsohn (1966) defended entertainment media, arguing that it had positive benefits as recreation and a break from a hard work.

Mendelsohn (1966) identifies the reasons popular entertainment media were perceived so negatively: the Hebraic-Christian notion of sin, which placed entertainment and even enjoyment in opposition with moral and ethical teachings; the notion of the Protestant work ethnic, which positioned popular entertainment as a waste of valuable time, equating it with laziness; the rise of secular-royalism which scorned entertainment products; the rise of liberalism, which attacked the media for corrupting the common man; the rise of ideological Marxism, which attacked entertainment for creating a false consciousness; and the rise of Freudian psychoanalytic movement, which raised a fear of fantasy gratification. Mendelsohn believes entertainment is compared to the 'evils of society', such as alcoholism, prostitution, criminality, and drug abuse:

> Further indication that entertainment is generally equated with evil in our society among the responsible sectors of our culture is the occasional distinction that is accorded to 'wholesome' or 'family' entertainment as contrasted with just 'entertainment' which, when the noun is not accompanied by a positive modifier, is presumed to be 'unwholesome' or unfit for the normal family. (Mendelsohn 1966: 18)

These feelings have diminished today, but even now popular entertainment is sometimes viewed as morally unacceptable for its excessive use of profanity and graphic depictions of violence and sex. Ironically, the evil in entertainment can be pinpointed to the type of stories that are imagined, and behind these stories are human beings with certain morals and values. Nonetheless, given the new centers of film production, global collaborations, and peer productions, the notion of a ruling class dictating fear in entertainment is long gone. However, stigma still surrounds the use of popular entertainment in education.

2.5   Era of convergence

As noted earlier, convergence that is key to the transformation of the media landscape is not a new concept in the field of entertainment; media professionals have been talking about it for years. Yet the old idea that all media will converge in a single platform has taken on significant importance. Jenkins, one of the key convergence theorists, defines 'convergence culture, [as the threshold] where old and new media collide, where grassroots and corporate media intersect, where the power of the media producer and the power of the media consumer interact in unpredictable ways' (2006: 2). According to Jenkins, the idea that convergence is strictly a technological movement is a fallacy. Both Jenkins (2006) and Lotz (2007) believe that convergence is a cultural and social phenomenon as well, one that involves a shift in both the production and the consumption of media. The modern convergence argument, which is also held by the entertainment industry, is that all media content will one day be delivered via a single black box into people's living rooms, or, in the mobile context, via a portable device that fits in the palm of the hand. At the same time, Jenkins believes that we should view convergence as a cultural logic (2006: 14–17). The cultural occurrence that Jenkins describes provides the foundation for transmedia storytelling, as well as for the transformation of education as it is currently known.

The transmedia phenomenon has been made possible by digitization of content and the development of broadband technology. As Miller (2008) tells us, 'the melding together of voice, video, and data in a single device or network promises to have a powerful synergistic effect.... And to the creators of entertainment, it promises to offer new types of entertainment experiences that would mean a greatly expanded marketplace for interactive programming' (p. 43). The 'synergistic effect' taking place is promising to offer new types of educational experiences as well. Jenkins (2006) explains that 'convergence alters the relationship between existing technologies, industries, markets, genres, and audiences' (p. 15). This has already been demonstrated by the participation, co-creation, and social networking activities found online. Convergence will change how the educational system operates and how students process information. Moreover, the shift in sociocultural practices such as digital storytelling, social media, etc. can alter and support new pedagogical practices that will benefit academia.

Society is witnessing a new breed of social and cultural practices, which also are creating new opportunities for media enterprise as well as the 'user movement'. Grassroots and socially responsible video production is also on the rise, as is niche programming of all sorts. Individuals can create content with a 'personal' point of view and distribute it on Facebook, Twitter, Tumblr, or other social media sites, or, they can be join an online community and create content with a 'social' point of view. Users' transliterate skills will continue to increase as they engage in the creation of content, and as they distribute that content, releasing entertainment and edutainment to the rest of the world via the Internet. Ultimately, these co-producers of content will compete with media conglomerates, and this healthy competition could lead to better content overall. It promises, according to Anderson (2006: 150–151), 'to free us from "the tyranny of lowest-common-denominator fare" and establish in its place "a world of infinite variety"' because, he explains, 'the compromises necessary to making something appeal to everyone mean that it will almost certainly not appeal perfectly to anyone – that's why they call it the *lowest common denominator*' (p. 118).

The user as a producer has been made possible by desktop production tools that have simplified the production process and have brought the studio into the home. Pool (1983) says about the effects of technology on society that 'freedom is fostered when the means of communication are dispersed, decentralized, and easily available, as are printing presses or microcomputers. Central control is more likely when the means of communication are concentrated, monopolized, and scarce, as are great networks' (p. 5). Central control is not an issue when communication is dispersed and decentralized, because every product goes to market and consumers determine its fate. Anderson (2006) explains that 'in the scarcity-driven markets of limited shelves, screens and channels that we've lived with for most of the past century, entire industries have been created around finding and promoting the good stuff' (p. 122). In reality, a lot of content that is considered 'good stuff' may not be that good, and users are left choosing among a lot of 'average stuff'. That model is changing: 'The general principle of the last hundred years of entertainment economics was that content and distribution were scarce and consumer attention was abundant. Not everyone could make a movie, broadcast on the airwaves or own a press. Those who could and did had control of the means of production. It was a seller's market, and they could afford to waste attention' (Anderson 2006: 165).

On the Internet, limited shelf space is not an issue, and niche content is made available for everyone. Thus consumers have more choices and the evaluation process is more democratic. Anderson believes that the audience will determine the fate of content, rather than a studio executive who decides what goes to market and what does not, and talks about 'pre-filters' and 'post-filters'.

'Pre-filters' determine what goes to market by the studios and 'post-filters' find the best of what is already in the marketplace by the audience. Anderson (2006) argues, 'when I talk about throwing everything out there and letting the marketplace sort it out, these post-filters are the voice of the marketplace. They channel consumer behavior and amplify it, rather than trying to predict it' (p. 122). In this new, more open, democratic marketplace everything gets green-lighted by the people who produce it or select it, increasing the opportunities for exposure for all types of content.

2.6   The Internet: media and content

Lifestyles may change and new media formats may appear, but history has shown that old media never die. Just as television did not replace radio (radio just adapted by focusing more on music programming), and cinema did not replace theater, the Internet will not replace this either. Also, it is unrealistic to compare, for example, the TV to the Internet because of the politico-economic transformations caused and accelerated by the Internet in terms of cyber protest, hacktivism, and social-media enabled uprisings and revolutions (see Karatzogianni 2006; 2009, and Karatzogianni and Kuntsman 2012).

Today's consumers have embraced the new technology products, and media have similarly adapted. Television networks stream their programs online through web syndicators, such as Joost and Hula, which buy broadcast rights to and aggregate commercially produced shows from studios and networks. Internet users can download or stream their favorite videos or TV shows directly onto their computer screens and watch them whenever and wherever they want. Apple's iTunes allows users to download music and video to their iPods. With a plethora of content options available for 'viewsers' ('viewers' + 'users', a portmanteau word referring to the viewer/user of the Internet) niche programming takes center stage, allowing for more choices in entertainment. The implications of separating content from the physical object of the CD or DVD and or the constraints of physical delivery have been ardently discussed. The digital distribution of media has broadened the scope of the content-centric entertainment industry. In the past, consumers had to buy an entire album or CD to hear their favorite song. Now they can simply download it from iTunes. And as a result, the business model has fundamentally changed, as the consulting firm Oxford Analytical noted in a report entitled, 'Unbundled Media Content Poses a Challenge':

> The unbundling of content and services across all media types and forms of technology has disrupted traditional content supply chains by increasing the power of content authors and producers, and content consumers, at the expense of the intermediaries who own and manage the traditional content distribution and supply chain. (Oxford Analytical 3 April 2006)

It is the consumer who benefits from the unbundling of content. Distributors, now with less power, are forced to compensate by offering content at a lower prices, or even for free. As a consequence, they are now seeking alternative revenue sources to make up for the lost distribution fees. Similarly, the entertainment industry is seeking new sources of revenue, and entering the education market as a potentially fruitful way to expand their reach (Oxford Analytica 3 April 2006).

My research goes beyond the television or the movie screen to explore transmedia storytelling as a form of education, information, and entertainment. The Internet is the perfect entry point into a world of converging narratives, specialized content and advertising. And what is even more alluring – this exhilarating world is just a mouse click away.

2.6.1 Audience and advertising

Bermejo (1997) notes that 1995 was the year Internet audience size began to be measured, and at the time there were twenty-five million users in the world, a fact that did not go unnoticed by the advertising industry. The Internet audience can be viewed from two perspectives. First, by the institutional classification of 'audience', which focuses on the relation of the audience to various media, and second, by the user involvement and participation, which the Internet has facilitated. 'Viewsers' expect a certain amount of value from their online interaction. My present focus is on the active nature of the audience.

The Internet user is actively seeking to satisfy a specific need, which is in contrast to the generally more passive consumption of the television and film audience. In this respect, the Internet 'viewers' are constantly engaged with the medium, and this is what makes it so attractive as an advertising medium. Internet users are actively involved with content in real time. The Internet empowers the user, giving them opportunities that go beyond information and entertainment into an entirely new arena of socialization. Technologies certainly impact humans; however, looking at the Internet from a Uses and Gratifications (Katz et al. 1974; McQuail 2005) approach versus a technological deterministic one supports the notion that people have changed the way they live, work, study, and even communicate. Niekamp (2008) conducted research to determine whether the user experience on the web is similar to those of other media. The study looked at two facets of audience activity (selection and involvement) and considered user motivation. Niekamp conducted an online survey of 208 volunteer web users that was similar to previous uses and gratifications studies of television viewers. Niekamp argues that television viewers exhibit two broad types of motivation: their media consumption was either *instrumental* or *ritualistic*. Users with instrumental motivation seek to gain something from each interaction with media content; ritualistic users, on the other hand, use media to escape and/or pass time. In addition, the study found that both instrumental web users and ritualistic web users are to some extent selective before going online (Niekamp 2008). Niekamp believes it is online content which distinguishes whether the user will be instrumental or ritualistic, and explains that 'the results in most instances were consistent with expectations based on uses and gratifications theory, except for greater selectivity of web content among ritualistic users' (p. 68). It is important to note that since both ritualistic and instrumental users are selective, it is likely that in the future learners will be selective when choosing learning options as well as module content.

Now we turn to a practice that is evolving – the branding of transmedia storytelling franchises. Branding sheds light on production processes, converging narratives, and audience behaviors, and has implications for learner behaviors and practices in the education context.

2.7   Branded story worlds

Branded entertainment or the convergence of advertising and entertainment content is referred to by Donaton (2004) as the intersection known as 'Madison and Vine', for Madison Avenue (in New York, the center of the advertising industry) and Vine Street (in Hollywood, the capital of entertainment). The intersection I describe in this book is that of entertainment and education, or what I like to call: 'Hollywood and Harvard'.

The entertainment industry, as Wyatt (1994) has documented, finds marketable content in high-concept films. The term 'high concept' basically refers to original stories that can be explained in one sentence and that have wide audience appeal. *The Goddess Within*, for example, can be described as 'the story of a modern-day Greek goddess destined to relive a myth when she moves to Greece to win back her ex-boyfriend, but who first must uncover the secret behind an ancient artifact known as the Apple of Discord'. High-concept stories are the most marketable and expandable to transmedia franchises. *Star Wars* and *The Matrix* are prime movie examples (Jenkins 2006), and recently, for television, *Lost* (Smith 2009). These intellectual properties fared well because they created story worlds that were ideally suited for interactive media. As a result there was brand extension and fan loyalty. In 2007 George Lucas bought the rights to the Star Trek franchise, and Lucasfilm subsequently launched a mashup site which encouraged viewers to create video using music and images it had uploaded to its website. ABC's *Lost* took fandom to a new level with an international fan community. A number of websites sprang up that allowed users to share and retrieve the show's content, for example 'The Lostpedia Encyclopedia', which is a wiki-powered index. On these websites, fans could interact with each other in order to understand and draw meaning from the show's complex story lines. The *Los Angeles Times* heralded *Lost* 'a model for a new media age' (Fernandez 2006). It is also a new model for branding transmedia storytelling projects.

In transmedia, story worlds traverse various media formats with ease, and while each transmedia extension can be experienced as a single entity, each must in some way contribute to the core narrative. Gomez believes that expandable narratives work best, and he is inspired by the works of J.R.R. Tolkein: 'he supplemented his novels with maps, languages, poetry, illustrations – all of it added up to a universe that felt as real as it was emotionally compelling for me' (quoted in Meyer 6 January 2010). Richer experiences can lead to 'richer', that is, financially profitable, brands, but profitability should not be the only goal. Gomez believes a good transmedia producer will make the story better *and* make more money. However, transmedia is more about art, about communicating the story in profound ways. For Gomez, it is 'about creative development, coordinated production and strategic distribution' (see Reddy 2010). Each individual narrative in the entertainment franchise becomes a brand that can be promoted differently to each target market, attracting a wider audience for the franchise as a whole. Consequently, the overall revenue potential for media markets increases as the property's brand values are expressed.

Scolari explores transmedia storytelling, which he abbreviates as TS:

> From a semiotic perspective, TS is a narrative that includes a series of stories expressed through different media. This narrative articulates an expression (TV serials, comics, video games, etc.) with a hierarchy of values that act as the content of the fictional world. These values are expressed in all the different texts that integrate the space of a certain TS experience. For example, the values of *24* are completely different than the values of *Harry Potter*; the former expresses values like nation loyalty, confidentiality, betrayal, competition, etc., while the latter narrative universe emphasizes friendship, cooperation. (2009: 600)

Scolari clarifies that a brand should not be viewed merely as set of values (2008c); rather, values must be articulated via aesthetics. In transmedia, every fictional world has a distinctive set of coherently structured narrative traits. Examples from television are *Numb3rs*, a series characterized by the use of advanced mathematics and by narrative complexity; and *Desperate Housewives*, in which a seemingly perfect suburban neighborhood is seen through the eyes of a dead neighbor. Scolari explains, 'in TS, then, the brand is expressed by the characters, topics, and aesthetic style of the fictional world. This set of distinctive attributes can be translated into different languages and media: It is a "moveable" set of properties that can be applied to different forms of expression' (2009: 600). Scolari compares traditional branding with online branding. Traditional branding employs iconography, such as logotypes, to create an indelible brand identity in the marketplace; whereas online branding focuses on the user's interactive experience (2008a; see also Niekamp 2008).

Branding expert Jonathan Baskin, in his book *Branding Only Works on Cattle* (2008), questions the effectiveness of traditional branding efforts and asserts that in getting consumers to purchase the product, consumer behaviors are just as, if not more important, than branding. He says that the current approach to branding is outdated. Brand strategists are no longer needed; instead, the management team should be involved in exploring the brand as an outcome of business practices. And this practice should not be the sole responsibility of the marketing department. Baskin tells his readers, 'your entire business is the brand, or, more specifically, brand is behavior. What matters is what you do, what your consumers do, and how all of those behaviors *intersect* with, influence, conflict with, and ultimately yield purchase behavior' (p. 31). Baskin's concept of life behaviors correlates with the participatory culture of today. Jenkins believe that 'a participatory culture is a culture with relatively low barriers to artistic expression and civic engagement, strong support for creating and sharing one's creation, and some type of informal mentorship whereby what is known by the most experienced is passed along to novices' (Jenkins et al. 2006: 3).

There is a value in shifting focus from brands to consumers' behavior, especially since culture sharing is not unique to the Internet. Today, people freely share information offline as well. Baskin argues:

> If we choose to define brands as internal states of mind, and believe that consumers have relationships with brands as expressions of self and ego, then there's a direct conflict with all of today's experience of media.... Today's consumer behavior is different. Not only are items purchased based on the input and affirmation of the community, but they are shared therein and thereafter. (2008: 72)

In branding behaviors, brand awareness becomes less abstract and more solution oriented. What consumers think and feel about the company that makes the product is not the priority, though they do not forget its importance. Baskin argues, 'by far the greater number of business successes come from recognizing and supporting existing behavior'

(p. 206). Behavior practices associated with e-learning invite story creation and instruction, which can be seen in the rising use of digital storytelling practices in higher education. E-learning also provides an ideal
platform for TmSE because it offers narrative forms on a single platform
that supports existing behaviors.

A new model for branding story worlds stems from what Lash and
Lury call a global culture industry. They argue that the global culture
industry works via brands, whereas the global culture industry worked
through commodities:

> Goods as commodities are all alike. They are distinguishable only by
> the quantities of money for which they exchange. Brands are not alike.
> Brands have value only in their difference – their distinctiveness –
> from other brands. Commodities only have value in the way they
> resemble every other commodity. Brands only have value in their
> difference. (2007: 6)

Moreover, 'the commodity is produced. The brand is a source of production. The commodity is a single, discrete, fixed product. The brand
instantiates itself in a range of products and is generated across a range
of products. The commodity has no history; the brand does' (p. 6).
Contextualizing the brand in this way aligns with the branded story
worlds. Converging narratives put into production as a 'range of products' are generated 'across a range of products', and have a history in
past stories or other platforms.

To sum up, consumer behaviors and the branding of story worlds
via values, aesthetics, and what may be considered a moveable set
of properties distinguish new transmedia branding from traditional
product branding. This 'movable set of properties' or the 'movement of
things' (Lash and Lury 2007; Scolari 2009) supports transmedia storytelling practices. These new practices require new literacies in media,
story construction, and applications of media tools and marketing. The
principles and practices of online marketing in both entertainment and
academia are examined next.

2.8 Digital marketing

In the digital era, the changes in media consumption patterns are
making it more difficult to predict consumers' actions, and moviegoers
are mobile, making them harder to track. At the same time, digital
film marketing, both advertising and publicity, is becoming more

sophisticated. The website of Market Research states: 'In 2007, studios of the MPAA [Motion Picture Association of America], and their subsidiaries, spent $754 million advertising films online', and it is predicted that this number will increase substantially. According to Digital TV Research, the United States will remain the dominant market for online advertising spending, which is expected to increase from $26 billion in 2010 to $58 billion in 2017 (Kemp 2012). Yet, despite these increasing numbers, poor box office performance creates challenges for the entertainment industry.

In the coming years, Hollywood will place more emphasis on new media channels. Online marketing is becoming an increasingly effective way to reach the young moviegoing public. The young market enjoys accessing information and content via web portals, social networks, blogs, user-generated sites as well as by downloading films. Nearly all movies are marketed on social media, via Facebook, blogs, or online communities. One of the first films that had marketing success via the Internet was *The Blair Witch Project* (1999), a story about three filmmakers who disappear in the woods. The film's website put up information that fooled moviegoers into believing that the filmmakers actually had disappeared. That was more than ten years ago, and this gimmick has become a standard marketing tool. Campbell (2009) cites more examples: As part of their marketing campaign for *Gattaca*, Sony placed fake ads in major newspapers around the country for a company that sold made-to-order children. Ironically, many people believed the company was real and called the phone number in the ad. By 2004, similar fake companies could be found in movie ads all over the Internet. The ads for *The Manchurian Candidate*, *Resident Evil: Apocalypse*, and *I, Robot* all featured fictional-corporation sites. The most disturbingly hilarious was the website created for the movie *Godsend*, about grieving parents' attempt to clone their dead child, which featured an ad for a fake child-cloning company. Many people thought the ad was real and called the Godsend Institute to either enlist their services or to sign in a petition to have the website shut down. Although this disturbed some people, it was also an ingenious controversy-driven way to promote a film.

Paramount Pictures is a major proponent of cross-media marketing. According to Berens (2008), two of the company's interactive marketing campaigns stand out: *Rain of Madness*, a fake documentary produced to promote the film *Tropic Thunder* (2008), and *Eagle Eye Free Fall*, an alternate reality game created to promote the thriller *Eagle Eye* (2008). In both cases, rather than recycle footage from the feature, Paramount created original content to extend and tease the target movie audience. *Free Fall* placed the player in the character Jerry Shaw's shoes and recreated the movie's intensity. In the game, players were contacted by characters from the movie and then become a part of the movie. As soon as a player signs up, his, or her, cell phone rings. The person on the other end sends players an e-mail containing instructions to use their computers to hack into security systems. One false move by the player and the virtual police arrive. The filmmakers used players' actions and their backgrounds against them, to create an experience that emulated what would happen if they actually found themselves in the situation, making the stakes in the game seem very real. *Eagle Eye Free Fall* was something the audience could relate to (Berens 2008). The idea of technology turning against mankind, in a world that is so reliant on it, is a tangible idea for an interactive cross-media production. A great many good movies do not have box office success because they do not get promoted as much as the mainstream films. And many good scripts never get made. A downside to movie marketing is that the trailers are often better than the movies themselves, which can leave moviegoers unfulfilled. Movie websites are getting better at engaging users by creating online communities and interactive experiences, but, these, too, may be better than the actual film.

Next, we look at sociocultural convergence as it relates to social networking, peer-to-peer file sharing, communities and collaboration, and minorities and minority groups in order to recognize what needs to advance within education. Political economy and sociocultural convergence interconnect when viewed in a media convergence light, and it is difficult to discuss one without the other.

2.9 Social convergence and peer production

Today, communication is many-to-many and social media is more than a socialization tool; it has also become an edutainment and information device. Watching television while also communicating via the Internet or a mobile device is a form of social television; however, social networking via Internet-connected TV sets is the final destination. Facebook has changed the way businesses, faculty, administrators, and students communicate outside the classroom. Social media, via the posting of user-generated video, has allowed anyone to become a video producer. Social networking websites, such as Facebook and Twitter are extremely popular and provide a bridge for social television.

Social television allows users the ability to interact around television content in real-time, increasing audience participation. In reality, television has never really been a completely private experience. People turned off the TV and then talked with other people about the shows they had watched, making viewing a social experience as well, one often summed up in a metaphor: 'the water-cooler conversations' that happen the next day in the office. And of course, viewers have always interacted with their television sets, even if just by talking back to them. But as social media enter the living room via social networking, the formerly 'passive' experience of watching TV will change (Rubel 2009). Broadcasters that embrace social networking will create added value for consumers, and advertisers will benefit as well.

Conventional broadcasting does serve to connect people to one another by creating experiences mass audiences can share. The most recent buzzwords, however, 'social television', or 'interactive television', represent a new mode of communication that dramatically enhances consumers' sense of being part of a community that transcends national boundaries. Interactivity has reshaped people's lives, and television's intrinsically social nature is at the heart of the paradigm shift. Simply put, television gives people something to talk about. And the user's *experience* is key.

Those of us who believed 'content is king' need to think again. As the writer Corey Doctorow famously said, 'Content isn't king. If I sent you to a desert island and gave you the choice of taking your friends or your movies, you'd choose your friends – if you chose the movies, we'd call you a sociopath. Conversation is king. Content is just something to talk about' (quoted in McDonnell 2010). Still, content may be 'just something to talk about', but without it there would be nothing to talk about. Therefore, it may be more appropriate to say 'content is king' and 'conversation is queen'. Rest assured, content will not be dethroned any time soon; content and conversation go together, and this is true in e-learning environments as well (see Chapter 3). However, as mentioned previously in the section on branded story worlds, what may be 'king' is 'behavior'. It is what consumers do that is mainly important.

As the television set changed the way people lived by bringing them to a central location, the living room, so has the Internet, by dispersing them throughout the house. Social television may bring the family back into the living room and reunite them with their online friends. One thing is certain, the distance between people will collapse and communication will take place at new levels. People's shared experiences will be enhanced in shared virtual spaces and people will communicate with mediated others. As Biocca and Harms state:

> While other species may sometimes respond temporarily to mediated others, we are the only species that engage *in sustained and prolonged interaction with representations of others*. In a society where mediated interaction is increasingly common, we may spend more time in social and parasocial interactions with mediated others than in face-to-face interactions with people 'in the flesh'. (2002: 14)

Mediated interactions will continue to increase, and so will mediated stories and mediated education. It is likely that most of mankind's experiences will one day be mediated, and stories will reflect these experiences. The advent of social interactive television is simultaneously creating opportunities for transmedia storytelling and in e-learning environments.

2.10   Peer-to-peer file sharing

File sharing allows computer users to directly access and distribute digitally stored information, such as movies, computer programs, electronic books, and, notably in the early days of the Internet, music. Prior to the Internet, music was sold on cassettes and CDs. The recording company owned the copyright and the exclusive right to distribute the music, and strictly speaking, it was illegal to copy it. Consumers could and did make copies of CDs to share with friends, but this was a minor problem compared to pirating (the large-scale copying of intellectual property for profit). Pirating was a major concern for the record companies, but at the time, most music-pirating operations could be tracked and shut down fairly easily.

Enter Napster, a free music-downloading Internet service which made it possible for people to bypass the established sales and distribution channels of the music market and obtain, for free, and share MP3 music files with each other online. Napster was immediately popular, and even though it was not making money, the music industry complained of copyright infringement, and sued. Seventy million members were using Napster before it was shut down by the courts in 2001 for copyright violations (Agence France-Presse 2006). Although Napster was shut down by the courts, it had shown potential of peer-to-peer file-distribution programs that were decentralized – and made 'illegal' copying much harder for the industry to control. As McClelland and Markel explain:

> Napster wasn't endemic of a population of thieves. Rather it was indicative of a new and irreversible paradigm that would soon dictate the public's expectations for online media consumption, exemplified by that fact that, in the same year as Napster's demise, Apple CEO Steve Jobs launched iTunes: a legal download service that not only revived his company's flagging financial health, but ushered in a period of unprecedented growth. (2009: 1–2)

Apple understood the potential of online media consumption and was able to act without regard for preserving the old business model. It emulated Napster's technological innovation and made it legal by charging a nominal fee for each download, and today, Apple is the largest music distributor in the world. It is safe to say that the new technology disrupted the music business and revolutionized media's traditional value chain (McClelland and Markel 2009). Following Napster, new free downloading companies have sprung up, but they operate without a central server, making it difficult for the media industry to track them and gather the proof they need in order to file individual law suits.

Along with decentralization has come an attitude shift among young technology users. I have had conversations with college students who express no concern that file sharing is a form of copyright infringement. In fact, students openly state that the reason they share files is because it is convenient. Einav (2004) similarly found that the preponderance of students she consulted with did not have moral misgivings about copyright, or even about revenue loss. 'On the contrary', she says, 'they see big media companies as money making conglomerates, full of executives earning six figure salaries, who are making a hefty profit as is. They also believe that when they pay, their money doesn't channel directly to the artists but to the managers and offices that want to increase their profit' (p. 155).

Einav adds that the majority of students also do not consider file sharing to be stealing; instead they believe they are promoting the product by sharing it with other students. She notes that avoiding the high cost of music CDs is not the main reason file sharing caught on amongst college students. Rather, the key appeal is its 'convenience, immediacy, and instant gratification' (p. 152). In contrast, she notes that students are willing to buy DVDs of films with compelling and good quality content (though the price has to comparable to or lower than a DVD rental).

Einav contends that owning the entertainment product has the added benefit that one can enjoy it over and over again. However, I would like to add that films do not benefit from replay in the same way that music does. Einav argues that college students also feel that it is unfair to have to purchase bundled content some or most of which they do not actually want. What is more, she notes, college students still go out to see movies in theaters; however, file sharing activities have replaced DVD rentals (2004).

Today, consumers have the opportunity to preview content before they purchase it, making them more selective than ever before, and they are no longer forced to buy an entire CD to get their favorite song. This in consistent with Niekamp's (2008) uses and gratifications research, which found that even ritualistic television viewers are more selective.

Students' views about file sharing are revealing because the practice is important to transmedia storytelling and academia alike. The ability to file share opens up resources that were once costly, and thus the sharing of these resources provides students with content and information to support both their entertainment and educational needs. Next, we explore how multidirectional production and these new forms of interaction support alternative forms of knowledge creation and consumption of converging narratives.

2.10.1 Peer production and user-generated content

The concept of community-based production was taken to a new level by the Spanish production of the sci-fi film *The Cosmonaut*, a project by Riot Cinema Collective. The website describes the group's concept as a 'collaboration, which is funded by a crowd' (Cosmonaut Organization 2009). The production responsibilities were spread amongst a very large group, and the film falls under a creative commons license, meaning everything will be fully available to the public for re-mix (the term 're-mix' is used to describe any subsequent alteration of the media). *The Cosmonaut* was distributed via the Internet (in an HD download) and was also available on DVD, television, and in theaters, all at the same time (Cosmonaut 2009). This is the first movie in the world that puts all the filming of raw footage in the hands of the audience. I like to describe it as a *reverse* example of a transmedia production process. Additionally, this transmedia project uses the Internet, social networks, and communities to exploit the story across media platforms; there is already a community-based transmedia storytelling expansion in the works. This is a film project that draws on the synergy between lots of people with a passion for filmmaking. The list of film supporters on the website is impressive and includes two retired Soviet cosmonauts.

The movie tells the story of Stan Arsenievich, a Soviet cosmonaut who gets lost trying to become the first Soviet citizen to land on the moon (El Cosmonauta 2010). By making the film as they have, its producers have, in effect, taken a stand against the old guard of film producers who initially resisted the Internet and did everything possible to shield their own profits and to criminalize consumers for downloading and remixing content. In some respect, commercial producers have become more flexible, and they will no doubt need to continue to rethink business practices.

On a much smaller scale, television was already encouraging user-generated content, setting the stage for today's online participatory culture. Rosenbaum (2008) reports that the early 1990s were the formative stage of user-generated content and cites the example of *Broadcast: New York*, a syndicated weekly half-hour television program. He describes the scenario: The show ran a promo on the air inviting the audience to share their ideas with the show's producers. It created a segment called 'Viewer's News', and it became an instant success. Cameras were loaned out to viewers, who produced their own stories (Rosenbaum 2008). This was audience participation at the local level in the TV medium and provided a glimpse of what was to come on the Internet.

It was Benkler (2006) who connected open-source software (i.e., software whose source code is made available to the public and can be used, modified, and shared by anyone) to user-generated content. Benkler explains that people enjoy collaborating within their interest communities and that they are motivated by passion, not profit: 'Human beings are, and always have been, diversely motivated beings. We act instrumentally, but also noninstrumentally. We act for material gain, but also for psychological well-being and gratification, and for social connectedness' (p. 6).

One of the gifts of distributed networks is their ability to connect people and give them choice. People can conduct all sorts of activities without permission from gatekeepers or institutions, and here, content and information are not owned but shared. On one side, you have the abundance of sharing communities, and on the other, the scarcity that the ownership of intellectual property imposes. This new economy is a sharing economy and everyone benefits from it. Additionally, it appears that online people are relying more and more on what others have to say, and sharing has become more prevalent as a social practice. When consumers log onto Amazon.com, they can read the customer reviews before deciding to make a purchase. Amazon also tracks customers' searches and purchases and recommends similar products based on their interests. The old paradigm valued knowledge as power; in the new paradigm, the acceleration of technology, sociocultural practices, and economic conditions make knowledge *sharing* extremely important. In some disciplines, knowledge becomes obsolete quickly; it is imperative – and thanks to technology, now possible – to keep abreast of the changes. Along with knowledge, creativity is needed, and today it, too, is valued more than ever. A creative mind is one that can provide solutions to difficult problems; however, it has to be nurtured to fully develop. In order to nurture the mind, academia must understand the sociocultural practices of sharing knowledge and build an infrastructure to support these new activities.

A democratization of storytelling is underway and is making its way into diverse disciplines and audiences. The sharing of converging stories is actually the sharing of points of view, and this creates insight and deeper meaning, and 'for a story to be a story, it must be shared' (Orech 2007). However, while storytelling is a natural fit for television, the Internet may be a better medium for sharing information, as Johnson explains:

> As a vehicle for narrative and first-person intimacy, television can be a delightful medium, capable of conveying remarkably complex experiences. But as a source of information, it has its limitations. The rise of the web has enabled television to offload some of its information-sharing responsibilities to a platform that was designed specifically for the purposes of sharing information. (2006: 120)

Furthermore, it is clear that technology- and community-driven user generated content and user-generated videos sometimes classified as mashups are on the rise and this can be due to the millennial generation.

According to the Pew Research Center (2010), the millennial generation (born after 1980 and aged 28 or younger) began arriving on college campuses around 2000. This generation has grown up with peer-to-peer file sharing and the co-creation of content; therefore, punishing youth and their households for copyright infringement seems a bit primitive. There is no loss to anyone when money is not being made from video creation. Today, if a child wants to use popular music or movie footage to make a video and then upload the video to YouTube, he or she would need to first obtain permission from the copyright holder, and securing the rights would be close to impossible and expensive. In a book like this one, a diverse group of individuals are quoted, referenced, and their ideas get built upon. In many ways, a video remix creation follows in the same vein; however, with a remix video someone has decided that fees should apply. Certainly, the archaic copyright law needs to be revised to accommodate today's remix culture. As Lessig (2008) advocates: 'Copyright law has got to give up its obsession with "the copy". The law should not regulate "copies" or "modern reproductions" on their own. It should instead regulate uses – like public distributions of copies of copyright work – that connect directly to the economic incentive copyright law was intended to foster' (p. 268).

Lessig believes that the law should be much simpler; amateur creativity should be free from regulation, and fair use guidelines should apply. File sharing, he says, should be decriminalized, at least in noncommercial uses. If no one is making a profit, then the original author only benefits from the additional exposure. Lessig (2008) holds up YouTube as an example of the ineffective copyright law as it stands today: 'Perversely, the law today says the amateur's work is illegal, but it grants YouTube immunity for indirectly profiting from work an artist has remixed' (p. 256). Ironically, YouTube does make a profit. Lessig also emphasizes that creative work is a public good. I agree. This basically means the consumption of the good by one person does not reduce its availability for consumption by another. Thus, creating something from somebody else's work does not prevent creation by someone else, nor does it take away from the profits of the original piece of work.

Online culture is community driven and likes to share, and government should take that into account when making policies that relate to this thriving, amateur participatory culture. Lessig (2008) sums it up perfectly when he writes, 'Our government is fundamentally irrational for a fundamentally rational reason: policy follows not sense, but dollars' (p. 294). And, everyone knows that Hollywood has plenty of dollars. Nevertheless, creative and remix practices do need to be addressed because they are moving into education. In the following section, fandom and virtual communities are examined for the purpose of understanding their social environments. The sociocultural context in which fans act is synonymous with other activity- and inquiry-based learning environments. But inquiry-based learning does not involve any preset outcomes. It is more dynamic, less predictable, and learners evaluate and decide its value.

2.11 Fandom culture and communities

Fan fiction has recently gained visibility in academic writing, and it is an integral part of the new media landscape. Fan fiction is a form of creative expression; some even consider it an art form. Fans are avid followers of mediated genres, and their subculture is the most involved audience segment. Members of fan communities associate with one another and bond with each other over their devotion to a specific media product. The proliferation of fiction in conjunction with the advent of the Internet has created virtual fan communities that are easily accessible by a global audience.

In his 1992 book *Textual Poachers: Television Fans and Participatory Culture* Jenkins celebrates fan culture. In fan fiction people take narratives and extend them, turning them into their own creative intentions. Jenkins believes that fans do not simply read texts; instead, they reread them and create new cultures. In *Convergence Culture* Jenkins (2006) describes the five characteristics of fan culture: *appropriation*, what the fan does when using the source in his own creation; *participation*, which describes the open collaboration among members of the community, for example, creating events; *emotional investment*, which typifies a person who is really invested in an object and wants to talk about it with likeminded others; *collective intelligence*, which arises when everyone is invited to contribute to the communal understanding of the group; and *virtual community*, one which may have face-to-face meetings and some of the people may know each other. In general, these are also characteristics of e-learning environments. And via TmSE these five characteristics provide a basis that enriches the practice.

It is well known in media studies that the modern form of fan fiction grew out of the science-fiction community, around the Star Trek franchise in particular. *Star Trek* started as a television series that went on to capture the imagination of millions of fans all over the world. The activities of fans, which are sometimes referred to as *fan labor*, include fan art, music videos, and the writing of fictional stories, most recently in video form. The derivative works produced are based on the characters within the story universe that the fan has chosen to be an ardent follower of. However, fans can encounter legal problems because they use content without permission.

Jenkins correlates fan fiction to transmedia storytelling which seizes opportunities to fill in the gaps of unfolding stories:

> Readers, thus, have a strong incentive to continue to elaborate on these story elements, working them over through their speculations, until they take on a life of their own. Fan fiction can be seen as an unauthorized expansion of these media franchises into new directions which reflect the reader's desire to 'fill in the gaps' they have discovered in the commercially produced material. (2007)

The desire to 'fill in the gaps' and to collaborate in virtual communities, makes transmedia narratives expandable and adaptable. According to Jenkins (2006), transmedia storytelling came about in 1999 with *The Blair Witch Project*. A year before the film hit the theaters, it had built up a fandom following on the Internet. Besides fooling people into thinking it was a true story (as mentioned earlier), the film's website documented 'witch sightings', and a pseudo-documentary about the witch aired on the Sci-Fi Channel. After the film's theatrical release, the website narrative continued in the form of comic books in which another person claimed to have met the witch, prolonging the fandom. All these efforts were designed to make everything look real, when in fact nothing was.

Nonetheless, it was an important moment that highlighted fans' interaction with media, which bears directly on transmedia storytelling on the Internet. The behaviors of virtual communities of fans can be found in other online communities, as well. Next, we consider the collective intelligence of a broader range of communities, in particular as relates to online learning environments and relevant to pedagogy.

2.12   Communities of practice and collaborative learning

Communities of practice, or learning communities, are groups of people that share an interest in something; they are mutually engaged around a joint venture, and by interacting, that is, by sharing experiences and resources, they learn how to do or understand something better. According to Wenger (1998) 'a history of mutual engagement around a joint enterprise is an ideal context for this type of leading-edge learning, which requires a strong bond of communal competence along with a deep respect for the particularity of experience' (p. 214). When these conditions are met, knowledge creation can exist.

Communities of practice are not interest-based communities or fandom communities where people come together for mere enjoyment.

Communities of practice come together to embrace something common like a craft or profession. According to Brown and Duguid (2002), storytelling helps communities of practice, not to achieve shared knowledge but to develop a common framework, which can lead to a shared interpretation. However, there is no reason why both shared knowledge and shared interpretation is not possible. Furthermore, Lévy (2000) argues that knowledge communities aggregate power, which gives them an advantage when negotiating with media producers; thus, he sees knowledge as restoring democratic citizenship and as an alternate source of power. He believes that via the Internet people make use of the talent of others through what he has coined 'collective intelligence'.

Triggerstreet Labs (aka triggerstreet.com) grew out of Trigger Street Production, a company formed by the actor Kevin Spacey in 1997. It is an online community, where peers showcase their original short stories, plays, books, comics, and screenplays and also receive feedback on their work (Everything Spacey n.d.). I uploaded *The Goddess Within* on triggerstreet.com, and embarked on a year-long, learning exercise with the community that involved participation, collaboration, and self-directed learning, supplemented by offline study. Triggerstreet Labs community members read the works of others in exchange for having their story reviewed. Each member benefits from the collective intelligence of the group and gains insights. During this process, I learned screenplay format, script structure, character development, dialogue construction, and much more. The support I received from the online community, along with my dedication, made for an intense experience that would be difficult to duplicate offline.

Although online knowledge communities are on the rise, many people still wonder if the Internet provides 'real' knowledge or just worthless information and entertainment. With entertainment production, some people question whether broad collaborative efforts can truly make an impact on the media marketplace, and whether individual mashups should even be considered art. Knowledge communities around scientific research, it should be noted, have proven to be beneficial. Nevertheless, it is the individuals who are responsible for what they send and receive, upload or post, search and share, and commune with, who should determine what is meaningful.

Learning is a social act, and through conversation and social interaction among participants learning can be achieved. More importantly, collaboration has been associated with retention and comprehension. Johnson and Johnson (1986) point out that 'there is persuasive evidence that cooperative teams achieve at higher levels of thought and retain information longer than students who work quietly as individuals' (pp. 31–32). Carlson and Zhao (2004) believe that collaborations promote a more integrated understanding of module content by linking knowledge of individuals together. This may be true, but different environments as well as the different knowledge individuals foster provide different outcomes.

The benefits of collaboration have been recognized in both academia and business. In an educational setting, collaborative learning environments are ideal for story-based curriculums as well as TmSE. Collaboration is discussed in more detail in the section on e-learning in Chapter 3. Presently, we turn to the collaboration of minorities, minority groups, and minority educators, who now have a platform to tell their distinctive stories as well as expand the perception of their learners.

2.13   Minority talks, Beavis and Butt-head walks

Beavis and Butt-head, a ground-breaking animated cartoon series on American television that originally aired on MTV is taking a walk, that is, their ideologies are being replaced by minority storytelling. Digital media provides a platform for all kinds of people with all kinds of stories, and these converging stories tend to represent their values and beliefs.

Stories have always reproduced culture and society. Stories can tell the code of institutions (Kelly 1985; Mumby 1987) as well as inform, persuade, and contribute to knowledge production, norms, values, and beliefs. Too often, in the past, stories about minorities have been expressed negatively, which leads to the dominant society's lack of understanding of the minority culture. However, there is a strong possibility that this will change as minority groups migrate online and form communities, and their voices will become more powerful. In both classrooms and online, minority teachers from a variety of backgrounds and cultures can contribute to understanding by sharing their different points of view.

Teachers are cultural agents. In the education context, the term 'agent' acknowledges the shift in perspective as well as practice that can turn teachers, as well as artists, into the drivers of group change. Humanities rarely investigates the social outcome of interpretation; however, digital storytelling may help force humanities to recognize what I call 'the collective effects of creative agents'. That is, humanities will begin to interpret the social and cultural impact of the creative efforts of both minority and non-minority groups. Convergence has encouraged people to share their personal stories, and these stories feed back into mainstream culture – in some instances becoming the basis of Hollywood movies. Likewise, these stories may be produced as group collaborations outside of Hollywood. Both ways, collective stories will migrate, and this migration will impact higher education. The result of 'minority talking' and 'Beavis and Butt-head' walking is an authentic reality brought on by real stories versus their Hollywood incarnations. Converging stories help construct identities. Stories told by groups of people help create social structures and are a vehicle for powerful voices to be heard.

Moreover, educators with a diverse set of voices and points of view can benefit the educational mission by using their authentic voices in learning environments, in the same way that stories are expressed authentically. The voices of minorities are being heard through their stories, bringing their experiences to people who might otherwise never know them. Storytelling is being turned over to the audience, and that audience is a diverse group of people that includes minorities. Kuntsman (2004) believes that cyberspace 'can bring together physically dispersed people, provide a space of communication for socially marginalized groups and serve as a resource for community organizing' (p. 3). In this respect, 'socially marginalized groups' can produce more authentic stories, and this collective authenticity has the potential to change the world.

What narratives will prevail? The television age specialized in a single narrative that was dominated by Western ideologies; the future holds an *emergent global narrative*, made possible by social media. Social media is an affordable alternative that supports many voices, and therefore, a superb method for delivering a global story. This type of storytelling can move civilization from a globalized monoculture to one of polycultural clusters, where minority groups can eventually be heard. It is very likely that narratives will move societies from the era of Disneyization to differenziation as well as online groupization. Lash and Lury (2007) contend that 'in a global culture industry, production and consumption are process of the consumption of difference' (p. 5). Lash and Lury (2007) compare 'classical culture industry' and 'global culture industry': 'Classical culture industry occupied the space of the symbolic: global culture industry the space of the real. Culture industry is Hollywood's dream-machine, global culture industry brute reality' (pp. 11–12). Hence, the global culture industry is likely to provide authentic stories through diverse voices.

To summarize the book so far, Chapter 1 presented my methodology, introduced media–education convergence theory, and provided an overview of the media landscape Chapter 2, explored media convergence's impact on storytelling, marketing, and production, and previewed narratives from folk culture to transmedia storytelling to digital storytelling. In the next chapter, educational convergence makes a case for the use of multimedia and multimodal edutainment experiences in e-learning environments. It is extremely important to be *au fait* with educational convergence, because it is in the process of revolutionizing the educational structure.

3
Media Convergence's Impact on Education

This chapter looks at the history of educational media and information literacy, and highlights the value of learning through play, because play is a biological desire of all human beings and when combined with education it has tremendous potential as it relates to learning. All students today need to be skilled in multimedia; therefore, a multimedia and multimodal theory of learning will be looked at. However, the main focus is on the Net Generation (Net Gen), known as the Digital Generation (D-Gen), Millennials, and Generation Y. The chapter also discusses transliteracy via transmedia storytelling; evolving narrative forms in higher education; how edutainment, or entertainment-education, and social change are enhancing learning; and how change can occur from watching popular television shows that incorporate social messages into their content. The chapter ends with a transformational business-to-business model for TmSE. We begin with a look at the institution of education.

3.1 The education system

As mentioned earlier, in the political economy approach the aesthetic view is answerable to economic and institutional constraints. These constraints are found in the educational system in general, and higher education in particular, which like many organizational systems, tends to resist change. Kerr views colleges and universities in a conservative light:

> About eighty-five institutions in the Western world established by 1500 still exist in recognizable forms, with similar functions and with unbroken histories, including the Catholic church the Parliaments of

the Isle of Man, of Iceland, and of Great Britain, several Swiss cantons, and seventy universities. Kings that rule, feudal lords with vassals, and guilds with monopolies are all gone. These seventy universities, however, are still in the same locations with some of the same buildings, with professors and students doing much the same things, and with governance carried on in much the same ways. (Kerr 1982: 26)

Change in educational institutions has proven to be extremely slow; however, as the market demands change, the educational system will have to adapt to keep up. According to Schneider:

> Even though the U.S. spends more of its gross domestic product on higher education than do other countries, and contains many of the world's best universities, the country's performance on measures of postsecondary attainment for its citizens, particularly young ones, is declining compared to other countries. Graduation rates provide further proof that American higher education as a whole is failing to live up to its reputation as the world's best. (Schneider 3 November 2008)

There is a lack of educational training within the film discipline as well. For one to produce meaningful work, one must experience a meaningful event, or at the very least, be exposed to one through education. Many Hollywood films are innovative, but none of them has confronted society as a complex whole (and perhaps, it is asking too much from cinema), and films could do more to deal with pertinent issues. Events such as 9/11 and the 2003 Iraq war that was justified by lies have not gone entirely unnoticed by the industry, but in relation to their impact on the world, the response from the film community has been tepid.

Nonetheless, it is not Hollywood who has failed to educate learners because this is not their main role, it is the educational institutions that have failed their learners. Hollywood promotes entertainment. They have never claimed to educate although it seems they are well suited to do so. Further, a poor education and educational system will only produce learners who will eventually produce films that can only touch the surface of mankind's existence. On the flip side, films have become more visually engaging via technology and plot innovation, and it is time for higher education to change its perspective, not only in film studies, but in philosophy. Atkinson states, 'It's time for a foundation or wealthy individual to endow an entirely new college founded on teaching 21st century skills, not 20th century subjects' (Atkinson 11 March 2011).

Once higher education understands the benefits of merging entertainment and education, a new form of addiction may spring up – and it could very well be a learning addiction.

3.2 The history of educational media

According to Egenfeldt-Nielsen (2010), educational media were created at school museums in New York beginning in 1890, and in the 1910s, instructional films began being used in schools. During the 1930s, however, following the Depression, the market took a downward swing. McClusky (quoted in Saettler 1968) believes this was due to the 'widespread skepticism against combining entertainment, commercial interests and education' (p. 27). According to Egenfeldt-Nielsen (2010), there was a general feeling among both educators and educational institutions that using film in the classroom was a low-level way of teaching. He believed this was due to both the lack of focus in the instructional films being produced and to the negative perception educators had (and have) of entertainment media in general. According to Gauntlett (1995), academics believe that television oversimplifies, desensitizes, and generates passivity.

Egenfeldt-Nielsen (2010), however, did not think it was the educational content itself that was problematic; he argued that it was the 'sales methods and propaganda used by proponents of instructional films [that] alienated educators and eroded the confidence in the instructional film'. He contends that this was in addition to 'regular technical problems', copyright issues and confusion regarding restrictions of use along with a '"saturated market" [because] a lot of universities, school museums and companies engaged in both distribution and production of subsidized instructional films directly or indirectly with government funding'. There was also a difference between 'commercial interests, directors of movies and the subject experts who were consultants on the production' (p. 28). McClusky (quoted in Saettler 1968) recommended that there be an independent market of developers, with a strong committee that could provide advice and validate the product, but as Saettler (1968) notes this progression did not happen.

In the new edutainment market, the creation of content should be a commercial venture, independent from government funding. The independent edutainment market could position itself to include a committee of entertainment professionals and academics, similar to the major Motion Picture Association of America (MPAA), but instead of rating movies, it would rate and approve learning content. Copyright issues remain a concern, which must be addressed whether edutainment evolves or not, because Internet users are increasingly interacting with intellectual property.

The University of Iowa in 1933 was the first educational institution to deliver educational television; however, the programs were ineffective (Egenfeldt-Nielsen 2010). In 1967, legislation was enacted that required broadcasters to broadcast educational content for young audiences (Calvert 1999; Federal Communications Commission 2003). However, there was little success until 1969, when *Sesame Street* aired for the first time. It was considered a pioneering show due to its urban setting and racially diverse cast (Public Broadcasting Service n.d.). According to Calvert (1999), some of the early challenges in educational television had to do with the differences in viewers' ages and knowledge levels, as well as the fact that programs were live, which led to the inability to build on previous ones. In the 1980s, educational content in the United States almost died out because of new legislation; however, it reemerged with the advent of newer legislation in the mid-1990s. Since then, channels such as the Discovery Channel, the History Channel, and Nickelodeon have emerged and become successful (Calvert 1999; Miller 2002).

Van Riper (2011) contends that Walt Disney's fascination with fantasy and his interest in reality led to the production of films meant to entertain as well as educate. In 1948, Walt Disney coined the term *edutainment* to describe such productions. However, it was Bob Heyman who, while producing documentaries for the National Geographic Society around 1973, popularzied the term (New World Encyclopedia n.d.). According to Smoodin (1993), Disney films ranged from 'shorts' that were eight minutes long to 'featurettes' of different lengths to fully developed feature length films. Disney Studios' films included 'traditional live-action documentaries; dramatization of historical events; animated illustrations of historical, scientific, and political concepts; and complex hybrids of animations, staged dramatization, and local footage' (Van Riper 2011: 2). Disney created content for diverse audiences. The company produced a large volume of films with edutainment content and then recycled and repackaged that content, which gave the company a 'ubiquitous presence in postwar American popular culture' (Van Riper 2011). Disney's *True-Life Adventures* nature documentaries were initially released in theaters, and then aired on Disney's Sunday-night television show; clips were used in the production of *Nature's Better Built Homes* (1969), and finally, the series was released to schools. The factual content found in Disney's edutainment films added significant value; it was 'part of the lessons the films are designed to impart' (Cousins 1950: 20).

According to Van Riper (2011), Walt Disney's term *edutainment* described the kind of content he wanted to produce, which was 'information-rich, yet lively and engaging' (p. 4). The Disney library contains films that blur the line even further, such as the animated feature *Donald in Mathmagic Land* (1959), which used a 'fictitious character's journey through a patently imaginary world to teach mathematical concepts' (Van Riper 2011: 4). Moreover, as Riper informs, Walt believed that a cartoon was an ideal medium to create interest and teach (ibid.: 114). Walt Disney was both an educator and entertainer, and he produced a plethora of edutainment content covering issues pertaining to war and propaganda, science, technology, mathematics, health education, nature, and American history.

Although edutainment has a long history, it has yet to be fully adopted as pedagogy or even a learning tool, and this is due to many factors. One could argue that some teachers do not have the know-how to integrate media with learning, or that they are not proactive enough to aggregate edutainment content to use in their modules. They may still consider edutainment inferior. However, the environment is changing, and because of the combination of educational technology, media-rich environments, transmedia producers, as well as the next generation of learners, edutainment is finding solid ground. Today, learners are skilled at multiplatform navigation, and following their favorite stories across the mediasphere is second nature to them. It is predicted that higher-education institutions will form more partnerships and collaborations with the entertainment industry; therefore, educational and commercial interests will be intertwined into the fabric of academia (Glenn 2008: 4). Combining entertainment, education, and commercial interests failed in the past; however, as they say, timing is everything, and the time now is ideal for merging these interests. The entertainment industry is already creating cross-platform stories, creating a strong foundation for moving into the educational market. Moreover, technological inefficiency is a thing of the past. Massy and Zemsky (1995) predict that technology will open up the education market to entrepreneurs, who will meet the needs of learners by adopting the advances that higher education institutions have avoided. At the moment, higher education has both the students and the product. The challenge for institutions is to use this advantage by incorporating technology to reach out to learners and prospective learners in new ways. Today, the entertainment industry is well positioned to branch out into the educational market. Ironically, Walt had no Internet, but today the Walt Disney Corporation does.

3.3   Media and information literacy

Traditionally, literacy has focused on learning to read and write; today, there is a different kind of literacy known as *media literacy*. Although there is at present no single agreed-upon definition of media literacy, fundamentally, it means the creation and understanding of communication. A 'media-literate' person is one who does not take media messages at face value. Media-literate individuals are comfortable using the Internet, mobile phones, and program guides, and they also use technology to create their own video or audio content. This type of literacy means that they have the skills to stay connected in a media-penetrated culture which encourages self-expression. Media literacy empowers citizens in a democracy, and it is now considered a 21st-century approach to education. The website of the Center of Media Literacy Organization states: 'Media literacy provides a framework to access, analyze, evaluate and create messages in a variety of forms – from print to video to the Internet' (n.d.). Media literacy advances thought through active engagement versus passive use, and it probes even further by analyzing the media, their messages, and their strategies. Zettl provides a definition of media literacy:

> Media literacy is concerned with helping students develop an informal and critical understanding of the nature of mass media, the techniques used by them, and the impact of these techniques. More specifically, it is education that aims to increase students' understanding and enjoyment of how the media work, how they produce meaning, how they are organized, and how they construct reality. Media literacy also aims to provide students with the ability to create media products. (Zettl 1998: 90)

How various media produce meaning and construct reality is a subject for a book of its own; however, their ability to do just that makes it imperative to study the topic. Christ and Potter (1998) believe that for those who work in higher education, defining media literacy requires teachers to think pensively about what and how they teach. Aufderheide (1997) believes the main underlying framework for all media curricula includes five basic perceptions: 'media are constructed, and construct reality; media have commercial implications; media have ideological and political implications; form and content are related in each medium, each of which has a unique aesthetic, codes and conventions; receivers negotiate meaning in media' (p. 80).

The Internet has given young people access to more forms of media than any other generation before has had; however, these young people may not possess the skills necessary to analyze and evaluate the information they are getting. The idea is help them to adapt media constructively, and to become active and effective media-literate users. On the Reading Online Organization website, Freebody and Luke describe their multiliteracy model:

> To say that literacy is a social practice is also to say that it is constrained, mediated, and shaped by relations of power – relations that may be asymmetrical, unequal, and ideological…. It was our position that determining how to teach literacy could not be simply 'scientific,' but rather had to involve a moral, political, and cultural decision about the kind of literate practices needed to enhance both people's agency over their trajectories and communities' intellectual, cultural, and semiotic resources in multimediated economies. Literacy education, then, is ultimately about the kind of literate society and literate citizens or subjects that could and should be constructed. (Freebody and Luke 1999)

Freebody and Luke are accurate in their observation that media literacy is a social practice that involves inequalities of power; however, the Internet is probably the first medium that has the ability to talk back.

According to Jenkins et al., new media literacy skills are needed in the new media culture and these are *simulation* – the ability to interpret and assemble dynamic models of real-world practice; *appropriation* – the ability to experience and remix media content; *distributed cognition* – the ability to interact with tools that expand intellectual capacities; *transmedia navigation* – the ability to follow stories and information across multiple modalities; and finally, *collective intelligence* – the ability to pool knowledge and evaluate it with others toward a common goal (Jenkins et al., 19 October 2006). Jenkins (2006) also believes fostering social skills and cultural competencies requires a more systemic approach to media education, which is an important aspect of learning online.

Scholars have come to agree that a media-literate person is one who has acquired a number of skills, such as understanding the decision-making processes of media enterprise and the motivations behind media production. However, not all media-literate people are at the same level. The more media-literate a person is, the greater his or her ability to decode complex messages. Potter (1998) believes that a person who attains high media literacy is able to sort through all the choices of meaning, and choose the one that is most significant from different perspectives – emotional, cognitive, oral, and aesthetic. Likewise, Bunckingham (1993) contends that people with high media literacy are able to appreciate television rhetoric, irony, and satire; they understand the television genre and are skeptical of media-offered interpretations. In contrast, people with low media literacy are in a 'mindless state' while viewing and do not actively process messages (Potter 1998). However they can follow narratives, understand editing techniques, and television grammar (Buckingham 1993). Also, media-literate people can create their own digital stories and upload them onto the Internet.

Hinchey (2003) believes media literacy will become an element in education whether we like it or not; however, she contends that 'internationally as well as nationally, extensive coalitions for years have been defending, endorsing and promoting media literacy as essential, yet it remains off the radar screen of many educators, including administrators, who can play a crucial role in enabling or thwarting curricular activities' (p. 269). As media saturation increases, people will increasingly need to make sense of it critically. And conceptualizing media literacy, narrative, and technology will enhance e-learning environments.

3.4 Learning through play

In the United States, entertainment is separate from education, and work is separate from play. Ironically, the computer is the first medium that allows the user to do both: work and play, because it allows the convergence of two entities. According to Med (2010), a good example of combining work and play in an educational environment comes from the University of Alberta, where medical students made a remix of Justin Timberlake's hit song 'Sexy Back'. They called it 'Diagnosis Wenckebach' and uploaded it onto YouTube (Med 2010 20 March 2007). A 'wenckebach' is a cardiac arrhythmia, and the students had to thoroughly understand it to create a video around it.

Although this form of learning through play is unusual for Americans, it is not unusual for the Japanese. Lessig states that Japanese culture encourages the remixing of material from a young age. He quotes cultural anthropologist Mimi Ito from a phone interview (24 January 2007):

> Japanese media have really been at the forefront of pushing recombinant and user-driven content starting with very young children. If you consider things like *Pokèmon* and *Yu-Gi-Oh!* as examples of these kinds of more fannish forms of media engagement, the base of it is very broad in Japan, probably much broader than in the U.S. Something like *Pokèmon* or *Yu-Gi-Oh!* reached a saturation point of nearly 100 percent within kids' cultures in Japan. (quoted in Lessig 2008: 78)

Essentially, this practice of active engagement through play is supported by Japanese society. Nevertheless, as Ito states, 'kids are not playing Pokèmon for the explicit goal of learning skills or gaining knowledge'. But the kids who play *Pokèmon* are gaining various skills and literacy. Ito cites new research which is showing that 'complex language skills and visual literacy' are gained through 'complex gaming environments' like *Yu-Gi-Oh* and *Pokèmon*, and this is a by-product of engagement (Ito 27 February 2010).

Once kids are engaged with media content there are opportunities to create learning environments that go beyond being just by-products of social engagement. Entertainment content can be designed with learning objectives in mind, and still be made to be engaging. And this goes for adult computer-oriented games as well. Ito believes:

> Today's networked media offers an unprecedented opportunity to support learning that is highly personalized and learner-centered, driven by passionate interest and engagement. But very few kids, parents, and educators are taking advantage of this opportunity. The reason for this is that too often we separate the worlds of kids and adults, play and education. (ibid.)

If we accept the notion that convergence affects social and cultural processes (Jenkins 2006), then it is only logical that these environments (play and education) will find a way to merge and become more fluid. It should also be mentioned that these are mediated story worlds that Ito is referencing. Thus, stories have the ability to engage and educate, whether they are games or moving images, but they need to be understood as part of an educational strategy that involves learner-centered curriculums.

In learner-centered curriculums teachers are more aware of how students actually learn, or at least, prefer to learn. According to Bransford et al.,

> learner-centered environments include teachers who are aware that learners construct their own meanings, beginning with the beliefs, understandings, and cultural practices they bring to the classroom. If teaching is conceived as constructing a bridge between the subject matter and the student, learner-centered teachers keep a constant eye on both ends of the bridge. (2000: 136)

A story-centered curriculum keeps one eye on the narrative experience and the other on the learning objective. An author can build learning layers into the story worlds. As a result, students can dig deeper into the narrative and will therefore gain more knowledge. In these new learning environments, the user discovers more of the story world and shares this knowledge with others. According to Lessig (2008), the difference between the US and Japanese environments is evident: 'American kids have it different. The focus is not: Here's something, do something with it. The focus instead is: Here's something, buy it' (p. 79). The Internet, however, is facilitating a new interaction that represents a more *Pokèmon*-like environment for everyone.

The scientific community has shown that human beings have a biological desire to play. Brown (2009) believes that 'we are designed to find fulfillment and creative growth through play' (p. 13). He is mainly referring to play in the real world that engages the five senses. But Brown also believes that video games offer some of the benefits of play, and that films do have something to teach. Through entertainment interactions people can experience events that they have never encountered and learn something from them. And they can try new things which do not threaten physical or emotional well-being: 'By living through Rick and Ilsa's doomed romance in Casablanca, we learn a little bit about love and how to live our lives with honor and a sense of irony when love is lost' (pp. 34–35).

Furthermore, people who sit in movie theaters suspend disbelief and are transported to another world – this is also a form of play. When film has engaged moviegoers, they leave the theater with new insights about their own lives.

According to Prensky (2001), 'fun "create(s) relaxation and motivation" and "relaxation enables a learner to take things in more easily, and motivation enables them to put forth effort without resentment"' (p. 11). These are qualities that learning environments should strive for because there is nothing wrong with a little relaxation, motivation, and even enjoyment. It is important to note that this book does not encourage play for the sake of having fun. In fact, many computer games, for example, are anything but fun – they are extremely difficult to master. And not all stories are pleasant. Nevertheless, fun does not have to be excluded from learning, and neither does entertainment from education. Convergence is shedding light on the importance of play in education. The next section discusses pedagogical tools for a new pedagogic strategy within multimedia and multimodal online learning environments.

3.5 Multimedia and multimodal theory of learning

In a world in which communication is both digital and cross-cultural, academics are sensing the inadequacy of texts that use primarily one semiotic channel to express meaning. Moreover, multimodality and multimediation theories have encouraged scholars to view modes of representation and communication and to determine their meaning-making potential. As technology progresses, students will become experienced in reading and consuming multimodal texts. However, throughout history, there have always been some who express concerns about new communication 'technologies'. During the 16th century, for example, the Church viewed the printing press as a harmful communication advancement which could not be trusted (Lea 1902). And 'when books appeared, many faculty members feared these dangerous new teaching machines, which clearly ceded much of the instructor's knowledge and power to the student' (Landow 2006: 313). Today, Internet technology is embraced by faculty members, and the focus has turned to how semiotic resources (language, image, word, and sound) combine to produce textual meanings.

As Kress and Van Leeuwen (2001) put it, 'Multimodality and multimediality are not quite the same thing' (p. 67). They contend that *medium* refers to the channel of communication, the physical materials (airwaves, print, etc.) used to convey information; *mode* refers to semiotic resources, such as speech, written texts, and video. According to Page (2010), a mode can be defined as 'a system of choices... What might count as a mode is an open-ended set, ranging across a number of systems including but not limited to language, image, color, typography, music, voice quality, dress, gesture, spatial resources, perfume, and cuisine' (p. 6). A mode is perceived by one of the three human perception channels: *visual, auditive*, and *touch*. When more than two modalities are involved, the term *multimodality* is used to convey communication content. Therefore, meaning can be derived from the different modes and media combined. Pool was the first to discuss convergence, and in his book *The Technologies of Freedom*, he explored the concept of convergence as it relates to media and modes:

A process called the 'convergence of modes' is blurring the lines between media, even between point-to-point communications, such as the post, telephone and telegraph, and mass communications, such as the press, radio, and television. A single physical means – be it wires, cables or airways – many carry services that in the past were provided in separate ways. Conversely, a service that was provided in the past by any one medium – be it broadcasting, the press, or telephony – can now be provided in several different physical ways. So the one-to-one relationship that used to exist between a medium and its use is eroding. (Pool 1983: 23)

The digital revolution is the force behind the convergence of modes; it has affected communication and made it electronic. However, social features of communication remain. Kress and Van Leeuwen (2001) argue that 'communication never just "communicates", "represents", and "expresses", it also always, and at the same time, affects us. The two cannot be separated. Even when communication seeks to do the opposite, the very fact of negating materiality affects us – by failing to engage us affectively' (p. 71). Further, each person tends to respond to a preferred sensory modality, and this may be communicated via different speech patterns. Iglesias (2005) contends that humans hold a predominant representational system which can show up in speech. He believes the three most common are auditory, visual, and kinaes-thetic, and provides examples: An auditory person tends to use words like 'listen', 'talk to you later', and 'I've heard good things about you'. A visual person uses words like 'good to see you', 'let me look at it', and 'see you later'. A kinaesthetic person will say things like 'I'll be in touch', 'hold on', and 'I've got a good feeling about this'. Olfactory people use phrases like 'smells fishy to me', while gustatory people, who are sensi-tive to taste, will say 'I'm so close, I can taste it' (p. 204).

Multimodality insists on the use of multiple resources in communica-tion, and different media technology offer different semiotic resources that educational designers can employ. Communication design involves selecting and coordinating communication channels. From a conver-gence viewpoint, content, semiotic resources, and communicative intentions are connected. Engebretsen argues:

> In the design, discursive content, semiotic resources and communica-tive intentions are joined together. But the interaction between these parts cannot be understood as a successive process, where one first defines content and thereafter selects a suitable form. Different semi-otic modalities point towards different types of discursive content; different types of 'knowledge'. (2010: 3)

Therefore, knowledge can be gained from one thing or from a combina-tion of things, or even through several media or one dominant medium. Kress attends to the changes in the contemporary communicational landscape:

> It is no longer possible to think about literacy in isolation from the vast array of social, technological and economic factors. Two distinct yet related factors deserve to be particularly highlighted. These are,

on the one hand, the broad move from the now centuries-long dominance of writing to the new dominance of the image and, on the
other hand, the move from the dominance of the medium of the
book to the dominance of the medium of the screen. (Kress 2003: 1)

The significance of images was also pointed out by the theorists McLuhan
(1964), Debord (1995), Benjamin (1989), Baudrillard (2001), and Kress.
Kress (2003), who believes that 'the effects of the move to the screen as
the major medium of communication will produce far-reaching shifts
in relation of power, and not just in the sphere of communication. The
world told is a different world from the *world shown*' (author's italics,
p. 1). He elaborates:

> The two modes of writing and of image are each governed by distinct
> logics, and have distinctly different affordances. The organization
> of writing – still leaning on the logics of speech is governed by the
> logic of time, and by the logic of sequence of its elements in time, in
> temporally governed arrangements. The organization of the image,
> by contrast, is governed by the logic of space, and by the logic of
> simultaneity of its visual/depicted elements in spatially organised
> arrangements. (Kress 2003: 2)

The Internet *centers* all channels and modes, and these different communication and technological tools offer different affordances. Conole and
Dyke (2004) believe a clear understanding of these affordances is needed
if they are to be effectively used in education. Thus, any creative use of
media and technology must consider the aspect of affordance, singularly
as well as in combination. In all likelihood, *screen education*, a term that
I would like to use to refer to e-education/e-learning when it has fully
evolved to include a TmSE approach, will be quite different from traditional forms of education. In the future, the affordance of the screen
will align more closely with students' needs. Experienced researchers,
including Zull, Iglesias, and Shank, have realized that efficiency in
learning is determined by the alignment of students' interests as well as
the level of modality and interactivity associated with the module.

According to research from Cisco Systems (2008) 'students engaged in
learning that incorporates multimodal designs, on average, outperform
students who learn using traditional approaches with single modes'
(p. 13). The study separated effects related to basic skills from those
related to higher-order skills; however, these skills were not defined.
Basic skills are understood by educators to be the ability to learn and

recall facts; higher-order skills include critical thinking, analysis, and problem-solving. The average scores on the basic skills assessments increased 21% when students were engaged in non-interactive, multi-modal learning (which included the use of text with visuals, text with audio, and watching and listening to lectures or animation that effectively used visuals) in comparison to traditional, single-mode learning. When the situation shifted to interactive, multimedia learning, such as engagement in simulations, modeling, and real-world experiences found in collaborative groups, results were not quite as high, with an average gain of 9% (Cisco Systems Inc. 2008: 13). The Cisco Systems study does not clarify whether the research was conducted for an online or traditional learning environment, or a combination of both. It is, therefore, difficult to determine the exact implications for e-learning; still, this research does show some of the benefits of a multimodal approach to learning.

Mayer (2001/2009) and Mayer and Moreno (2003) have identified principles related to multimedia and modality. I single out three for discussion: (1) the *multimedia principle*, the idea that using words and pictures together improves retention; (2) the *modality principle*, which says that learning takes place when there is a combination of narration and animation than from animation and on-screen text; and (3) the *redundancy principle*, which is the notion that 'students learn better when information is not represented in more than one modality – redundancy interferes with learning' (cited in Cisco Systems Inc. 2008: 12–13). According to the redundancy principle, presenting words in two sense modalities, such as on-screen text that is identical to narration, overloads the visual channel. Correlating narration with animation, however (the multimedia principle), does not create visual overload because words go through the auditory channel. The basic idea is not to overload either the visual or auditory channel. The Internet is one channel with many modes of communication. According to the current redundancy principle, the Internet would be considered highly redundant and may negatively impact learning. Today, the principles outlined above need to consider both multimodal and multimedia because the Internet environment merges modes and media in a single platform. Further evaluation of Internet text, hypertextual arrangements, and the structure of websites is needed. As technologies evolve, they introduce nuances that cannot be overlooked and continued research is needed to determine best practices. Nonetheless, the use of multimedia and multimodal designs to enhance learning is showing positive signs.

The way information is presented is important and may greatly affect long-term memory. A screenplay may have pictorial superiority over a textbook because of its picture-inducing capability. According to Medina (2008), 'when it comes to memory, researchers have known for more than 100 years that pictures and text follow very different rules. Put simply, the more visual the input becomes, the more likely it is to be recognized – and recalled. The phenomenon is so omnipresent it has been given its own name: the pictorial superiority effect, or PSE' (p. 233). Medina contends that when people read, they try to visualize the text. This is the reason for using a screenplay-to-understanding as the basis of the empirical research for this book. It is telling that the Irish playwright George Bernard Shaw once said that 'words are only postage stamps delivering the object for you to unwrap'. As Medina (2008) explains further, 'Text and oral presentations are not just less efficient than pictures for retaining certain types of information; they are way less efficient. If information is presented orally, people remember about 10%, tested 72 hours after exposure. That figures goes up to 65% if you add a picture' (p. 234). The brain, says Medina, sees words on a page as lots of miniature pictures. He contends that 'data clearly show that a word is unreadable unless the brain can separately identify simple features in the letters. Instead of words, we see complex little art-museum masterpieces, with hundreds of features embedded in hundreds of letters' (2008: 234). This has implications for understanding writing efficiency: 'Reading creates a bottleneck. My text chokes you, not because my text is not enough like pictures but because my text is too much like pictures. To our cortex, unnervingly, there is no such thing as words' (ibid.).

Medina's arguments support the idea of using less text in educational environments, and less-dense text is characteristic of the screenplay form. It was for this reason students were asked to read a hypertext screenplay in the e-module case study rather than a textbook. According to Kress (2003) and Medina (2008), writing is image and images are full of meaning. Kress (2003) believes that 'writing will more and more become organized and shaped by the logic of the image-space of the screen' (p. 20). There is a preference for image in communication, which is intensified by new media. The preference of image is also moving into education and this can be highlighted by websites, user-generated video, and the contemporary textbook. According to Kress:

New textbooks are not 'books' in the older sense: carefully structured, coherent expositions of knowledge, knowledge to engage with

reflectively and to 'absorb'. The new 'books' are often collections of work-sheets; no careful development of complex coherent structure here, and no deliberate carefully reflective engagement with these pages. These are books to work with, to do things with, to act with and often to act on. ...

Writing is undergoing changes of a profound kind: in grammar and syntax, particularly at the level of the sentence, and at the level of the text/message. Writing now plays one part in communicational ensembles, and no longer *the* part. Where before all information was conveyed in writing, now there is a decision to be made: which information, for this audience, is best conveyed in image and which in writing? (2003: 21)

It seems that the alphabet is being taken over by the digibit, making literacy without images unthinkable. Kress (2003) contends, 'The former constellation of *medium of book* and *mode of writing* is giving way, and in many domains has already given way, to the new constellation of *medium of screen* and *mode of image*' (p. 9). Learning may no longer be driven by language alone. The new age of multimedia is ushering in an environment based on visual communication. While the field is still evolving, the researchers mentioned above have shown that retention can be accomplished through visual communication, and that visual clues activate more parts of the brain than traditional text-based learning. The findings support TmSE as it relates to moving image extensions and perhaps even screenplays.

In the context of multimodal education, I like to refer to mode as does Page (2010: 6) as 'a system of choices used to communicate meaning in a learning context'. Kress et al. (2001) contend that 'how humans make meanings, represent and respond to these meanings, and rework the meanings of others...is perhaps clearest in its effects on our conceptions of learning, and above all, on what we might best be able to use as evidence for documenting the processes of learning' (p. 9). Moreover, Page (2010) believes 'the stories that harness the rapid development of new technologies are part of this semiotic expansion, and in themselves are often characterized by multiple resources as they integrate words, image, sound, hyperlinks, and animation (for example, as seen on web-based homepages, or creatively exploited in digital fiction)' (p. 2). Multimodal theory regards semiotic resources as interest-based and the result of people's sociocultural learning and meaning-making.

Furthermore, multimodal representation is unique when it relates to the Internet since there is one core channel of communication, if you will, with many types of modes of communication within. This gives it more flexibility in terms of providing shared experiences as well as more meaningful acts of communication. Marshal McLuhan (1964) famously said that 'the medium is the message'; today, it may be more appropriate to say the 'meaning is the message', or the 'mode is the message'. We draw meaning from our experiences, and thus meaning is different for different people, just as a story impacts people differently. Educational convergence will give rise to a new ecology of learning based on customized and personalized programs and sociocultural practices. There are benefits to mediated learning environments, but the real challenge facing educators today is to establish collaborative learning environments, teaching practices, and curricula as well as to technology to fit pedagogy. The Internet is a place where learners can trans-engage with a diverse set of communicative digital modalities, and it adds new dimensions to multimodal learning that warrant continued research.

3.6 E-learning

E-learning has been defined in a number of different ways in the literature. It is referred to variously as electronic learning, web-based training, online learning, computer-based learning, or any learning supported by a computer and is connected to the Internet. In general, the term 'e-learning' is broadly used to describe learning experiences and content delivered or enabled by technologies (Ong et al. 2004). The Internet provides a platform for unlimited options for the delivery of modules, and it is also affecting how students learn.

Currently, online learning happens anytime and anywhere, and dialogue is open-ended. In other words, communication happens on a daily basis in the forums whereas in traditional education the dialogue ends when the in-class session concludes. In this scenario, students are required to wait until the next in-class session to have an open discussion with their peers and instructor. In face-to-face (f2f) teaching, the modes of communication are open, allowing for more meaning and emotion to be conveyed through various channels (expression, intonation, posture, etc.). In online communication text-based communication is one dominant; however, pictorial icons can be used as emotional cues. Additionally, f2f teaching uses synchronous communication, and contributions are more spontaneous. On the other hand, e-learning uses asynchronous communication, and the time and place of communication are decided on by the learner. This allows the learner to respond with more thought-through comments. In addition, learners must wait their turn in f2f communication, whereas in online environments this is not necessary. In an online environment the learning material is available 24/7, and the platform gives way to learning environments which facilitate the sharing of information outside the constraints of time and place. Asynchronous learning is constructivist, that is, it is student-centered and emphasizes collaboration and peer-to-peer interactions. Constructivists view 'learning [as] an active process of creating meaning from different experiences' (NDT Resource Center n.d.). In other words, students learn best by trying to make sense of something on their own with the instructor/tutor as a guide. In the e-journal *Journal of Technology Education*, Gokhale (1995) writes that in e-learning environments, 'the instructor's role is not to transmit information, but to serve as a facilitator for learning. This involves creating and managing meaningful learning experiences and stimulating students' thinking through real world problems'. In that respect, a tutor is like the person who stands in the wings while a play is in progress and feeds actors their forgotten lines. Educators must understand how e-learning changes the role of the teacher from 'instructor' to 'tutor', and of the learner/student from 'listener' to 'doer'.

Moreover, an emergent culture synthesized and materialized around the Internet provides several benefits to e-learning environments. It allows a connection between information, people, places, corporations, institutions, and even documents or works. Hypertext and hypermedia on the Internet can be classified by the ability to make connections with other 'documents or works'. Farkas (2004) explains the difference between hypertext and hypermedia. 'Hypertext' and 'hypermedia' refer to websites that employ hyperlinks to take users to other places within the document. Hyperlinks take the form of buttons, underlined words or phrases, and other 'hot' areas on the screen. 'Hypermedia' refers to the presentation of video, animation, and audio. Hypermedia is a form of penetrable media, and module assignments should be designed to benefit from the connectivity factor. Landow states:

> Whether it is true that readers retain less of the information they encounter while reading text on a screen than while reading a printed page, electronically linked text and printed text have different advantages. One should therefore prepare an initial assignment that provides the student with experience of its advantages – the advantages of connectivity. (2006: 286)

It is crucial that new forms of communication and connectivity be used holistically. Rather than having students write research papers, learners may be asked to create digital stories or even podcasts. Moreover, Landow (2006) argues that 'electronic linking shifts the boundaries between one text and another as well as between the author and the reader and between the teacher and the student' (p. 52). Hypertext interlinks a variety of types of material and encourages independent exploration. It allows the student to make connections and formulate inquiries, unlike in traditional education, where all the specific subject matter is contained in the module. Dillon and Jobst (2005) worry that learners may find the hypertext learning environment confusing because they cannot see the structure of the lesson; to alleviate this problem a graphic organizer, which is much like the table of contents of a textbook, can provide structure. Similarly, a storyboard, a series of illustrations that block out a visual sequencing of the narrative can be used. This is a technique often used by film directors before they begin to shoot the film.

A hypermedia environment converges multiple forms of media, information, and narrative with multiple forms of participation in completely new ways. However, like new technologies, they tend to be compared to the older forms and are therefore sometimes misunderstood. Landow argues:

> We often approach an innovation, particularly an innovative technology, in terms of an analogy or paradigm that at first seems appropriate but later turns out to block much of the power of the innovation. Thinking about two very different things only in terms of their points of convergence promotes the assumption that they are in fact more alike than they really are. Such assumptions bring much comfort, for they remove much that is most threatening about the new. (2006: 315)

It is natural to compare the new to the old because the old is our basis for understanding; however, convergence is not just a technological issue and cannot be viewed strictly by their point of convergence. Nonetheless, in contrast to cross-media, multimedia can be categorized as media that are found on a computer screen. The cross-media channels (TV, film, books, etc.), which are also found on a computer, may better be described as *Internet-enabled content* (IEC), which is a term introduced here. IEC enables multiple entry points and allows students to design their own reading engagement paths to suits their individual needs.

According to Schank, 'computers have the power to alter the very nature of education, to transform what is taught and how it is taught, but will not do so unless those in charge of the larger system of education see the need and the opportunity' (2001: 5–6).

He elaborates:

> When the ancient Jews wanted to educate the masses, they read to them every Saturday from the sacred scrolls. This made sense because most people couldn't read and there were very few scrolls. Today everyone can read and there are lots of scrolls. Why hasn't the method of instruction changed? Because we somehow have gotten it into our heads that the means of instruction available in 1500 BC was right. (ibid.: 6)

Ironically, digitized lecture modules are now available online, continuing the 'learning-by-telling' tradition. According to the Scholastic website, John Dewey (1859–1952), an American educational reformer, philosopher, and psychologist, coined the phrase 'learning-by-doing'. For Dewey it was important that education not teach dead facts, but rather integrate skills and knowledge into the learner's life. Dewey eloquently said, 'Education is not preparation for life: Education is life itself' (n.d.). Although philosophers, researchers, and educators beginning with Plato have known for a long time that learning-by-doing is what works, the approach has not been implemented on a large scale.

Holt elaborates:

> What we have mistakenly come to think of as 'bodies of knowledge' or 'fields of learning' or 'academic disciplines' or 'school subjects' are not nouns but *verbs*, not things that exist independently somewhere out there, but things that people *do*. No one can say, '*Here* is Biology, *here* Mathematics, here Philosophy.' No one can *point* to Physics, or show us Chemistry. In reality no dotted lines divide History from Geography or Physics from Chemistry, or Philosophy from Linguistics, and so on. (2004: 13)

For Holt, disciplines, subjects, and fields of knowledge are what people actually do. There is no dotted line dividing one domain from the other. As technology has progressed, the different media, such as print, radio, and television, have converged in one medium – the Internet – and moreover informal and formal learning environments are coming together to create all sorts of new learning experiences. According to Burnett:

> The disciplines that have been the bedrock of education must incorporate the lessons of the informal into their purview. For example, the study of language and composition should not take place outside

of the experience of popular culture. The study of the sciences cannot be divorced from ethical and philosophical issues. If we are to take the effort seriously, then the creation of new learning communities will bring with it a transformation of what we mean by disciplines. (2005: 3)

Burnett is describing the convergence of the informal and the formal, that is of popular culture and educational culture, science and ethics and philosophy, and this will undoubtedly change these disciplines as they are currently taught. Burnett further contends that 'the context for this change is not just the individual nature of history of one or the other discipline. Rather, the social and cultural conditions for the creation and communication of ideas, artifacts, knowledge and information have been completely altered' (ibid.).

Burnett understands the social and cultural conditions of convergence and the implications of change; however, a more holistic understanding of the implications is required. The evolution of educational convergence will in all likelihood emulate the evolution of media convergence, though at a much slower pace. As new media evolved, old media changed to adapt to it. As new forms of education evolve, traditional education will also have to adapt. Disciplines will be redefined and organizations will be restructured. Isolated fields of learning may become more process oriented and blend academic disciplines. Some things might be learned in the classroom setting, while others may be better learned elsewhere; either way, however, learning will be more practice oriented. Schank (2001) puts learning-by-doing into a story perspective.

3.6.1 Story-centered pedagogy in e-learning

In 2002, Schank and his team of educational-design innovators developed a story-based curriculum for Carnegie Mellon University's Silicon Valley Campus. They created a new kind of master's degree program, whose primary methodology was learning-by-doing. According to Schank, the program offered no classes and gave no examinations. Instead, the course work consisted of series of projects done by a team of students working under a mentor. In addition, the program could be delivered either face-to-face or online, and a website was used to help get the students started by offering background knowledge and assignments. The students were expected to produce the kind of deliverables that they would need to produce in the real world. This master's program was extremely successful, and students from the standard program that was offered at Carnegie Mellon main campus in Pittsburgh, could take courses remotely by teleconference. Based on its success, the Open University in Andorra and La Salle University in Barcelona have adapted the story-based curriculum approach for their MBA programs, offering students business experience via a story-based curriculum. The stories are designed to help students develop relevant business experience, based on what business people believe the key issues to be. There are seven modules in the MBA Story-Centered Curriculum used at La Salle. One of the modules is entitled 'Marketing: Launching an Internet Business', where students are asked to plan a new business online. The team writes and presents a business plan and marketing strategy, and then plans the operations (Schank n.d.).

It is well-known in academia that different pedagogical strategies need to be employed to reach students, hence the diverse sets of learning theories. Edutainment practice can help increase engagement in e-learning environments through storytelling as pedagogy. Schank argues for Story-Centered Curriculum; however, narratives have educational value in themselves. To understand its true potential in learning environments, we need to look at the notion of story-as-action. Zull argues:

> To the brain, movement is more than physical movement of parts of the body; it is also mental movement, or imagined progress...the brain's ability to imagine actions, orchestrated by the executive centers in the front cortex. Those imagined actions give us pleasure when, for example, we read a story. Our body isn't moving, but the story is. And, according to this theory, this is why the brain enjoys a story. It goes somewhere! (2002: 234)

Zull believes the pleasure in learning comes from learners' 'perception of progressing toward a goal' (ibid.). Structural anthropologist Claude Lévi-Strauss (1995) argues that people store memories as narratives. Based on this evidence, it seems clear that taking an innate approach to education via the story form will be beneficial.

That said, education, entertainment, and storytelling are converging in new ways and creating new forms for reaching students. This new 'educationsphere' will no doubt dominate higher education in the future, but at the moment, it is stirring up a lot of uncertainty among faculties as well as concerns over whether it creates authentic learning environments.

3.6.2 Faculty and constructivist-learning environments

Much like the unbundling of media content discussed in Chapter 2, the traditional duties of a college professor's job are being separated out as well. 'The unbundling of the faculty role is changing the very nature of the "faculty" position itself, causing many faculty to retool and receive training in how to integrate technology into their instruction, how to communicate with and mentor students online, etc.' (Howell et al. 2004: 35). According to Paulson (2002), universities are now dispersing tasks, assigning them to more than one person or to specialized teams of professionals. These positions are often filled by non-tenure-track staff or graduate and sometimes undergraduate assistants, freeing up tenured faculty to concentrate on research. In distance education, the instructor often acts as module manager (Roberson and Klotz 2002; Scagnoli 2001) and is still responsible for teaching, facilitating, grading, and problem-solving. Howell et al. (2004), and de Alva (2000) note that traditional faculty privileges, such as tenure, are being eliminated.

The future is in electronic education that merges education and entertainment and stimulates *browser-activity* learning, a term I have coined to mean activity-based learning that connects the learner to content on the Internet. Browser-activity learning has the potential to evolve constructivism (the theory that one constructs his own learning by making connections) in even more specialized and individualized directions. It is also true that designing for constructivist-learning spaces challenges instructional-designers because the content is often not prescriptive, and to a certain extent the learner determines the direction. The classical forms of instructional design are therefore considered easier to develop because they have fixed outcomes. Nevertheless, learning objectives should be set and metacognitively guided when incorporating technology such as the Internet in order to encourage specific learning outcomes.

Moreover, assessment criteria must be accurate since there is no face-to-face interaction with e-learners, which would allow for more information regarding the academic ability of the learner. Today, learners have the ability to construct their own knowledge, and teachers have the ability to measure performance differently. Landow argues:

> If the Web's greatest educational strength as well as its most characteristic feature is its connectivity, then tests and other evaluative exercises must measure the results of using that connectivity to develop the ability to make connections.... If one wishes to develop student skills in critical thinking, then one might have to make one's goal elegance of approach rather than quantitative answers. (2006: 287)

It is important to make the most of new technologies that cultivate new learning environments rather than to hold fast to old theories and practices. I propose a model of education for constructivist e-learning/ teaching in higher education which may be more authentic in nature. The model includes experience and activity-based learning (case studies, scenarios, simulations, internships, research projects, collabora- tions, and field trips, etc.), interest-based learning, learning-by-doing, learning by browser-activity, narrative-centered learning, self-directed and student-centered learning, multimodal representation, knowledge construction, collaboration, authentic and real-world tasks, reflective practice, and finally, next-stage module development. 'Next-stage module development' simply means that a module can be designed for a different purpose. For example, a communications professional may need to understand numbers, whereas a finance person would need to be able to do precise calculations. Therefore, the idea is to have two modules designed differently for the same finance module. Each of the two modules would have different learning objectives and outcomes; this has the potential to increase long-term retention because the design of each module would be specific to the learner's interests and what he or he needs to know. Researchers such as Zull (2002) and Shank (2011) are amongst those who believe that when students are interested in learning, then they will learn.

The continued development of niche education will allow students to be even more selective about their educational choices, in much the same way niche media content offers a wider variety of choices. The future holds new forms of learning which are socially constructed by one's self. Students will choose and build their own knowledge bases according to their interests, and will also determine the relevance and usefulness of the information they receive. Instructors will design modules that promote conversations between students and a moderator, and students will be collaborators in their own learning. Effective and meaningful learning will continue to take place; it will just be different. Next, we look at edutainment in electronic education while keeping in mind how learners retain information. Emotional engagement, motiva- tion, and retention are the central factors.

3.7   Emotional engagement, motivation, and retention in e-learning

A recent study conducted at the University of London brought to light an important fact: the human brain is hardwired with basic emotions. The study compared people from Britain to Nambia and found that 'basic emotions such as amusement, anger, fear and sadness are shared by all human beings' (Nauert 27 January 2010), and that although people communicate differently, humans share an extensive range of emotions, which are expressed through language, sounds, and facial expressions. Research spearheaded by Professor Scott from University College London reveals that 'sounds associated with emotions such as happiness, anger, fear, sadness, disgust and surprise are shared among different cultures' and that 'emotions form a set of basic, evolved functions that are shared by all humans' (Scott 26 January 2010). Not only are emotions the same, 'their vocalisations – are similar across all human cultures' (cited in Nauert 27 January 2010). Hence, 'it is evident that human emotion is universal, only experience is different' (Kalogeras 2013: 4). This is an important finding, and not surprising to me, as it relates to narrative instruction.

Jonathan Gottschall, an English professor and scholar at Washington and Jefferson College in Pennsylvania, is known informally as literary Darwinists. Gottschall asserts that the themes found in stories from around the world do not arise from each specific culture, but instead come from 'universal themes reflecting our common underlying biology' (quoted in Hsu 2008: 4–5). As journalist Hsu contends:

> Storytelling is one of the few human traits that are truly universal across culture and through all of known history. Anthropologists find evidence of folktales everywhere in ancient cultures, written in Sanskrit, Latin, Greek, Chinese, Egyptian and Sumerian. People in societies of all types weave narratives, from oral storytellers in hunter-gatherer tribes to the millions of writers churning out books, television shows and movies. And when a characteristic behavior shows up in so many different societies, researchers pay attention: its roots may tell us something about our evolutionary past. (2008: 2)

It is worthy to note that even Jesus told stories to emphasize his points, 'I will open my mouth in parable' (Psalm 78:2–4).

During the exploration of cognitive knowledge, it was discovered that emotional and cognitive development is connected. Developmental psychologists found that cognition and emotion became integrated as children grow (Smith 2003). Smith contends:

> Our minds must make decisions based on limited information, and we do so based on resemblances, probabilities, and temporary fits. We do not rely on a careful system of 'if-then' logic to categorize our world. Classical predicate logic provides a clarity of argument that still dominates much philosophical discussion (including discussion of emotion), but this mode of reasoning is a poor model for the complexities of many real-world processes. (2003: 16)

According to Smith (2003) cinema studies as well as cultural anthropology have neglected emotion as a topic of study because it is difficult to report on internal states of minds. Unlike memory or perceptual tasks, emotions cannot be simulated by computers. It was studies related to the effects of mood on memory that required cognitivist scientists to consider emotion as a research area. Just like other disciplines, film theory has neglected the emotional effects that films have on the audience; however, Smith (2003) states that mostly 'everyone agrees that eliciting emotions is a primary concern for most films ... [and that] ... cinema is a place to feel something'. Paradoxically, 'emotions are carefully packaged and sold, but they are rarely analyzed with much specificity by film scholars' (p. 4). Moreover, Smith states, 'the temporal unfolding of the filmic stimulus is crucial to the way it appeals to the emotional system, [and] producers share a set of narrational conventions that allows the story to be told and understood' (ibid., p. 11). Together, these things evoke feelings in the audience, but people may feel different things based on their experiences.

Although people have similar biological capacities to feel, there are also the politics of emotion to consider; that is to say, emotion is dependent on aspects of race, gender, class, psychology, and disability issues as well as the digital divide. The emotional experience brought on by digitality and that of multiplatform stories is not a universal one; there is inequality, but the very essence of multiple forms means that emotion is triggered in some form.

According to Smith (2003), individuals' emotional responses to specific situations depend on the way their experiences have shaped them. This should not take away from discussing emotional response with any particularity, nor should awareness of this variation in people's emotion network 'paralyze film criticism' (p. 12). The neuroscientist Marco Iacoboni has studied the workings of the brain. In his book *Mirroring People* (2009), he asks, 'Why do we give ourselves over to emotion during the carefully crafted, heartrending scenes in certain movies? Because mirror neurons in our brains re-create for us the distress we see on the screen. We have empathy for the fictional characters – we know how they're feeling – because we literally experience the same feelings ourselves' (p. 4). Iacoboni believes that this is attributed to motor neurons found in the human brain called 'mirror neurons', which fire when we act and when we watch others act. This indicates that the audience people connect on a visceral level. It seems that stories capture the big picture, and movies make sense to the brain.

Stories contain universal themes that resonate on an emotional level with all human beings. According to Iglesias:

> It has been said that emotions unite people and ideas divide. This is why the writer is advised to make the reader feel the theme instead of making him think up-front. An idea expressed only intellectually is just an essay. But when it's wrapped inside an emotion, it's more powerful and more memorable. Great storytelling is the creative, *emotional* demonstration of the truth you want to express. Never explain intellectually. Dramatize emotionally. (2005: 43)

What is more, says Smith, 'Film structures seek to increase the film's chances of evoking emotion by first creating a predisposition toward experiencing emotion: a mood' (2003: 42). Movies can affect us profoundly because they invite us to laugh, cry, and empathize with the characters, or in some cases, to even feel disgusted by them.

The study of human memory stretches back twenty centuries. Early attempts to understand memory can be found in such works as Aristotle's discourse *On the Soul* (Sachs 2001). During the course of his studies, Aristotle came to realize people memorized better when they were emotionally involved. Numerous studies have shown that students' attention span during lectures is about fifteen minutes (Wankat 2002); thereafter, attentiveness drops significantly, and the result is less retention of the material (Prince 2004). Conveying information with moving images, however, has been shown to be far better than lecturing by itself to maximize retention (Mayer 2001/2009; Mayer and Moreno 2003; Chatterjee 2010). To be au fait with the big picture, feature films can hold audiences' attention for up to three hours. This is typically the maximum length for an epic film, which should not be confused with the actual human capacity for engagement.

Fisher (1987) believes that all communication is a form of storytelling. His *Narrative Paradigm* asserts that people are essentially storytelling animals, and that reason, therefore, is best appealed to through stories. Moreover, we all have the same innate ability to determine the 'narrative rationality' (interpreted value) of the stories we hear. First, we examine the story's *narrative coherence*, that is, whether it holds together and makes sense. Then, we check *narrative fidelity*, to determine whether the story aligns with our own beliefs and experiences. Persuasion is achieved when there is narrative coherency, fidelity, and what Green and Brock (2000) describe as 'transportation'. Green and Brock's transportation theory refers to cognitive, emotional, and imagery engagement with story. They argue that attitudes and beliefs of viewers who are transported (absorbed) into a story are more likely to be influenced by, and possibly move towards, the attitudes and beliefs the story portrays. In theorizing edutainment, one must therefore consider the aspects of emotional engagement and persuasion that are embedded in stories.

Before we move forward it is important to revisit the terms 'entertainment' and 'engagement'. Entertainment is often defined as diversion: it is fun, light in nature, and engaging. Engagement is characterized as emotional involvement in or commitment to the story. Edutainment therefore can lead to engagement. According to Deutsch, 'learner engagement can be defined as the learner's act of investing effort and commitment to meaningful activities in anticipation of learning outcomes' (Deutsch 6 February 2009). However, when learners' anticipation of learning does not meet their expectations, this 'act of investing effort' can and often does lead to disengagement.

The importance of using narrative practice in e-learning therefore cannot be overstated. As important as the design of instructional material and learning activities are in facilitating and engaging learners; motivating learners to learn remains another key challenge. Motivation in e-learning can be understood in relation to the individual, institution, and content, not to mention rewards and recognition. Zull (2002) believes that rewards in the form of grades, gold stars, and scholarships, for example, are off the mark when it comes to engendering learning. He writes, 'We may get people to do things with extrinsic rewards, but we can't get them to learn' (p. 53). At the same time, he recognizes that 'extrinsic rewards can sustain a learner at times of pressure and difficulty' (p. 54). According to Keller (1999), 'to develop motivational systems, the educator must assume that motivation is influenced by others and is not purely a matter of self motivation' (p. 10). In online environments the lessons are designed and packaged, and everyone receives the same module. Students may have the option of picking a topic for a project-based exercise, but only within pre-set parameters. E-learning would benefit by the incorporation of learner-controlled options, which could increase 'motivational systems'. In asynchronous e-learning environments there is a lack of emotional connection, and this can result in a lack of motivation (Wu et al. 2002); yet if instructors can engage students emotionally and sustain their engagement throughout the learning experience, the outcomes could be tremendous (Chatterjee 2010). The challenge is that in e-learning there is no face-to-face communication between learner and instructor. Many studies have shown that learners often feel isolated. I believe the feelings of isolation can be overcome by engaging students. Keller (1999) argues that 'ultimately, each human being is responsible for his or her motivational condition, but it is abundantly clear that the environment can have a strong impact on both the direction and intensity of a person's motivation' (p. 29).

The learning environment is a very important factor. Like the researchers and scholars mentioned earlier, LeDoux (1996), Zull (2006), and Medina (2008) have pointed out that people learn better when they feel emotionally connected, whether with content or with other people. Zull believes that feelings always affect reasoning and memory and writes that 'much depends on the feelings of our learners' (2002: 86–87). In Figure 3.1, Zull provides a simplified adaption of Kolb's Experiential Learning Cycle, which begins with *experience*, advances to *reflection*, and then progresses to *developing abstractions* and *active testing* of these abstractions. At the base of the cone rests *emotion*.

Top left in the diagram shows the cortex and its four neocortex subdivisions, and indicates the extensive connections between the four neocortex and the limbic cortex, where emotion rests. The right side of the diagram depicts a cone shape, with the four elements of the learning cycle on the top resting on a shared base of emotion. LeDoux (1996) believes that emotions overpower cognition, that is, that people's emotions influence their thinking rather than the other way around. If it is truly emotion that guides learners, then why not give learners what

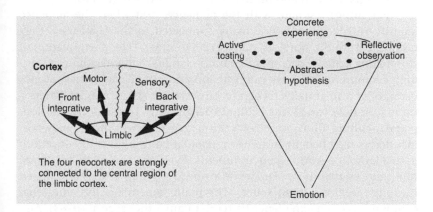

Figure 3.1 Learning cycle and the cone of emotion
Source: Copyright © 2002 Stylus Publishing, LLC.

they want, or better yet, what they actually need? Zull (2002) argues, 'Since living is about what we want, we are not surprised to find that learning will also be about what we want. We will always be motivated to learn things that fit into what we want and to resist those that don't' (p. 65). Based on this and other information I have gathered, I conclude that alliance with learners' interests and goals are the key things that seem to support learning and retention. Schank (2011) says it simply: 'When the stuff that is being taught does not relate to the inherent goals of the student, it will be forgotten' (p. 11). Perhaps, in films, the inherent goal of the character, along with the invitation to feel, are the two ingredients that should not be overlooked as they relate to merging entertainment with education.

Instructors who continue to use PowerPoint presentations, reading assignments, quizzes, and other teacher-centered tools will not engage students emotionally. Kopp (1982) discusses how to design the boredom out of instruction; he believes instructors should employ interesting graphics and animation to gain learners' attention, even if doing so introduces incongruity or even conflict into the lesson. It should be noted that conflict is essential to good stories. Learners' curiosity can be aroused using mystery, by trying to solve problems, and the use of techniques to stimulate a sense of inquiry in the learner, all of which are characteristics of compelling stories. Both visual and auditory learning styles can be stimulated by moving image in the form of entertainment, documentaries, and instructional videos. Davies (2000) has said that 'the hemispheres of the brain work together when emotions are stimulated, attention [is] focused and motivation [is] heightened' (p. 148).

When stories resonate with the audience, and when the audience identify with and feel emotionally connected to the characters, they become part of the story. As Wallace (2000) states, 'The phenomenon of storytelling actually becomes a common language that facilitates meaningful communication; we can hear and understand each other's stories because we can usually recognize ourselves in the stories of others – no matter how varied our cultural backgrounds' (p. 436). In addition, popular-culture films are already attractive to a worldwide audience; instructors may benefit from using popular-culture films in education, particularly in e-learning environments. Everyone can relate to a good film, and edutainment can serve to unite a group and foster shared learning. Medina (2008) states, 'The brain remembers the emotional components of an experience better than any other aspect' (p. 83). And those 'emotionally charged events persist much longer in our memories and are recalled with greater accuracy than neutral memories' (p. 80).

The bottom line is that 'emotions get our attention' (ibid.). It should be noted that brain experts (Medina 2008; Zull 2006) state that episodic memories are stories, and episodic memory is 'in charge of remembering "episodes" of past experience, complete with characters, plots and time stamps (like the 25th high school reunion)' (Medina 2008: 126). Therefore, it might be fruitful in education to make episodic lessons around narratives instead of strictly tasks.

Storytelling is an ancient tradition used in cultures of all kinds to inform and educate. Storytelling, an ancient technology, was replaced by modern technology and, as such, lost its importance as a tool for educating people. Humans across cultures enjoy stories which are associated with entertainment and not education. This defeats the purpose as stories have a genuine purpose and cognitive role that cannot be overlooked. Recently, neuroscientists have come to understand the importance of stories. Advances in research and cognitive science have revealed that our brains are hardwired for stories and so are our emotions. It has been said that storytelling is the language of the brain, because we think in narrative, and emotion is the language of the heart, because we feel sensation. It is my belief that these two universal human traits are key factors to innate learning. Neuroscientist Antonio Damasio contends the way to make "wisdom understandable, transmissible, persuasive, enforceable – in a word – [...] storytelling" (Damasio, 2012: 4). It is my belief that storytelling is the only word that can connect and engage all learners across cultures.

Chatterjee wrote a white paper on entertainment, engagement, and education in e-learning approaches in corporate training. Her survey was delivered to a small sample of e-learning developers across the world. The respondents were from the United States, United Kingdom, and India. Not surprisingly, the findings make a strong connection between the need for entertainment and engagement in education. Respondents were asked how important it is to entertain using instructional strategies, such as 'interactive scenarios, stories, and games etc.'; 67% said they thought it was 'important'; 26% said 'very important'; and 7% thought it was 'not important' (Chatterjee 2010: 4). When different age groups were asked who needed to be entertained, those aged 8 to18 years reported 85%; those aged 18 to 25 years reported 73%; the 25- to 35-year-olds reported 23%; and the 35- to 45-year-olds reported 12% (ibid.: 5–7). The findings reveal that people within all age groups need some form of entertainment while learning. Not surprisingly, the younger age groups indicated a greater need for entertainment because when today's younger learners enter higher education, they will have been exposed to entertainment as a key factor of their learner engage-ment. Furthermore, this study found that the top four programs used in e-learning are scenarios, games, questions, and stories (ibid., pp. 7–8). Also, when the respondents were asked why they thought entertain-ment was required in training they cited, 'it creates better retention of learning, it makes the learner happy and more receptive to learning, it helps learners get over learning fatigue, and it provides a context for learning' (ibid.: 8–9). Moreover, when respondents were asked what defines learner engagement in the context of e-learning they indicated that the relationship between engagement and retention level as being very strong (ibid.: 9). The website of the NDT Resource Center (n.d.) provides a list of learning methods, and the retention levels associated with each: lectures 5%, reading 10%, audiovisual 20%, demonstration 30%, discussion group 50%, practice-by-doing 75%, and teach others/immediate use of learning 90%. Although the audiovisual method was not defined, it is probably safe to say that it did not incorporate edutainment. Further, 'teach others' was rated the highest, and therefore creating a digital story that others can learn from can be considered a form of 'immediate use of learning'. In addition, it seems that retention improves from viewing other digital stories (audiovisual). Ironically, 'lecturing', which is still one of the most common practices in higher education, resulted in the least retention. And practice-by-doing also scores favorably for recollection. Plato wrote:

> According to my view, any one who would be good at anything must practice that thing from his youth upwards, both in sport and earnest, in its several branches: for example, he who is to be a good builder, should play at building children's houses; he who is to be a good husbandman, at tilling the ground; and those who have the care of their education should provide them when young with mimic tools. (Jowett trans. n.d. Laws, Plato; 360 BC)

Zull also believes learning takes place by doing, that it is action that generates learning (2002: 228). I discussed learning-by-doing previously as it relates to e-learning; creating narrative is also a form of doing. Stories are active and create meaning just as does activity-based learning. Moreover, when students create videos as part of their coursework, their motivation and engagement increase (Burn et al. 2001; Hoffenberg and Handler 2001; Kearney and Schuck 2004; Ryan 2002), and new opportu-nities to engage their creativity arise (Reid et al. 2002). Experience may be the better teacher, however an intriguing story is second best.

As the percentages cited in Chatterjee's white paper show, 'practice-by-doing' (also known as learning-by-doing or activity-based learning) cannot be overlooked and should be incorporated into learning environments. In addition, learning-by-doing and learning-by-story edutainment seem to be excellent ways to stimulate engagement, persuasion, motivation, and retention. To sum up, for effective learning to take place, content to which learners respond on an emotional level is vital to education.

3.7.1   E-learning and the net generation

The Net Gen are native speakers of digital language and are thus often referred to as Digital Natives. And for anyone who is compared to this generation they are referred to as 'Digital Immigrants'. Oblinger and Oblinger describe Digital Natives on the Educaus website: 'The Net Gen is more comfortable in image-rich environments than with text. Researchers report Net Gen students will refuse to read large amounts of text, whether it involves a long reading assignment or lengthy instructions'. Thus, writing will not only be 'shaped by the image-space of the screen' (Kress 2003: 20) but by the logic of the Net Gen learner. College students of today have been raised on moving images, and they have become immune to the static image of print. This makes them the most suited for fast-paced video narratives or movie scripts. Prensky argues:

> Digital Natives accustomed to the twitch-speed, multitasking, random-access, graphics-first, active, connected, fun, fantasy, quick-payoff world of their video games, MTV, and Internet are bored by most of today's education, well meaning as it may be. But worse, the many skills that new technologies have actually enhanced (e.g., parallel processing, graphics awareness, and random access) – which have profound implications for their learning – are almost totally ignored by educators. (2001: 5)

Interestingly enough, the findings make a strong connection between the need for entertainment and engagement in education. The outcome of the shortening of students' attention spans is their need to receive information quickly and concisely. This generation, brought up with computers seeks information on demand. They do not want to be burdened by having to memorize facts and figures. Instructors need to understand that Digital Natives like to multitask, function best when they are networked, and prefer graphics and hypertext, which provides random access, to text (Prensky 2001). Prensky elaborates that 'Children raised with the computer think differently from the rest of us: they develop hypertext minds, they leap around. It's as though their cognitive structures were parallel, not sequential' (p. 3). Nisbett (2009) highlights research by social psychologists that has shown that people who grow up in different cultures think differently. According to Zull, the brain adapts to its environment through plasticity. New research shows that the brain changes based on external stimulation and this affects the thought process, and this goes for the immediate, surrounding culture as well as the mediated one (Nisbett 2009; Zull 2002).

People have different learning styles and learning preferences. The shift in cognitive styles (away from focused attention to short attention spans) is distinguished by Hayles as 'deep attention' and 'hyper attention':

> Deep attention, the cognitive style traditionally associated with the humanities, is characterized by concentrating on a single object for long periods (say, a novel by Dickens), ignoring outside stimuli while so engaged, preferring a single information stream, and having a high tolerance for long focus times. Hyper attention, by contrast is characterized by switching focus rapidly between different tasks, preferring multiple information streams, seeking a high level of stimulation, and having a low tolerance for boredom. (17 January 2008)

According to Hayles there are advantages and disadvantages to each cognitive mode. Deep attention is beneficial for solving complex problems found in a single medium; however, its flexibility is limited. Hyper attention is beneficial for negotiating fast-changing environments that require multitasking skills. The disadvantage of hyper attention is impatience for long periods of time on a non-interactive object (ibid.). One can see the disjointedness of these two styles in higher education. Deep attention is the norm and is encouraged, whereas hyper attention is misunderstood and is not yet widely accepted. The hyper attentive style characterizes millennial students and those born after the millennials which poses a challenge to the current educational system. Many educators have a preferred cognitive mode, and their expectations and those of the millennial generation that has learned to think differently are mismatched.

Students who demonstrate hyper attention are not supported by educational institutions, which are dawdling in their efforts to amend their traditional practices. A major concern in higher education is the prevalence of 'Digital Immigrant instructors, who speak an outdated language (that of the pre-digital age)', and who must struggle to teach a population that speaks a new language:

> Today's students have not just changed *incrementally* from those of the past, nor simply changed their slang, clothes, body adornments, or styles, as has happened between generations previously. A really big *discontinuity* has taken place. One might even call it a 'singularity' – an event which changes things so fundamentally that there is absolutely no going back. This so-called 'singularity' is the arrival and rapid dissemination of digital technology in the last decades of the 20th century. (Prensky 2001: 1, 2)

The difference between the millennial and post-millennial generations and those preceding them is that the Net Gen identifies with media and technology. Today, learning with new media involves a social process of participation in a shared culture.

In 2005, the Kaiser Family Foundation reported that young people (aged 8 to 18) spent an average of nearly six hours and twenty-one minutes a day with media, and managed to cram more than eight-and-a-half hours of media content into that time by multitasking. Today, those numbers have increased. In 2009, among all 8- to18-year-olds, the average amount of time spent with each medium in a typical day was as follows: TV, 4 hours and 29 minutes; music/audio, 2 hours and 31 minutes; computers, 1 hour and 29 minutes; video games, 1 hour and 13 minutes; print, 38 minutes; and movies, 25 minutes. The total daily media exposure was ten hours and forty-five minutes, 29% of which was spent multitasking, leaving the total daily media use at seven hours and thirty-eight minutes. This is almost the amount of time that adults typically spend at work each day, except that young people use media seven days a week instead of five (Rideout et al. January 2010). Moreover, given the amount of time young people spend interacting with more than one medium simultaneously, today's youth cram in a total of ten hours and forty-five minutes worth of media content into those daily seven and a half hours. This is an increase of almost two-and-a-quarter hours of media exposure per day since the last study. The above numbers do not include cell phone use or time spent using the computer for homework (Rideout et al. January 2010). This study also shows that students multitask while doing homework, which results in reduced efficiency because simultaneous task completion is not as efficient as doing tasks in sequential order. One could argue that multi-tasking is not in all actuality possible because when a student switches tasks, and then returns to that task, they must continue sequentially from where they left off, which basically makes everything more time-consuming. Hayles believes the strong preference young people have for multitasking may be based on their need for stimulation, rather than the need to be time efficient, as was originally presumed (Hayles 17 January 2008). Moreover, all this multitasking does not allow much time to think. Prensky argues that the Net Gen has lost their ability to reflect:

> One key area that appears to have been affected is *reflection*. Reflection is what enables us, according to many theorists, to generalize, as we create 'mental models' from our experience. It is, in many ways, the *process* of 'learning from experience.' In our twitch-speed world, there is less and less time and opportunity for reflection, and this development concerns many people. (Prensky 2001: 5)

Nevertheless, there is some evidence that reflection is overrated:

> Classical methods and concepts of organizational learning are all variations of the same Kolb (1984) based learning cycle: learning based on reflecting on the experiences of the past. However, several currently significant leadership challenges cannot be successfully approached this way because the experience base of the team often is not relevant for the issue at hand. (Scharmer 2000: 2)

Here, Scharmer differs from Prensky (2001), who believes digital natives need the capacity for reflection. However, Scharmer's references to team collaboration in the business setting, not the education setting. All the same, what is indisputable is that the environment is constantly changing, and what worked in the past may not work as well in the present. According to Scharmer (2000), in the new economy traditional methods of learning are no longer effective because the previous experiences are no longer relevant to the new challenges found in the market-place. A challenge for education is to create more experience-based learning opportunities and to develop new ways to include some form of reflection into their practice. As already mentioned, stories are one way to put reflection back into learning because they engage learners, allowing them to think deeply about the topic.

3.8 Transliteracy through transmedia storytelling

Story is the heart of transmedia narrative and of transmedia edutainment. Transmedia Storytelling Edutainment is a critical-creative pedagogy that is derived from an overarching narrative concept that uses multiple platforms, formats, and story extensions, whether they be fiction or non-fiction, to educate. The stories can be both popular and non-popular; however, well-known stories developed between entertainment and academia which support the subject matter are often better in capturing the learner's interest.

Transmedia and transliteracy have an interesting relationship. As Thomas et al. argue, 'transliteracy is the ability to read, write and interact across a range of platforms, tools and media from signing and orality through handwriting, print, TV, radio and film, to digital social networks' (Thomas et al. 3 December 2007). Today, effective communication requires the ability to interact across multiple media and social platforms, such as wikis, blogs, tagging, social networking, virtual worlds, videos, and podcasts.

Narratives in higher education are evolving. At the core of the new pedagogical models is *learning through stories*. Bruner (1990) defines 'narrative' as 'a unique sequence of events, mental states, happenings involving human beings as characters or actors'. But these constituents do not, as it were, have a life or meaning of their own. Their meaning is given by their place in the overall configuration of the sequence as a whole, its plot or fibula' (p. 43). More importantly, digital narrative-learning environments are supported by researchers and educators.

Furthermore, constructivist-learning emphasizes an active role for learners as they acquire new concepts and create their own stories. As we saw earlier, learning is not just about knowledge; it is about engagement, motivation, and even social interactions. Learning through stories can take many forms, including narrative presentations, narratives constructed for scenario-based learning, narratives constructed for character-centered learning (learning through the character's story), or the emergent narratives found in virtual environments (which will be discussed later). According to Mott et al. (1999) narratives provide a way for people to organize and structure new knowledge and experiences: 'One can envision a narrative-centered curriculum that leverages the organizational features of our innate metacognitive apparatus for understanding and crafting stories. This insight has led educators to recognize the potential of contextualizing all learning within narrative-centered approaches' (p. 2). I argue that the educational story needs to be rewritten to include the narrative/visual mode, which can be original, adapted, and even remixed. Successful online instructors master tools and applications; however, online instructors must also blend science with art (the skill of teaching with the art of student engagement) in order to be highly effective.

Currently, there are two main pedagogical models based on story-telling: scenario-based curriculum (Bareiss and Singh 2006) and story-centered curriculum (Schank 2007), which was thoroughly discussed earlier. With these curricula, students are placed in either made-up scenarios or in a story world, where they take on certain roles and perform tasks in accordance with those narratives. Sharda's approach to using stories in e-learning is based on the story creation principles outlined by Robert McKee, author of the highly acclaimed book *Story* (1997) and creator of the story creation model movement-oriented design (MOD). Sharda believes, as all good storytellers do, that every story has a beginning, middle, and end. In his model, these are coded respectively (B), (M), and (E). The beginning of a story entices the user to learn more, the middle delivers the educational component, and the end concludes the unit. The last unit should link to the next story (Sharda 22 April 2010). A story, whether in film or education, that does not have a strong beginning, middle, and end will in many cases be ineffective.

Sharda notes that 'when creating e-learning content, often the authors overload it with useful information without linking these with an effective narrative; consequently the learner's interest wanes' (Sharda 22 April 2010). Similarly, Beard et al. (2007), De Fossard (2008), and Robin (2010) believe that well-known media act as hooks and introduce students to more complex, less well-known ideas. Quinn believes that the learning experience should be positive in the beginning, get negative when it is time to dig deeper into the material, and then get positive again at the end (3 April 2006). Ironically, this notion emulates the progression of a motion-picture storyline. In the beginning, there is equilibrium; that equilibrium is disrupted while the character overcomes the problem (negative), and then the character eventually reaches his/her goal, having learned on the journey (positive). This also emulates the three-act structure of screenplays (beginning, middle, and end). McKee (1997) makes the same point as Quinn, but from a narrative perspective. He believes that narrative must include a minimum of three stages: an inciting incident (which gets the story moving), progressive complications, and finally, resolution. Screenwriters are well aware of the fact that rising conflict and emotional engagement is what maintains the audience's interest in any story.

It is also important to explain the concept of emergent narrative here, which was introduced by Aylett in 1999. An emergent narrative is conceptualized in virtual reality, and, rather than follow a plot that has been worked out in advance, the story is shaped by the interaction between the user and the virtual environment. The author creates a story and the user touches the material to create different versions of the story. Further, in interactive computational narratives, students are immersed in captivating experiences. These narratives are designed to involve students in story-centric problem-solving activities across a range of disciplines:

> In mathematics, narrative could shift the focus from mechanical, algorithmic problem solving, e.g., arithmetic, to a more analytical approach to real-world problems that emphasizes analyses. In the sciences, an inquiry-based curriculum featuring dynamic narratives of the highly nonlinear process of scientific discovery could foster an in-depth understanding of how real-world science plays out. In social studies, biographies could shift the focus from rote memorization of facts and dates to an analysis of compelling historical figures, their motivations, and the geographical contexts in which they lived. (Mott et al. 1999: 2)

Emergent narratives can play a key role in e-learning environments because of their natural fit on the Internet. Mott and his colleagues believe narrative-centered learning environments provide the following activities: co-construction of knowledge through narrative exploration 'by considering how characters' intentions affect their actions in the evolving narrative, [and] by reflecting on narrative experiences and their underlying subject matter' (p. 2).

If interactive computational narratives can immerse students in captivating experiences, then introducing *seductive details* into those experiences can make them even more appealing. Garner et al. (1989) coined the term 'seductive details' to refer to interesting but 'irrelevant' material that is added to make something more appealing. Harp and Mayer (1997) use the terms 'seductive text' and 'seductive illustrations'. For both Garner and his colleagues, and Harp and Mayer, seductive story details are those that are not related to the cause-and-effect explanation of how something may work, and this is what makes them 'irrelevant' to the story. Ironically, the story's hook can be considered a 'seductive detail', meant to capture learners' attention. De Fossard (2008) states, the 'hook' is the entertaining background or the entertaining characters in story that can attract and hold student interests. In writing the *The Goddess Within* screenplay, I discovered that the seductive details made the story more interesting and engaging. According to arousal theories, adding interest even when the material is irrelevant helps learners to pay more attention. Arousal theorists predict that lessons containing seductive details will help students perform better on 'tests of transfer than students who learn without the seductive details' (Mayer 2001/2009: 93).

Mayer believes 'that seductive details may interfere with the process of knowledge construction' (2009: 95). However, he has not studied narrative in text or in motion pictures. And in a personal e-mail to me, he wrote, 'I think narrative can help prime appropriate prior knowledge if it is done well or can be a seductive detail if it is done badly' (13 May 2011). Mayer's work has considered narrative in educational games, but not in traditional storytelling, which may have other affordances. In my view, seductive details that are appropriately ingrained within the narrative are actually the elements that increase the story's relevance, and therefore also increase viewers' engagement and retention, as discussed earlier. That being said, all good books about screenwriting recommend the use of seductive details to make the story more engaging.

Now, the kaleidoscope lens zooms in on plot. Iglesias (2005) tells screenwriters that the 'story is your creation, your art. Plot is the vehicle for telling your story in an entertaining way, your craft' (p. 78). An educational program may benefit from utilizing both story and plot, the story being the theme of the module, and the plot being the design of the module. Plot arrangements evoke in the viewer pleasant sensations of anticipation, curiosity, and surprise – preferably relegating emotions like tension and fear to the characters. Interest is the opposite of boredom; if the student is interested in a lesson, then attention will naturally follow. Zull (2002), Iglesias (2005), and Schank (2011) believe that interest encompasses all the other storytelling emotions, and say that curiosity arouses interest. Online educators should seek lessons that inspire and sustain curiosity, interest, and positive emotions. You must grab the student's attention and hold it from the beginning of the module to the end.

Tan (1996) asserts that 'interest' encourages theater goers to investigate a film and discover more about the story world. Tan believes interest guides cognitive and emotion processing of narrative information. On the other hand, Kintsch (1980) believes students enjoy lessons that they can easily understand or make sense of. In his view cognition affects emotion. From discussion with students and from my point of view, it is interest that guides learners, and easily understandable information alleviates the emotion of frustration; however, this alone does not encourage further investigation.

Iglesias states (2005) that 'stories are metaphoric models of our lives', and as such, there is an 'innate desire for logical plotlines that follow a clear cause and effect progression to a climax and a resolution' (p. 81). He elaborates:

> We have an inner emotional need to make sense out of things, the world, and the universe. We know that everything has a cause, and when we know the cause, we understand the effect. E. M. Forster once gave this example: 'The king died, and then the queen died.' This is just a chronicle of events. But if you say, 'The king died, and then the queen died of grief,' it's a more satisfying sentence because you add a cause. The cause links the two events, which gives us emotional satisfaction and interest. Thus, a clear plot where we understand how each event causes the next will hold more interest than one whose events are episodic and random. (Iglesias 2005: 81)

Causation practice added to the educational-design process could help make lessons more engaging. Additionally, linking two events may be just as important as 'scaffolding' (adapting material to take into account what the learner already knows) (Wood et al., 1976). Educators who create e-learning material that add up to meaningful point(s) through cause and effect may be providing added value; however, this concept warrants further investigation. Nonetheless, good stories keep the audience wondering about what will happen next. Iglesias (2005) defines curiosity as 'the emotional state of wanting to learn more about something, the intellectual need to answer questions and make sense of things' (p. 44). In films, 'each act answers a different question' and builds to the central question which gets answered in the end (p. 86). To reiterate, there are three acts to a screenplay: the beginning, middle, and the end. Nonetheless, designing modules that have a strategically structured format, like the one found in film, may lead to more knowledge construction.

However you look at it, the cause-and-effect sequence of narratives is easy for viewers to process, and whether narratives are real or imagined, they do not lose their interest-generating power. Bruner (1990) explains the relation of the empirical and the imaginative: 'The fact that the historian's "empirical" account and the novelist's imaginative story *share* the narrative form is, on reflection, rather startling. It has challenged thoughtful students both of imaginative literature and of history since Aristotle. Why the same form for fact and fiction?' (p. 45). The screentext I used in the e-module merged the historical account of the Trojan War with the imaginative story *The Goddess Within*, which in turn became the inspiration for the development of more creative project-based stories. All the same, it is the sequencing of events, and not whether the story is fact or fiction that determines the meaning-making potential of the story. Burner (1990) explains, 'For stories have to do with how protagonists interpret things, what things mean to them. This is built into the circumstance of story – that it involves both a cultural convention and a deviation from it that is explicable in terms of an individual intentional state. This gives stories not only a moral status but an epistemic one' (p. 5).

Stories impart an emotional understanding of the world versus an analytical one, but they can do both. Sociocultural influences affect emotional expression, but they cannot reconstruct our human emotional system. According to Bruner (1990) and Mott et al. (1999), humans depend upon common modes of discourse or frameworks for understanding and negotiating differences in meaning and interpretation. Drawing together all the evidence shows that there is memory loss for information that does not get structured narratively.

Storytelling is an ancient practice, an innate human ability, and it can be used in a broad range of disciplines in higher education to create more than a 'mood'. Heiden and Fassbender (2010) point out that story 'often triggers the motivation to learn more about the background facts, especially in a historical, scientific, or technological context' (p. 2). Experts in all fields, argues Zull (2002), tend to represent their knowledge in narrative form, meaning that proficiency in an area means being familiar with its narrative as well as constructing new narratives. 'We should tell stories, create stories, and repeat stories, and we should ask our students to do the same' (p. 228). Moreover, 'stories engage all parts of the brain. They come from our experiences, our emotions, our ideas, our actions and our feelings. They allow us to package events and knowledge in complex neuronal nets, and part of which can trigger all the others' (ibid.). The value of stories in education is undeniable:

> Plato once argued that all storytellers should be banned because they're a threat to society. They deal with ideas, but not in the open,

rational manner of philosophers. Instead, they conceal their ideas inside the seductive emotions of art. Whether we write novels, sitcoms, comic books or screenplays, we are artists. Aristotle believed that all art serves two purposes to delight and to teach. As screenwriters, we delight through story and we teach through theme. (Iglesias 2005: 40)

Yet 'to delight and to teach' is not confined to screenwriting. Film audiences also react to promotional messages that 'delight' and inform, such as movie trailers and reviews, which prepare audiences to expect the emotion associated the film. For example, the trailer for a thriller carries a very different emotion than one for a comedy. It may be necessary to set the tone in e-learning environments as well. By creating emotional messages, and utilizing elements of film structure, educators can promote their modules and programs.

As noted earlier, visual information also supports learning. According to researchers Schoenmaker and Stanchev (2000), 75% of a human's capacity to learn can be ascribed to visual perception. Hart and Steven (1995) integrated short videos into classroom instruction and found that it enhanced comprehension because more parts of the brain are activated by the visual clues. The use of video makes a subject more appealing and more fun. Beard et al. (2007) reported that 'instructional television was more effective when it did not instruct, but was seen as an extension of the teacher and supported curriculum-related projects' (p. 8). One of the questions about instructional videos is how long they should be. According to Beard and his colleagues (2007), it may be hard to understand long videos; Millar talked about memory overload and suggested that information reception is not as great as originally thought (quoted in Beard et al. (2007)). Zull (2002) argues, 'given the centrality of images, it seems that teachers could make extensive use of images to help people learn. If we can convert an idea into an image, we should do so. And whenever possible, we should require our students to show us their images. It should go both ways' (p. 146).

When considering the short attention span of Digital Natives, adapting edutainment into a curriculum fits the present day environment more than ever before. Digital Natives (like Digital Immigrants), it must be remembered, can sit through and pay attention to movies that are approximately from ninety minutes to two, or sometimes three, hours long. There is something to be said about this type of prolonged engagement. Further, 'conscious watching' can enable students to see how they relate and respond in various circumstances by living through the experiences of the characters. Woltz (2005) explains, 'When you experience a movie, or anything else in your life with conscious awareness, you increase your capacity to access your inner wisdom. Inner wisdom is more than knowledge. Whereas knowledge is simply acquired information, wisdom requires understanding on a deep level' (p. 45). She elaborates, 'knowledge informs us, wisdom transforms us' (ibid.). Emotional connection as well as emotional distance can facilitate a learning interaction. It is important to reiterate that the language of film is universal and appealing for e-learning environments that often consist of a diverse student body.

Moreover, in education, film, and their cross-media educational components can be rated, in much the same way the Motion Picture Association of America rates films (G, PG, PG-13, R, etc.). A newly created, didactic educational value system would help educators determine whether material is appropriate for their module. For example, an e-resource might be categorized by discipline; one that is appropriate for English and Theater could be coded 'ET'.

It would behoove subject-matter experts to determine how to incorporate edutainment values into their curriculums. Modules should be student-centered, flexible, and allow for self-directed and interest-based learning within defined parameters. These parameters should broaden as the level of education increases, allowing for more flexibility and specific interest-based pursuits. It is imperative that instructors stay abreast of technology, popular culture, and subject matter. The difficulties students have with learning are often not related to the subject matter itself but to the way it is taught. Here are what I call the Ten Mandates of Transmedia Edutainment in Higher Education.

1. Instruct/moderate with passion and provide an inspirational performance.
2. Incorporate storytelling in the form of a popular film and have students create digital stories (learning-by-doing).
3. Aggregate the best content. Bring in short instructional videos on the subject matter (must be current and interesting).
4. Incorporate multimedia and new forms of reading material (i.e. hypertext and hypertext screenplay).
5. Develop personalized creative material that is unique to the learning objectives, using elements of edutainment.
6. Allow room for student-centered, self-directed, and interest-based learning around a story-based curriculum.

7. Define the material to be taught based on the needs of the learner; then identify the order of presentation, while keeping in mind story-based principles.
8. Design conversations for discussion and collaboration.
9. Design coursework with flexibility and provide cases with real-life situations, taking into account the continuing path of learners. Curriculums should be defined by the needs of the next learning stage, and what comes next varies from student to student.
10. Design creative assessments around different literacies that accurately measure learning outcomes.

The Internet with its wide range of communication tools and platforms allows students to learn in entirely new ways that appear more authentic and attuned to learners in terms of constructing knowledge in present day. But of course, there are challenges and concerns ahead for both e-learning and TmSE, and we turn to those next.

4
Challenges, Concerns, and Critiques of Transmedia Storytelling Edutainment

This chapter looks at learning disabilities, cultural representation, and the portrayal of minorities in film. As the integration of technology and media into scholarly activities increases, and as media and technology continue to evolve, new forms of literacy will be necessary. This chapter illustrates that the fusion of education and technology must be student-centered rather than technology-centered. It also sheds light on entertainment-education and social change, and highlights the role of transformational education and transformative learning. A critical-creative pedagogy is introduced.

4.1 Critical success factors

Higher education is changing in the digital age, and with change come challenges. Some of the main issues facing e-learning initiatives are instructional design, learner interface, navigation, type of content, pedagogy and models, learning theories, and constructivist-learning environments. As we saw in Chapter 3, instructional design is a critical success factor, and the success of e-learning depends on the effectiveness of both content and delivery. There are other performance issues to be worked out, having to do with bandwidth and software resources, such as PDF, Movie/Flash player, and so on; but this is a given. Creating quality learning content is the larger problem for the successful adaptation of e-learning in higher education. In this regard, visual interface and media have received a fair amount of attention. As for the interface, multimedia devices, such as mobile phones and iPods, will provide more platforms for content delivery and raise additional concerns for e-learning as well as TmSE. Producers are already creating 'mobisodes' (video programs designed to be viewed on a mobile phone) and are capable of producing educational narratives in various forms. Navigation and freedom go hand in hand in e-learning; therefore, e-content must be easily manageable and useable.

Interoperability and Standards are important to consider because storing and distributing content must be accessible. Video-based content requires larger bandwidths, which can be a significant constraint for TmSE. And to hold viewers attention, long videos must be interactive; however, interactive simulations that exploit learning are praised as being the most effective. The way content is organized and delivered is also key. Content must be shareable and reusable, at several different levels, because of the high cost of developing it. At the lowest level, content can be as simply borrowing a document and using it elsewhere. There are standard efforts, such as the Sharable Content Object Reference Model (SCORM), which are compliant with most of today's learning management systems (LMSs); however, SCORM is not foolproof. According to Aroyo and Dicheva (2004), in order to increase the effectiveness of educational functions, 'systems need to interoperate, collaborate and exchange content or have a re-use functionality. A key to enabling the interoperability is to capitalize on the (1) semantic conceptualization and ontologies, (2) common standardized communication syntax, and (3) large-scale service-based integration of educational content and functionality provision and usage' (p. 60). Interoperability is a key issue that needs to be considered for TmSE as well. The authoring of educational content and the creation of learning objects (like the screentext, for example), as well as their annotation, such as the creation of metadata (information about the item's content) are key points of consideration for authoring activities. Additionally, there are content licensing and copyright issues that need to be taken into account.

Desantis notes that the next generation of e-learning systems faces several hurdles. Among them is instructors' desires to customize their modules and the inability of the system to allow material to be customized to the extent needed. 'And highly-interactive systems are often too complex for pioneering professors to adopt and sustain on their own' (Desantis 1 May 2012). In a report issued in May 2012, Kevin Guthrie, President of Ithaka Research, notes that 'emerging types of online-learning platforms, which collect data about student performance to customize lessons, offer the potential to make instructors more efficient'. However, 'many of them are not yet widely used ... because professors want to retain control over the creation of their online courses' (quoted in Desantis 1 May 2012). Also under consideration are instructional models such as ADDIE, which is an acronym for a popular design model consisting of five phases – Analysis, Design, Development, Implementation, and Evaluation – that can be incorporated into constructivist-learning environments. Moreover, there is a growing concern that students may not possess all the necessary technical skills. Time management and motivation are key challenges as well. The future considerations for administrators are for technologies to change the cost structure by reducing tuition.

While technology is shaping the future of education, this can be seen both as a benefit to and a struggle for educational institutions. We have discussed many of the benefits; the drawbacks include costs, the fact that some instructors resist the changes, and the time needed to invest in learning new systems. Research from the Economist Intelligence Unit indicates that a core differentiator in the recruitment process will be technology, and technological innovation will play a major role in teaching methodologies. Online learning will continue to evolve and gain a global presence. As universities open up in foreign locations, distance education will continue to leverage advance technologies to provide education to individuals around the world (Glenn 2008: 4). This technology-driven environment also encourages international research partnerships. According to Glenn, funding and cost concerns will result in the formation of more 'corporate-academic partnerships' (p. 4). Administrators will need to adjust organizational practices in order to encourage resistant faculty members to embrace new technologies. Glenn believes that there are other, potentially disruptive challenges for the educational institutions embracing technology, and these include increased 'student plagiarism, cheating and distractibility' attributed 'to easy and ready access to mobile technologies' (ibid.).

Once instructional design and other technological-support issues are resolved, e-learning will begin to meet learners' expectations. Technology offers learners the ability to construct their own knowledge, and this is the key to successful cognitive learning. Collaboration tools are already a reality, and they are increasingly impacting the way teaching and learning are evolving. There will be more opportunities to engage students in flexible, collaborative, multimedia learning environments across various platforms. People do not live within a single medium; instead, they engage with multiple media, across various platforms. Educators must move quickly to incorporate cross-platform thinking into their digital learning environments. Those social networking tools that have already gained a foothold in education will continue to evolve and be used in modules, for alumni communication as well as by students and instructors. Blogs, wikis, video podcasts, mashups, collaboration software, and document management are also present and evolving. Online marketing, which is expanding its reach to include recruiting and even fundraising, will be a key driving force in the future. Likewise, technology-supported services such as module registration and a plethora of self-service initiatives are forthcoming; however, since technology is not foolproof, a physical presence for advice on services is still necessary.

Leading the way is multimodal teaching, which is supported by technology, and where instructors will teach and present information in more than one medium. Professors may have their modules filmed, and they can be accessed online by students; however, emulating traditional education is not the best practice for online environments and, therefore, students will have more options such as viewing the entire lesson or selecting a section that interests them. Technology-enabled, enhanced presentation tools that include video are also on the horizon. Web applications and freeware will reduce costs while improving efficiency; simulation software, online gaming, and narrative instruction are innovations likely to be adopted in higher education. The computer screen will not be the only interface available, as mobile devices will extend accessibility and reach. Transmedia education such as story-based scenarios which emulate real life will emulate TmSE practice via multiplatform delivery and interaction.

Based on his survey results, Glenn (2008) predicts:

> Courses will vary in length, rather than being semester-based, dynamic delivery of content will allow coursework to adjust to a student's performance level, traditional credit requirements will change, a greater number of interdisciplinary majors will be offered, more inter-university collaboration on individual coursework will be available (i.e., students from different institutions may work together on a given topic). (p. 7)

Organizational change in higher education is on the horizon, and new dynamics will create challenges for faculty members and administration alike. The changes will likely also affect the publishing business, as new forms of printed material move online. For example, text that is delivered in virtual form may be updated in real time, providing up-to-the minute information. There will undoubtedly be new forms of content and collaboration. Moreover, it is likely that:

> Students will be able to mix and match classes from various institutions to meet degree requirements, students will be able to customise their own degrees, a rise in partnerships between universities and corporations will lead more professionals to pursue highly specialised certification programmes, a rise in partnerships between universities and corporations will lead more students to seek specialised degrees. (Glenn 2008: 7)

Collaborating institutions will labor together in new ways, and there will be tremendous efforts made to manage and sustain specialized partnerships and programs. According to Glenn (2008), overall educational programs will be more engaging, more convenient, and more specialized and will allow learners to customize their educational experiences. Corporate sponsorships and partnerships will be the key in research and innovation as technology-supported teaching is adapted. This blurs the lines between knowledge creation and use.

A university's chief information officer (CIO) will be a key player and decision maker (Glenn 2008). In addition to technological and administrative issues, educational institutions will wrestle with copyright issues. Glenn quotes Lieutenant Colonel Sobiesk (US Military Academy, West Point), who contends that students will need to be proficient in 'intellectual property rights, online fact validation, and document sourcing and attribution' (quoted in Glenn 2008). In total, the challenges will be in adapting new practices for both learning environments and administration. These challenges are instigated by technology and adapted by digitally motivated students. In due course, this will lead to a different type of education, as well as a different type of workforce. Glenn (2008) contends, 'Sweeping technological changes will effectively change the skill-sets of the future workforce, as well as its approach to work in general' (p. 16).

In my opinion, the field of education has a bright future with opportunities that can lead to more effective learning environments. Despite the inevitable challenges that accompany change of any kind, progressing forward should be the hallmark of academia. Scholars in the teaching profession must develop the same passion for exploring teaching methods as they have for obtaining new knowledge in their particular fields. Also, there must be an alliance between faculty members and administration. In 1994, The American Association of

University Professors (AAUP) released a policy statement entitled 'On the Relationship of Faculty Governance to Academic Freedom'. It said that faculty governance is 'inextricably linked' to academic freedom and, therefore, neither is 'likely to thrive' except 'when they are understood to reinforce one another'. Indeed, a union between administration and faculty is more crucial today than ever before to ensure progress in the field of academia.

Critical to the success of TmSE is the development of subject driven narratives. Transmedia storytelling is a fairly new practice and transmedia storytelling edutainment is just a concept, therefore, more practice will be needed for critical evaluation. Transmedia is a complex interdisciplinary process; therefore, for criticism to be meaningful there need to be experiences to evaluate, like the feedback gained from the e-module. Since the e-module was positive, the field warrants more exploration.

4.2 Learning disabilities

Learners with handicaps may be challenged by the TmSE approach, as they would be challenged by traditional forms of education. Conley (2007) proposed that successful academic achievement in college requires not only contextual skills, such as the ability to understand policies and expectations, but also the ability to read, understand, and retain academic content. Cognitive strategies, such as the ability to think critically, are also required. Lindstrom (2007) notes that students with learning disabilities may struggle with reading and understanding complex content, note-taking, preparing written and oral presentations, conducting research, and monitoring their own learning experiences.

Hallahan and Mercer (2001) define 'learning disability' as a disorder in the basic psychological processes involved in using or understanding spoken or written language, which can result in a diminished ability to listen, speak, think, read, write, spell, or, calculate math problems. The term describes handicaps that involve perception, minimal brain dysfunction or brain injury, dyslexia, or developmental aphasia. The term does not apply to students who have learning problems which are predominantly the result of hearing, visual, or motor handicaps or to students who may be disadvantaged from an environmental, cultural, or economic standpoint.

To ensure that students with learning disabilities can achieve success in postsecondary courses, it is important to address the impact of these deficits on performance, and to provide these students with the appropriate accommodations and support (Lindstrom 2007). To cite a TmSE example, a computer could read screentext out loud so that a student with significant vision impairment could listen to a story. Similarly, a hearing-impaired person could be shown images of a digital story as well as read the text on-screen. Although it would be outside of this book to discuss all the different disabilities and their relevant solutions, there are six accommodations most frequently requested by students with disabilities at the postsecondary level, and they could easily be adapted by a TmSE pedagogical approach. According to Banerjee and Brinkerhoff (2010), Gregg et al. (2005), Lindstrom (2007), Skinner (2004), the six accommodations most frequently requested by students with disabilities at the postsecondary level are (1) extended time for exams and assignments; (2) separate, reduced-distraction rooms for exams; (3) note-takers; (4) alternative media; (5) foreign-language substitution; and (6) reduced course load. In fact, for some disabilities, 'alternative media' may already be included in the TmSE approach.

4.3   The cultural representation of film: *The Goddess Within*

The literature on cultural representation in film is quite diverse, but rather than focus on the traditional representation found in films, I have chosen to look at digital forms, which are the new mode of production and distribution. It is well known that films set a mode or style in their representation of others, and this will be discussed in relation to *The Goddess Within*, which as a produced piece of work would take a digital form.

Cultural representations in digital productions consist of multiple image layers that are flawlessly composited to convey multi-layered reality and polysemic meanings. Further, digital forms confess that their images are representations by way of animation and computer-generated imaging, whereas traditional films try to uphold reality by live action.

The Goddess Within employs computer-generated images of the goddess and other deities that blend live action and digitally created images. This leads to both realistic and fantasy representation and, therefore, the cultural representation of *The Goddess Within* is neither real nor hyperreal. The screenplay does portray characters who are corrupt in the university system, but based on recent history with country leaders, this is a legitimate real-world portrayal. For example, an article in the *J. S. Economist* (30 May 2012) showed Greece to be the number two corrupt country in Europe, second to Italy. According to the journal *Times Higher Education*, Greece's higher education system is dysfunctional and in desperate need of reform despite the fact that it was the birthplace of the academy. Mavrogordatos contends:

> Greece's system of higher education suffers from a crisis of values as well as outdated policies and organisational structures. The tragedy is that leaders, scholars, students and political parties that aim to promote the public good have been trapped in a system that subverts the goals they seek, corrupts the ideals they pursue and forsakes the public they serve. (24 May 2012)

The characters in *The Goddess Within* display through their actions the 'crisis of values' and 'corrupt ideals' that Mavrogordatos notes. Moreover, Mavrogordatos puts Greece's higher education system into perspective, and this is culturally represented in *The Goddess Within* via reality (live action) and fantasy (computer-generated images) set in an overall fictional world. The cross between the real and surreal may make this cultural representation of Greece easier for native Greeks to digest. Also, creative discourse provides a seamless expression of the facts, in much the same way digital media technologies flawlessly assemble images. This seems to indicate that when the truth is disguised, it is more readily received. And, as Albert Camus wrote, 'Fiction is the lie through which we tell the truth' (Goodreads n.d.). I wholeheartedly agree and would add that within the lie one can also find truth, because it is through the lie (story) that information and knowledge can be gained. In this respect, TmSE has a place in higher education.

It is hard to predict how cultural representation that takes on new media forms will affect the general public, let alone learners; however, much of the same concerns around cultural representation are similar in the actual stories, regardless of their form. Also, developing stories for educational purposes which are to be distributed to a global marketplace will need to be more sensitive to these issues. Transmedia edutainment may be a novel concept; however, edutainment media is not. In following sections, the examination narrows in on existing concerns with popular entertainment products, as these could easily extend into TmSE. We also look at edutainment media's past failures, even as its future possibilities are contextualized. Although the method of transmedia education is appealing because engagement is built into it, it is both the context of the story and the educational content that will determine its success. Certainly, all stories do not appeal to all individuals; however, they might have a better chance of penetrating on a larger scale over traditional forms of education. Next, we consider the representation of minorities in order to get a better picture of film in the classroom.

4.4   Minorities and representation

As the world becomes a smaller place, the issue of minority representation becomes even more crucial. The postmodern condition that dominates most societies and stories tends to represent minorities via stereotypes that exclude or ignore individual differences. Stereotypes are a one-dimensional portrayal of people based on their profession, age, race, religion, or sex.

According to Rockler-Gladen (2008), minority representations in the media, whether of racial, sexual, or religious groups, have certain elements in common. Minorities depictions in the media are frequently meant to make the majority of viewers feel comfortable, and this is done to guarantee high ratings. And since ratings govern content, representations that are controversial are removed. A classic television example that Rockler-Gladen presents is *The Cosby Show*, which Cosby himself had trouble pitching to network executives, many of whom believed that Americans were not ready for a family show that featured African American people. To make the show more acceptable to mainstream America, the show focused on universal family experiences. *The Cosby Show* rarely did anything that was specific to the African American culture. Another example Rockler-Gladen cites is the television show *Will and Grace*, in which the gay characters never suffered discrimination. *Will and Grace* also steered clear of controversial issues, such as gay marriage. Although there are exceptions, especially in the way minorities are represented in traditional media, these patterns of representations still hold true, however alternative media is changing this by providing a platform for new innovative stories (Rockler-Gladen 29 April 2008).

Filmmakers tend to rely on stereotypes because they are a quick way to establish a character. On a positive note, however, it seems that today's film industry is more sensitive to issues of gender and culture than ever before. Nonetheless, oversimplified portrayals of minority groups can affect how they are perceived in the broader culture. Children are particularly vulnerable being influenced by stereotypes because they have a limited experience of the world. In higher education, however, things are more even-handed. Since transmedia storytelling can be experienced on a cross-platform basis, the effect of stereotyping on perceptions can be extremely powerful.

It should be noted that the institution of education has been around for quite a long time and has yet to fully resolve the issue of learning styles or issues related to stereotypes and cultural differences. In this respect, it is too early for TmSE, which is a newly emerging field, to resolve representational issues. Nonetheless, teachers must come to understand cultures in order to understand how different learners actually learn.

Culture and environment can also affect the way students learn, and here, too, the educational system has not yet resolved all the problems. According to Morris, African American children's learning styles are characterized by cooperation, harmony, and socialization. They are more spontaneous, open-minded, and flexible than their European-American counterparts. They show a preference for visual information processing, and they are more field dependent and prefer interpersonal relationships (2 November 2007). Ethnic students in particular continue to fall behind in the classroom and Black-Americans have it worse. Jenks and Phillips (1998), in their article 'The Black-White Test Score Gap: Why It Persists and What Can Be Done', write: 'African Americans score lower than European Americans on vocabulary, reading, and math tests, as well as on tests that claim to measure scholastic aptitude and intelligence. The gap appears before children enter kindergarten and it persists into adulthood. It has narrowed since 1970, but the typical African American still scores below seventy five percent of Caucasians on almost every standardized test.'

Ethnic students, in particular, continue to fall behind in the classroom. Distance-learning has yet to embrace an administrative infrastructure or policies geared toward improving academic performance. Although there is research on student outcomes in e-learning environments, it is primarily focused on the comparing online formats to traditional formats. Several researchers have noted that student outcomes have nothing to do with culture or ethnicity (Dominguez and Ridley 1999; Ryan 2000; Gagné and Shepherd 2001; Cooper 2001; Shea et al. 2001).

Engagement issues are a strong predictor for success; however, it is difficult to compare and measure, for example, the benefits of engagement and information when oversimplified stories and stereotypes are used. The goal of TmSE is to have entertainment conglomerates create specific content for educational purposes and to be considerate of representational issues. Diversity enhances people's lives by creating understanding. And there is a plethora of diversity on the Internet to combat representational issues. The idea of a monoculture society is not an edutainment issue but something much more profound. Edutainment content may appear to accommodate cultural norms, although it may still only touch the surface. Freire (1996), in *Pedagogy of the Oppressed*, conceived of education as a dialogical pedagogy. He believed communication should provide an equal distribution that includes grassroots participation through sharing and reconstructing experiences. This participation is made possible by Internet technologies. However, technology-centered approaches to communication as well as to education should not be the focus.

4.5   Technology-supported approaches to pedagogy

Cuban (1986, 2001) acknowledges the technologies of the 20th century that were implemented in education and argues that technology-centered approaches, by and large, fail when it comes to effecting lasting improvements in education. That being said, there were high expectations that motion pictures, which were invented in the early 20th century, would improve education. Likewise, Thomas Edison, in 1922, predicted that film was destined to revolutionize education and that it would 'supplant largely, if not entirely, the use of textbooks' (quoted in Cuban 1986: 9). Edison wholeheartedly believed it was 'possible to teach every branch of human knowledge with the motion picture' (p. 11). Cuban points out that these predictions were not realized: 'Most teachers used films infrequently in their classrooms' (p. 17).

The Ohio History Central Organization strongly believed that radio was a technology that could be used for educational purposes. Benjamin Darrow, who established the Ohio School of the Air in 1929 described educational radio this way: 'The central and dominant aim of education by radio is to bring the world to the classroom, to make universally available the services of the finest teachers, the inspiration of the greatest leaders and unfolding events which through the radio may come as a vibrant and challenging textbook of the air' (Ohio History Central Organization 1 July 2005). Darrow's colleague William Levenson, the school's director, predicted in 1945 that 'a radio receiver will be as common in the classroom as the blackboard' (quoted in Cuban 1986: 19). Then came the idea of educational television, thought to combine movies with the benefits of radio coverage. In the 1950s, educational television was hyped as a way to create a 'continental classroom', and flaunted as a 'richer education at less cost' (Cuban 1986: 33). Nonetheless, the outcome showed that teachers used television in the classroom either rarely or never (ibid.).

In reference to education, Mayer (2009) clearly points out that film, radio, and television all had the same life cycle even though different technologies underlie the different media: 'First, they began with grand promises about how the technology would revolutionize education.

Second, there was an initial rush to implement the cutting-edge technology in schools. Third, from the perspective of a few decades later it became clear that the hopes and expectations were largely unmet' (p. 12). In previous times, edutainment was technology-centered rather than student-centered. The social and cultural aspects of learning were similarly overlooked. Mayer (2009) notes that the emphasis on technological advancements is what led to the disappointing results of the early forays into educational media. Students had to adapt to the 'demands of cutting-edge technologies' rather than technology being made 'to fit the needs of human learners' (p. 12). He believes the focus should have been on technology as a learning aid and human cognition, as the focal point.

The modern approach to educational media may not be wholly a technology-centered one. In fact, the pervasiveness of technology today is still often overlooked. McKenzie (2000) coined the term 'technotainment', which he characterizes as technology fortified with entertainment but lacking in value. This is basically the technology-centered approach. Education, on the other hand, is concerned with the development of cognitive structures, which is a pedagogy and, therefore, should be student-centered. Technology is considered a medium, not a pedagogy; therefore, this fusion (of technology and pedagogy) needs to be examined critically. Gandz notes:

> Education has much less to do with information gathering than with developing an individual's thinking and reasoning so that he or she can appraise that information, and separate the relevant from irrelevant and the important from the trivial. This requires that individuals develop useful models for absorbing or rejecting this mass of information, critically appraising its validity. (1997: 11)

It is crucial that technology support pedagogy and does not become the focal point. Gandz (1997) contends, and I wholeheartedly agree, that learners must have 'models for absorbing or rejecting mass information'. Although mass information can penetrate the unconscious and have profound effects, I believe that a conscious effort to create and use narrative in education is a positive model. Apple believes that technology is much more than just machines and their software:

> A form of thinking that orients a person to approach the world in a particular way. Computers involve ways of thinking that under current educational conditions are primarily technical. The more the new technology transforms the classroom into its own image, the

more a technical logic replaces critical, political and ethical under-standing. The discourse of the classroom will centre on technique, and less on substance. (Apple 1991: 75)

Apple is describing concerns that have not been adequately addressed by higher education as it adopts technology into its programs. Salomon (1983) addresses technology in a constructivist-learning environment as it relates to multimedia and hypermedia. He believes that because of the non-linear structure of the Internet and hypermedia, the learner is drawn in by the visual appeal of the content and, therefore, wanders aimlessly. Salomon and Almog (1998) believe that this may affect the notion of what knowledge is because students may 'prefer to learn from sources that present fields of knowledge in a hypermedia like structure'. Also, students may 'prefer to learn from sources that present fields of knowledge in a hypermedia structure, thus sidestepping the acquisi-tion of the logical, hierarchically structured connections and links that constitute science, as we know it' (p. 235).

Through the years, the education industry has failed by adapting a technology-convergence viewpoint, and this limiting view detracts from the possibility of substantial change. Consequently, viewing media and educational convergence as merely a technological phenomenon isolates the potential for considerable impact on the instructor-learner relationship. Norman (1994) who supports the student-centered view argues, 'Today we serve technology. We need to reverse the machine-centered point of view and turn it into a person-centered point of view: Technology should serve us' (p. xi). Simply stated, technology should serve learners and promote human cognition.

Therefore, it is essential to *engage* human cognition, which plays a much deeper role in the ability to learn and remember. Engaging with content is a key factor for the success of educational media and edutain-ment as pedagogy. And the entertainment industry, through transmedia storytelling, has already shown proficiency by serving the 'person-cen-tered point of view'. For this reason, the entertainment industry is in a much better position to move into the edutainment market. Nevertheless, education is moving into the mediasphere; and so now content creation is explored in relation to authentic approaches to learning.

4.6   The era of screen education: performance, digital text, and transformation

In his ground-breaking book, *Presentation of Self in Everyday Life*, Goffman (1959) adapted Shakespeare's famous line 'all the world's a stage' and developed the term *dramaturgy* to indicate the ways in which social life can be conceptualized as a series of performances. These ongoing performances are daily rituals of 'impression management' that encompass 'front stage' and 'backstage' behaviors. Applying this concept to e-learning, 'backstage' behaviors offer the opportunity to evaluate and reevaluate module material, making teaching, or the 'onstage performance', better each time around. Further, exceptional teaching engages learners, just as an outstanding theatrical performance engages an audience. Lepionka argues that 'online instruction, like classroom instruction, is performative, a foundation of edutainment' (Lepionka 1 September 2009). It is worth noting that once instructors come to terms with how performative their roles are, both online and in the classroom, then they may become as engaging as Hollywood movie star because of their ability to create emotive experiences that inspire students. Keller (1987) elaborates: 'Motivation is not a magical or purely charismatic process of charming the audience. The factors that promote a positive response can be tried, adjusted, and readjusted until the desired effect is achieved. This is exactly the process used by entertainers whose goals are primarily motivational rather than instructional' (p. 1).

In order to captivate an audience prior to filming, actors commit themselves to hours of rehearsal. The practice of 'rehearsing' could also benefit educators, although in education there is seldom that same level of commitment to developing the motivational aspect of a module. For Keller, motivation is key to learning; he contends that instructors can do two things to improve it: 'First, it is necessary to have an understanding of motivation; that is, to have an overview of the primary components of the motivation to learn, and of the kinds of strategies that will have a positive influence on these components. Second, it is necessary to know what types of strategies to use, how many to use, and how to design them into the course' (1987: 1). I would like to add that a sound e-learning strategy includes the incorporation of TmSE. Further, the dynamics of an e-learning environment, driven by content and supported by media and technology, play an active role in the learning process of Net Gen learners. Today, strategies to increase motivation need to balance media and technology, and just as online pedagogy has its own rules, so, too, will instructional design. In the digital age the textbook as we know it will soon be archaic, and new forms of material will engage students. Lepionka supports the use of the screenplay format over the textbook in e-learning environments:

> Your designed conversations with students may still include evidence-based narratives, but you will develop your manuscripts more like

scripts – with settings, stage directions and special effects in addition to players, speeches, and lines. As odd as it may seem compared to conventional textbook writing processes, screenwriting is appropriate for content that will be displayed on a screen. Your content will be displayed on computer monitors, laptops, PDAs, ebook readers, mobile phones, and any other so-called destructive technologies (so-called simply because they necessitate structural change) that the future holds. (Lepionka 1 September 2009)

It is evident that text is being shaped into new forms, such as portable document formats (PDFs) and e-books; however, the electronic advantages of these forms are not being utilized; or, they are being used inappropriately. Landow contends that there is a misuse of the PDF on websites:

A PDF version of text documents has the great value of preserving the exact appearance of the original document. It has strengths – but also the limitations – of print. Within an electronic environment, a PDF presentation of a document represents a refusal to employ any of the advantages of digital technology other than its ability to send copies quickly and cheaply over a network. It permits, however, neither searching nor linking, thereby creating an annoyingly inefficient means of conveying information. (Landow 2006: 316)

The PDF does permit linking, but it seems to be rarely used. Further, offline text is very different from online text, and thus, the linking of information must be studied further in order to understand its benefits and drawbacks. In any case, the empirical research, the screenplay entitled *The Goddess Within*, incorporated linking into the PDF in order to benefit from connectivity of the electronic form. *The Goddess Within* is a story about a *modern-day Greek Goddess who is destined to relive a myth when she moves to Greece to win back her ex-boyfriend, but first the protagonist (Athena) must uncover the secret behind an ancient artifact known as the Apple of Discord*. The characters are a personification of Greek gods (Athena, Aphrodite, Hera, Zeus, and Hephaestus); therefore more information about gods/goddesses/Greek mythology was made available by clicking on the hyperlinks within the PDF. The original myth, The Judgment of Paris was *adapted* and *extended* into the present day story *The Goddess Within* in the same way a transmedia narrative would be adapted and extended. In general, screenwriting with its sparse text, emotionally engaging dialogue and action lines are easier on the eye and more appealing to the heart and mind than traditional texts. People are accustomed to its format and its affective experience-generating capability.

The Net Generation, or any generation for that matter, seems to find text formatted like a screenplay, which is not copy heavy, engaging. This will be discussed more in the analysis. *The Goddess Within* screenplay was formulated by Campbell's well-known narrative theory, *The Hero's Journey*, which was extracted from his 1949 book, *The Hero with a Thousand Faces*. Campbell's established narrative theory, used in Hollywood screenwriting, draws on a familiar structure, which popular culture is accustomed to via its movie-viewing experience. On the Internet, a screenplay could be made available via its traditional text format, or it could combine the text with artwork, much like a graphic novel. In addition to the screenplay form, traditional text or textbooks could be read by a student to subsidize their learning content. This hybrid format bridges the gap between the works of literature and converging forms of knowledge. A likely scenario in TmSE in relation to screenplays would go something like this: a film is released theatrically, the narrative text in the form of screenplay transverses to the Internet where it is made available for the audience (students) to penetrate via hypertext and hypermedia. Thus, the screenplay text is linear, meaning it follows a specific path; however, along this path (via links) the student can immerse him- or herself into the story world, accessing edutainment via text or video. Instructional texts that are formatted into screenplay formats grounded by engaging stories might have something to offer e-education. The Digital Native language is a mediated language, and screenplays are written texts rooted in imagery, making them most appropriate for the screen. Scripts (whether for TV or film) form visuals in the receptor's mind; therefore, they might have a relevant place as a learning tool in screen education.

Moreover, online learning is a mediated experience, and video and screenplay (screentext) fit organically into that experience. Narratives derived from popular entertainment are more appealing in e-learning environments because they are well known due to their marketing campaigns and studio affiliations. Further, the thinking and feeling dimensions of media products cannot be overlooked, and learning can and should incorporate some of the experiences that come from popular media. Moving image or screenplay text on the Internet engages learning and enables reflection. Once you are engaged with a story, whether it is in print, moving image, or spoken by a physically present storyteller, you are bound to learn something. Plus, the emotional component found in story has the capacity to keep students motivated.

The hypermedia novel is a storytelling approach that also has similarities to the graphic novel. The idea behind this electronic book is to learn without being aware of it, just as with the screenplay format. Heiden and Fassbender (2010) discuss the benefits of hypermedia environments: 'Hypermedia-based e-learning environments can fill this emotional and motivational gap and are well-suited to fulfill the desire for background information that is directly related to narrative content' (p. 126). Indubitably, the exploration of the hypermedia novel begins with information that is specifically related to the narrative; however, as one digs deeper into the depths of the story world, one finds oneself engrossed in discrete topics via the connective capacity cultivated by the Internet. The model integrates different user roles (author, receptor, and publisher), allowing personalized storytelling and reception. Heiden and Fassbender (2010: 127) argue:

> The integration of modular story authoring and non-linear story reception in a Hypermedia environment (i.e. an environment that combines multiple forms of media – like text, video, audio, 3D animation – in one presentation) therefore seems to be a promising concept for edutainment because it effectively links narrative and informational content in an approach that uses multiple forms of media.

Moreover, Kress (2003), Heiden and Fassbender (2010), and Lepionka (2009) all support the use of alternate forms of text as learning material.

Currently, academic recognition of digital work in the humanities is lagging behind due to the slowness of institutional change and the misunderstood nature of the visual medium. As noted in Chapter 3, popular-culture entertainment associated with visual media is considered lowbrow, and is dismissed by some as garbage. We have seen that the learner's experience as well as the social aspects of storytelling have tremendous educational value. Yet, pedagogy is slow to respond to change, and some instructors have failed to keep abreast of technology innovation. Landow notes:

> I do not expect to see dramatic changes in educational practice for some time to come, in large part because of the combination of technological conservatism and general lack of concern with pedagogy that characterizes the faculty at most institutions of higher learning, particularly at those that have pretensions to prestige. (2006: 314)

Some of the fault may lie with the institutions of higher learning, which have failed to educate their educators, and which are resistant to innovation. Even though educational institutions have embraced the Internet by creating websites to display their offerings, it is evident that teaching has yet to embrace the web fully 'because many educational technologists and faculty users still think in terms of the book' (Landow 2006: 314). Additionally, educators' idea of technology consumption is putting theories on a PowerPoint presentation and reading the material to the class. Further, many faculty members still think strictly in terms of outdated theories that have no place in today's economy. Still, if we can get students to care about the learning experience, they will learn better – but first habitual thinking must change. If educational institutions can be more student-centered and customize education to fit the learner's needs then the results can be transformative. Pine and Gilmore argue:

> Experiences are not the final offering. Companies can escape the commoditization trap by the same route as all other offerings: customisation. When you customise an experience to make it just right for the individual – providing exactly what he or she needs right now – you cannot help changing that individual. When you customize an experience, you automatically turn it into a transformation. (quoted in Pollock 20 June 2006)

This is exactly what higher education needs to be. It should customize modules based on student needs in order to provide transformative experiences. According to Pollock:

> If the Experience Economy is the commercial expression of the networked Knowledge/Information Age, then it is fair to say that the Transformation Economy is the outer, transactional expression of the emerging Age of Meaning when finally the needs of a human's spirit and soul are met in the marketplace of ideas and personal services rather than in the cloister, temple or mosque. (20 June 2006)

Convergence provides the foundation for an emergent culture and within this culture surfaces the 'emerging age of meaning'. The principal activity of the transformation economy is the buyer seeking change and businesses of all kinds responding by providing fulfillment. The transformation economy relies on how well a business such as academia understands the individual aspirations of its clients, and how well it can guide them to achieving these aspirations. Mermiri believes within the experience economy, consumers seeks authenticity, but they also search for a stronger relationship with the products, brands, and services they consume (Mermiri 8 December 2009). It is safe to say then that in the transformation economy academic institutions need to connect with their students and provide them with sound benefits. It is thus, the bridging of the gap between education and entertainment for more meaning-making and emotional engagement. Mermiri contends, 'The issues of authenticity and transformation are particularly relevant in light of the current economic climate where people and businesses alike are re-evaluating their priorities both in terms of consumption and production' (ibid.). According to Gilmore and Pine (2009), authenticity also appeals to both senses and perception, which are closely connected to values and meaning. Mermiri adds:

> In this light culture and the arts have inherently and from various perspectives been considered authentic, with their emotional appeal to expression and creativity. Moreover, culture products (art, plays etc) invite and challenge audiences to give their own interpretation of what they're experiencing and what it means for them. Consequently the cultural product (whatever it is) will stimulate a different reaction for every person, and so will encourage an authentic dialogue between its consumer and producer. (8 December 2009)

When Mermiri's ideas about consumers are applied to the student experience, it looks something like this: student experiences can be enhanced with the infusion of a narrative through film or other cultural forms in order to evoke emotions and authenticity and, therefore, stimulate and engage students. Mermiri believes 'the arts are in themselves authentic, because of the inherent value, meaning and emotion they stir in people' (ibid.). Also, student-produced digital video can enable more authentic learning experiences (Kearney and Schuck 2004) and provide students with a sense of ownership (Kearney and Schuck 2005).

The current educational model is too expensive and poorly designed. A climate of receptivity to new ideas is on the rise, as demonstrated by three universities: Rice, Massachusetts Institute of Technology (MIT), and the newly created University of the People. Since 1999, Rice University has provided educational resources free of charge through its Connexions website, which is an open educational resources repository. At Connexions, the online trademark of Rice University, people collaborate, authors create material, instructors build and share collections, and learners explore content. MIT OpenCourseWare is a free web-based publication of virtually all MIT course materials for undergraduate and graduate subjects taught at MIT; however, MIT OpenCourseWare does not grant degrees or certificates and does not provide access to faculty.

The University of the People tuition-free online academic institution is 'dedicated to the global advancement and democratization of higher education' (University of the People). Many similar examples of institutional change are in the making. Above all, academic institutions will need to move away from focusing on a strict theory based approach and adapt a practitioner's approach in the classroom. Today, students prefer to learn by completing tasks, projects, and activities which provide them with valuable skills for the workforce. The university system must drastically change to adapt to these demands, as well as develop partnerships, not only with entertainment conglomerates, but with corporations in general. Effective and meaningful learning will continue to take place, it will just be different.

In the future it is likely that students will be guided, as opposed to dictated to, by instructors and institutions rather than have education 'delivered' to them in the traditional top-down manner. Students will shape their education by choosing their preferred content from one or many institutions. Mermiri states: 'In the transformation economy goods and services are co-created or co-produced through the interaction of consumers and producers' (8 December 2009). As we move into a transformation economy, it is likely that creativity and interactivity will be the epitome of culture. Heron (2001) contends: 'The old model of education, going back to classical times, dealt only with the education of the intellect, theoretical and applied ... Nowadays we have people who are learning by thinking, feeling and doing – bringing all these to bear on the acquisition of new knowledge and skills' (p. 208). Moreover, 'the emotional and the intangible (think and act) are becoming increasingly important factors for consumers, and businesses must respectively tap into those areas in order to offer their audiences the transformation they require' (Mermiri 8 December 2009).

To sum up: the integration of technology and media-rich environments into scholarly activities is evolving, and as media and technology evolve, new forms of literacy will be necessary. Along with that, edutainment opportunities will emerge as screen media transform into a truly immersive and interactive form on the Internet. Next, we look at entertainment-education in the context of social change in order to get a better understanding of what it is and how it can eventually be in the setting of education.

4.7 Entertainment-education and social change

Edutainment, as we have seen, is a combination of education and entertainment designed to inform and, in some definitions, amuse. (However, the argument made in this book does not include the amusement aspect of the definition.) Essentially, edutainment can be defined by what it does: 'Edutainment typically seeks to instruct or socialize its audience by embedding lessons in some familiar from of entertainment: television programs, computer and video games, films, music, websites, multi-media software, etc. ... There are also lessons that use edutainment as a basis for teaching in a more efficient and faster way' (Webster's Online Dictionary).

The terms 'edutainment' and 'entertainment-education' are often used interchangeably; however, there are differences between the two. As De Fossard (2008) explains, the primary purpose of edutainment is education, whereas entertainment-education programs are created for a general audience and appeal to the attention and emotions of the audience through serial dramas. In this scenario 'audience members can empathize with the characters and gain a sense of self-efficacy, which is vital to their ability to adapt to new behavior' (p. 19). De Fossard defines 'edutainment' as 'a form of distance education that enhances the possibility of reaching, engaging, and educating students who are denied any contact with teacher and where it might not be possible to measure the previous or ongoing educational levels of the students' (p. 18). De Fossard's definition of edutainment applies to underdeveloped countries, where distance education does not include the Internet (materials are mailed instead), and where there is no contact of any kind with the teacher. However, edutainment can also benefit e-learning environments, where students have moderate online contact with the instructor.

Entertainment products have the ability to inform and motivate social change, although Hollywood content for the most part is meant to entertain. Nonetheless, it would be unfair to say that Hollywood does not produce meaningful movies because numerous great films with noteworthy themes have been made; however, one cannot deny the plethora of poor films that are also available. Nonetheless, it is important to examine the field of entertainment-education, because it combines communication, education theory, and the communicative arts primarily to deliver social-development messages. Entertainment-education has existed for 1,000 years in the form of parable and fables; the leading modern-day theorist and practitioner in the field is Miguel Sabido. In the 1970s, Sabido began producing telenovelas (soap operas or serial dramas on television) that combined communication theory with pro-health-related messages to inform audiences throughout Latin America (Sensagent n.d.). Sabido developed a theoretical basis for the field;

Singhal and Rogers (1999, 2002) provide a definition: 'Entertainment-education (E-E) is the process of purposely designing and implementing a media message to both entertain and educate, in order to increase audience member's knowledge about an educational issue, create favorable attitudes, shift social norms, and change overt behavior' (cited in Singhal et al. 2004: 5).

Entertainment-education is not a theory of communication per se, although several communication theories provide the basis for it. It is rather a communication strategy for bringing about behavioral and social change. Sabido (2004) applied his communication strategy to the telenova because the format uses emotions to create identification, which can teach the television audience a desired social behavior, such as family planning or adult literacy. In contrast to North American soap operas, in which the storyline continues day after day, each Latin American telenovela has a beginning, middle, and end. It therefore provides an opportunity to incorporate information on a topic or explain a service such as family planning clinics. According to Sabido, at the end of every telenova episode, there are short epilogues that convey to the audience important information about infrastructure services. Without hurting ratings, the telenovela can easily add characters that the audience can identify with and learn relevant social behaviors from (pp. 63–64).

Sabido's model incorporates the work of psychologist Albert Bandura, of Stanford University, as well as of other theorists. Bandura is the originator of *social learning theory* (1977). Bandura's theory, as discussed by Vaughan et al. (4 December 2000), puts forward the notion that new behaviors can be learned through the observation and imitation of the behavior of others. The underlying idea is that by witnessing the behaviors of characters similar to themselves (on TV), individuals may increase their ability to perform a task successfully. Social learning theory claims that the audience will emulate the behaviors of characters, if that behavior is rewarded in the show, and avoid socially undesirable behaviors that are punished. This modeling by the characters can thus strengthen as well as weaken certain behaviors among members of the audience.

Entertainment-education's intent is to contribute to social change by increasing awareness, which can happen individually or collectively. It can influence behavior toward a socially desired end and create the conditions for social change at a system level. As Greenberg points out:

> The use of entertainment to educate in the form of modeling behaviors and imparting values deemed 'prosocial' is not new, but rather is

rooted in the ancient art of storytelling...Greek theater, epic poems, anthems, and childhood fables of disparate oral cultures constitute some of the earliest uses of this communications practice, albeit somewhat different from the use of E-E in feature length films and TV series. (Greenberg et al. 2004: 193)

Since the beginning of time, the very essence of storytelling has been entertainment and education. Building upon the entertainment-education strategy for social change, while combining it with trans-media education, enables the educational experience to reach new levels of effectiveness.

Entertainment-education is approached differently by a variety of countries that utilize the model for social change. Developing countries adapt entertainment-education as part of a strategy to inform the public about social issues, whereas in the United States, individual producers may seek out information based on their own personal interests, and then adapt the message to the entertainment content. Although there are some organized forms of entertainment-education taking place in the United States, none of them is centered on organized social change. However, several entertainment-education projects have been developed and implemented around the world in such countries as India, Kenya, Brazil, Philippines, China, Tanzania, Pakistan, Ethiopia, Turkey, Netherlands, and Mexico (Singhal et al. 2004). One of the most successful and prominent campaigns is South Africa's *Soul City*, produced by the Soul City Institute of Health and Development Communication. The institute's website describes the *Soul City* initiative as a health promotion and social-change project that 'reaches more than 16 million South Africans through multi-media and advocacy strategies' (Soul City Institute n.d.). *Soul City* is an ongoing intervention project in South Africa that deals with issues related to HIV/AIDS, tobacco, tuberculosis, land and housing, household energy, violence, and alcohol misuse. 'Its impact is aimed at the level of the individual, the community and the socio political environment' (Soul City Institute n.d.).

Even when the content of Hollywood entertainment does both entertain and educate, it is generally not produced as part of a deliberate social change initiative, and therefore to call it entertainment-education is misleading. Nonetheless, it is important to contextualize educational television or educational themes before moving forward. According to the online dictionary *Sensagent*, motion pictures with educational content appeared as early as 1943, with the film *Private Snafu* produced by Warner Brothers animation studio between 1943 and 1945. Snafu was a character in black-and-white American educational cartoon shorts which taught soldiers what not to do at war. Today, edutainment has shifted toward children's television series, such as *Sesame Street, Dora the Explorer,* and *Teletubbies.* There are also examples of educational engagement productions that are broadcast outside the United States, for example the United Kingdom's *Homework High* on Channel 4 (Channel 4 Learning n.d.), and the BBC's, *GCSE Bitesize.*

For adult viewers, individual situation-comedy episodes can serve as edutainment vehicles. In the United States, ABC's television series *Boston Legal* was about a group of lawyers who took on cases no one else wanted. The show engaged audiences because it dealt with real-life social issues that the media tended to overlook. Alan Shore (played by James Spade) was an attorney known for tackling interesting and difficult cases. One show took on the subject of Alzheimer's disease, and featured a courtroom scene in which Shore/Spade was extremely compelling in arguing the case. The show's storyline centered on an Alzheimer's drug called 'Dimebon', which had been available on the Russian market for 25 years, but had not been approved by the FDA for the US market. The character Denny (William Schatner) wanted to get the drug because it improved memory and thinking, but he could not. Shore argued the case in court and he was both powerful and effective in his persuasion. *Boston Legal,* in this particular episode on Alzheimer's, informed, educated as well as inspired. Alan Shore presented an emotional story as he argued his point in the courtroom.

In the courtroom, the jury and the judge want to emotionally participate in the 'story' being told by each side just as much as a theater viewer does when watching a film. A lawyer who presents a great argument using the principles of storytelling will have a much better chance of winning their case. This episode of *Boston Legal* provided viewers with a lesson on courtroom rhetoric as well as information on a very important disease.

Another example of entertainment combined with information was the American prime-time television drama *Thirtysomething.* According to Blau, the show's producers, Edward Zwick and Marchall Herskovitz aired an episode in which the main character, Nancy (Patricia Wettig), is diagnosed with cancer. Viewers immediately became alarmed (Blau 22 January 1990), and many felt the subject matter was too depressing. Zwick responded by saying 'illness is another aspect of life' (quoted in Blau 22 January 1990). Zwick also made it clear that the network (ABC) had never tried to influence any aspect of the plot and that the show's creative team was always left alone to make important decisions (Blau 22 January 1990). The show that aired is an example of a what can happen when a producer's personal values and ethics, not to mention socially informative storyline, come through. The American Cancer Society requested that their contact number be shown on screen at the end of the show for anyone who wanted to request information (ibid.). Here, the social initiative worked in reverse. The show was developed, the cancer storyline was added, and then the American Cancer Society got involved. A planned program could have allowed for more collaboration from the outset. Nevertheless, convergence changes the way we interact, consume, and learn. Convergence in this instance aligns values and ethics and information and education with media content and media organizations.

Beck (2004) notes that the popular American soap opera *The Bold and the Beautiful*, probably the most-watched television show in the world, broadcast in approximately 110 countries, features universal themes and health issues (p. 208). The soaps *One Life to Live* and *The Young and the Restless* have also highlighted the issue of breast cancer. Beck says about *The Young and the Restless*: 'The educational message embedded in the script addressed screening, diagnosis, and treatment for breast cancer' (p. 211) and notes that 'the PSA [Public Service Announcement] produced in conjunction with the storyline included a toll-free number for Cancer Information Service (CIS) sponsored by the National Cancer Institute' (ibid.). Another prime-time show that educated viewers each week on health-related topics was *House*, a weekly medical drama with comedic elements that ran on Fox TV. Television has had a plethora of issue-oriented episodes in shows produced by Hollywood, and in shows about doctors and set in hospitals, such as *House*, the issues-oriented messages are an organic part of the narrative.

The characters on the CBS show *Numb3rs*, as mentioned in a previous chapter, use mathematical equations to solve crimes. The equations are not for the average person to grasp, but they could easily be part of an edutainment lesson. *Numb3rs* aired an episode that took on the issue of the shortage of organ donors that had the United States glaring in the mirror. Writer David Harden's plot line centered on the black-market organ trade. Health officials did not approve of the storyline, refusing to believe that there is a US black market for organs. They were also concerned that Americans would no longer become organ donors. Ironically, there was an increase in organ donors after the aired episode (Associated Press 2007).

The government agency Centers for Disease Control (CDC) is a resource for Hollywood entertainment, and it has supported several storylines in popular series such as *Chicago Hope, LA Doctors, Beverly Hills*

90210, One Life to Live, General Hospital, Any Day Now, and *Sex in the City,* just to name a few (Beck 2004: 217).

Health messages tie in nicely with programming since they are universal concerns, but they are not the only concerns of society. In the United Kingdom, the BBC is a leader in educational and informational programs. Unlike the US broadcast industry, in which companies are privately owned, the BBC was created under a Royal Charter to be a free service to the public, with a main objective of informing, educating, and entertaining (Cody et al. 2004: 244). A commercial television station, the Independent Television Network (ITV), was later introduced in the UK to provide competition for the BBC. These networks have produced edutainment shows, such as *Coronation Street, Casualty, Doctors,* and the long-running soap *EastEnders. EastEnders* insistence on producing a "slice of life" soap led to a diverse range of important issues addressed over the years' (ibid., p. 248).

The goals of entertainment and prosocial programming may not always be compatible, but once the decision to incorporate an educational message is made, writers and producers strive for accuracy in the portrayal of the information. Furthermore, writers and producers know how to strategically weave in prosocial storylines without losing the program's entertainment value. Beck (2004) notes, 'Writers and producers make decisions about direction and content of storylines, and have the "final say" about what is included in the script. The role of public health in this process is most aptly described as a resource role' (p. 213). Beck is correct in saying that writers and producers have the final say, and they should because they are experts in knowing how to engage audiences worldwide, which is their first priority. It is the role of the health experts the show employs to educate the creative staff about health issues, but these experts have no creative control over what material is used in a storyline. Nonetheless, programs like the ones mentioned above represent a type of edutainment, and serve as models that can evolve and be built upon and then used as a teaching tool in TmSE. In a TmSE setting, however, the subject-matter experts would need to be involved in the creative process. In the future, the writer, producer, and the subject-matter expert will need to collaborate to create edutainment content for higher education.

Some popular-culture film narratives have already been used in higher education. For example, I used the 1997 film *Wag the Dog* in a mass-media module. The film is about a Washington spin doctor who hires a Hollywood film producer to invent a fake war to cover up a sex scandal before the presidential election. This film highlighted the government's manipulation of media and corruption, portraying events that blurred the lines between reality and fiction.

There have also been Hollywood films that can help students discover what it takes to be successful in college and in life. According to Downing, the film *The Matrix Revolutions* was used to give confidence to students to persevere in their collegiate studies and life. Students were asked the following questions: '(1) What was Neo Anderson's motivation for persevering against the controlling machine? (2) Have you faced a similar difficult obstacle and chosen to persevere? Why? (3) How does Neo's persevering compare to your experiences in life or college? (4) What wise choices will you commit to in order to achieve your collegiate and/or life goals?' After brainstorming, individuals and/or groups reported their insights via oral presentations or through journal entries (Downing 2 August 2010).

Downing mentions additional movies that used scene-specific material: *Witness*, which highlights the value of collaboration to achieve a challenging goal; *Ferris Bueller's Day Off*, which encourages students to be responsible for the quality of their education and, ultimately, of their lives; *The Emperor's Club*, which encourages students to make prudent and ethical choices in their education and in life; *Remember the Titans*, used to discuss the scripts we live by and to illustrate personal responsibility; *The Rookie*, which encourages students to persist in their accomplishments and claim their dreams; *What About Bob?* used to help students learn how to break large projects into smaller and manageable tasks; *For the Love of the Game*, used to help students concentrate in the midst of emotional distress; *The Empire Strikes Back*, used to help students understand the significance of their values and beliefs, and influence their choices and accomplishments; *Rocky IV*, used to help students understand that life is not always 'fair' but perseverance can lead to benefits; *Hoosiers*, used to help students see the importance of positive thinking; and *The Karate Kid*, used to help students understand the significance of sticking to something even when there is no immediate payoff (ibid.).

The Center for the Study of Political History and Political Culture at George Washington University and Mediapede, an organization devoted to enhancing the understanding of history through film, offer teaching guides for five films that are suitable for the teaching of history. Mediapede.org lists them as follows: '*The Crucible*, an adaptation of the Arthur Miller play about the Salem Witchcraft Trials of 1692; *The Last of the Mohicans*, an adaptation of the novel by James Fenimore Cooper about Indian-white relations; *Lone Star*, John Sayles' 1996 film looks at how Tejanos, African Americans, Native Americans, Mexicans, and

Anglo-Americans in Frontera, Texas, interact with each other and deal with the actions of generations past; *1776*, a savvy musical about the drafting of the US Constitution; *The Truman Show* [1998], the fictitious story of a thirty-year-old man whose entire life has been broadcast to a global audience as a TV show' (Mediapede Organization n.d.). Each teaching guide contains a summary of the story; age-appropriateness recommendations; suggestions for how to break down the movie for classroom instruction; discussions of sections of the film, depending on the subject of focus; suggested classroom activities and discussion; hyperlinks to related content; and specific film analysis and media literacy activities (Mediapede Organization n.d.). The e-module which I conducted was also linked to other sources, giving students the capacity to compare different versions of history as they are portrayed in other sources, which is part of the case study that can be found in Chapter 6. The above-mentioned teaching guides are excellent resources that could easily be emulated as transmedia makes its way into education.

According to Voeltz (2010), additional examples of films used to teach history, either in their entirety or through clips, are: '*Revolution* (1985), *Alamo* (1960, 2004), *Glory* (1989), *Sergeant York* (1941), *Saving Private Ryan* (1998), *The Day the Earth Stood Still* (1951), *Salt of the Earth* (1954), *Dr. Strangelove* (1964), *JFK* (1991), *Born on the Fourth of July* (1989), *The Hurricane* (1999), *Mississippi Burning* (1988), *Thunderheart* (1992), *Dances with Wolves* (1990), *Forrest Gump* (1994), *Black Hawk Down* (2001), *Gunner Palace* (2004), *Saving Jessica Lynch* (2003), *American Beauty* (1999), *Titanic* (1997), and *Walker* (1987)'. Oliver Stone (14 July 2000), known for his films *JFK* and *Nixon*, puts into context the relationship between historians, filmmaking, and the facts. He talks about the use of facts in his film *Nixon*: 'As far as facts go, I used them as best I could, but the truth is, you can't use them all. You are forced to omit some. And any honest historian will tell you that he does that, too' (p. B9). Stone talks frankly about historians:

> Let's face it – any historian knows that jealousy plays a huge factor in human affairs. We're especially vulnerable here in Hollywood to a public fantasy business that is fodder for the media. The outside world thinks of us all as rich and irresponsible. But the truth is, many of us work long hours (60- to 80-hour weeks for some directors) and are harried by the pressure to make films pleasing to large audiences within an expensive financial structure. I think many historians, whether they know it or not, are equally subject to this jealousy, and, thinking that history is their territory only, they come at filmmakers

with an attitude of hostility. To them we pervert the paradigm with emotion, sentimentality, and so on. But historians exhibit much pomposity when they think that they alone are in custody of the 'facts', and they take it upon themselves to guard 'the truth' as zealously as the chief priests of ancient Egypt; the prophesies must belong to them and them alone. I don't think anyone who knows of the jealousies extant in any cerebral profession, be it history or filmmaking, will question the petty infighting that results each year for prizes, awards, and tenure-all at the expense of true investigation or creation. (Stone 14 July 2000: B9)

By the same token, Giddens (1984) states, 'Literary style is not irrelevant to the accuracy of social descriptions ... [because] the social sciences draw upon the same source of description (mutual knowledge) as novelists or others who write fictional accounts of social life' (p. 285). In addition, complex information can be conveyed by recollecting the events of the past via film.

Moreover, math is also prevalent in films and there are several examples of these films used in educational settings. Oliver Knill, who teaches mathematics at Harvard University, describes this practice on his website. He has used such films as *The Hangover* (2009), 'simple arithmetic to Fourier theory'; *A Serious Man* (2009), 'the Uncertainty Principle in Quantum Mechanics'; and *The Double* (2011), 'a statistics lesson on hypothesis and p-value' (Knill 2006–2010). Knill also uses film as a teacher-training resource that explores the questions, 'What effective teaching elements can you identify in the clips? What is ineffective?' For this he uses a clip from *A Beautiful Mind* (2001), in which 'mathematician John Nash (Russell Crow) gives his first multivariable calculus lesson at MIT around 1951 ... [and] throws the book into the garbage and presents a problem which is above the level of a beginning multivariable calculus student' (Knill 13 September 2005). Other examples include a clip from *Kinsley* (2004), in which 'biologist Alfred Kinsey (Liam Neeson) gives his first lecture on human sexuality at Indiana University around 1948 ... [and] starts the lecture while entering the room', and *Mona Lisa Smile* (2003), in which Katherine Ann Watson (Julia Roberts), a history of arts professor at Wellesley College teaches her first lesson to students who just happen to know all the material before the lesson begins (ibid.).

Knill, then, uses film to teach math as well as the art of teaching. And it is a well-known fact that 'Harvard Business School has a long tradition in teaching complicated topics using stories, in the form of cases' (Ruggles 1 August 1999: 2), and several higher education institutions have already incorporated the case-study method into their programs. Some of the case studies that have been created have incorporated problems faced by media conglomerates. This method could evolve to incorporate stories in which characters of popular media appear; the stories could address some of the characters' problems, wherever appropriate, or the characters could be used in another context that extends the story.

Steven Johnson believes popular culture is making us smarter outside the classroom as well:

> For decades, we've worked under the assumption that mass culture follows a steadily declining path toward lowest-common-denominator standards, presumably because the 'masses' want dumb, simple pleasures and big media companies want to give the masses what they want. But in fact, the exact opposite is happening: the culture is getting more intellectually demanding, not less. (2006: 9)

Television and film narratives have become more complex, forcing the viewer to make sense of interwoven and difficult plots. Ironically, both media content and advertising demand that viewers make sense of both what is there and what is not. Johnson argues, 'Narratives that require that their viewers fill in crucial elements take that complexity to a more demanding level. To follow a narrative, you aren't asked to remember. You're asked to analyze' (2006: 63–64). Johnson further explains:

> There may indeed be more 'negative messages' in the mediasphere today, as the Parents Television Council believes. But that's not the only way to evaluate whether our television shows or video games are having a positive impact. Just as important – if not *more* important – is the thinking you have to do to make sense of a cultural experience... Today's popular culture may not be showing us the righteous path. But it is making us smarter. (ibid.: 14)

It may be in the educational system's best interest to adapt or even to help spearhead the development of media products that can put learners, who are a part of a wider popular culture, on a 'righteous path'. Either way, people are exposed to media, so why not use it wisely. Johnson believes that games are making us smarter too. He says it is the reward system that draws us into playing video games, not the subject matter, and points out that 'no other form of entertainment offers that cocktail of reward and exploration' (2006: 38). The desire to figure out the game and decipher the rules is compelling. Games force players to analyze situations and make decisions. Johnson contends that 'no other popular culture form directly engages the brain's decision-making apparatus the same way' (p. 41). Johnson's ideas challenge the conventional wisdom that the increasing number of negative messages in entertainment is hindering people's value systems. Although media alone do not create a downward spiral of society; however, there does appear to be a general decline in morals and values in society, and this raises some questions, especially if mankind is under the belief that entertainment content mirrors society. Nonetheless, the overall argument here is to use the power of media and transmedia storytelling practices to benefit society in a more strategic manner.

American media is engrained in contemporary culture, and this makes teaching through edutainment extremely popular. Today, it is easy to access a movie through DVD rentals, Internet downloads, cable and satellite television and, in the future, via TmSE content. Different audiences, like different academic disciplines, require different content. Dena (2009) defines and explains the process called *tiering*, which addresses 'different audiences with different content in different media and environments' (p. 239). She elaborates, 'tiering denotes the design of projects that facilitate different points-of-entry into a transmedia fiction through targeting different content (and in many cases media) to different audiences' (ibid.). Dena adds that 'some of the tiering practices, for instance, are specific to the knowledge and skills of both the practitioners and audiences' (p. 330). As the skills of the practitioner and the learner evolve, it will create opportunities for targeted content that can be located on the Internet. Tiering can also be incorporated into a TmSE strategy.

What is needed in the future is a partnership between entertainment conglomerates and educational institutions, rather than just clinging on to the current model in which socially responsible programming is often an afterthought. We need more strategic development of educational narratives. The Internet facilitates interaction by providing a place for conversation, and information sharing, as well as a platform for edutainment stories. Edutainment content can be integrated within a transmedia enterprise and also have a compelling Internet component, providing educational knowledge and interest-based learning via story worlds. TmSE delivered via the Internet has the capacity to reach new audiences in new ways. Story extensions tailored for this new audience can provide both entertainment and education. As mentioned earlier, Beard, De Fossard, and Robin have all noted the importance of a 'hook' to capture online learners' attention. 'In edu-tainment, this "hook" is provided through an entertaining background story, or through entertaining characters that can attract and hold student interests' (De Fossard 2008: 20). In the education setting, Robert Gagné's Nine Steps of Instruction (1985) puts 'gain attention' first. The 'hook' is also entertainment-industry jargon for grabbing a viewer's attention. Clark (2004) expanded on Gagné's instructional steps as shown in Figure 4.1.

Many instructional designers (Mayer 1999; Schaller and Allison-Bunnell 2003) feel that the traditional learning theories, which evolved in the industrial age, are no longer appropriate in the information age. But traditional learning theories do not rule out the use of entertainment (note Gagné's step one: gain attention).

Raines puts it into a story perspective: 'Once upon a time people told stories to share experiences and to teach. With the growing popularity of distance-learning modalities educators have been searching for ways to enhance social presence and reflective thinking in the online learning experience' (Raines 9 August 2010). Education scholars such as Raines (2010) have already acknowledged the human connection that digital storytelling provides. The use of story forms is thus a good strategy for enhancing social presence, reflective thinking, and bringing emotion into online education. In addition, the interaction with popular culture or industry-produced stories has the advantage of established engagement. Producing a transmedia component under a particular discipline with a subject matter expert is highly beneficial in the context of narrative instruction. Although Cole (1997: 136) believes that 'narratives must be authentic with respect to the lives, culture, plights, and language of the populations for whom the materials are designed', I do not believe this to be entirely true. American popular culture would not

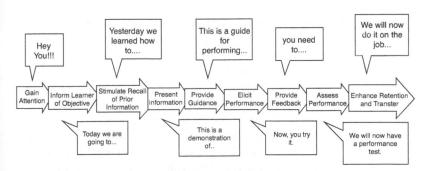

Figure 4.1   Robert Gagné's nine steps of instruction
Source: Clark 1 October 2004.

be as popular as it is around the world if this were the case. I do believe that narratives must be authentic to their story worlds, and when they are, people in all cultures will connect to them on an emotional level. Narratives designed specifically for use in education will be authentic by nature. Moreover, the interactive nature of the Internet is also authentic and keeps users involved: searching, seeking, and sharing information. This behavior is important to illustrate and understand because it is a form of active learning.

Clearly, the teaching of many disciplines could benefit dramatically from the availability of compelling and stimulating moving image. The Internet is the perfect place for the storing of material, which can easily be accessed in e-learning environments. The idea is to take the edutainment initiatives and disperse them on the Internet, so that they can be freely accessed. Transmedia storytelling allows for the creation of different layers of interaction depending on the users' different needs. Individuals who seek more education can interact with the educational layers, and individuals who want more entertainment can access those layers. Communication on the Internet is multidirectional and multicultural, and available in multiple forms. The edutainment content can be produced and extended by media conglomerates working from a new business model, or a reverse strategy is underway by innovative professors, such as Harvard's Professor Knill, who appreciates popular culture and strives to make a difference. Transmedia storytelling as an edutainment initiative already has a history and is waiting for the next narrative.

4.8 Transformational education: a model for social change

It is clear that the gap between entertainment and education must be bridged. The potential to transform the business of entertainment and the business of education depends on it. There is an enormous business and educational potential in converging the two practices, and the Internet is the perfect platform for a TmSE business model. It can serve as a repository for edutainment content produced by the studios and made available to higher education as an online e-resource. In this model, entertainment producers would work with subject-matter experts, and together they would produce TmSE content. Edutainment learning routes could be planned and provided by media conglomerates through their collaboration with subject-matter experts, or they could be selected by the instructors. The content would need to be catalogued by discipline, and learning outcomes would need to be provided. A description of how and where to use/reuse the e-resource should also be supplied. Currently, instructors must scan the literature to aggregate material for their modules and this can take time, which may be limited. Thus, a repository of edutainment content could be invaluable to instructors. Below, is a basic business-to-business (B2B) model for TmSE. It is based on a B2B outline provided by the Board of Innovation website (19 March 2009).

The Players:

A. The entertainment company
   The producers of edutainment content.
B. The higher education consumer
   The client, who receives the edutainment product.

Part 2: The flow from company to client

Product:
A digital TmSE product which is available as an e-resource on a website.

Service:
Instructions on how to use the learning material and assignment suggestions.

Experience:
The entertainment company sells more than learning material; they sell an educational experience.

Reputation:
Selling the status of 'Hollywood and Harvard' (entertainment and education) which is an essential brand experience.

Part 3: The flow from client to company

Money:
The payment scheme can either follow the Subscription Model or the Sponsorship Model or a combination of the two. The payment scheme based on the Subscription Model provides for a monthly and/or yearly fee to be paid by the higher education institution. The instructor would have access to a wide range of learning material, which would include instruction and assignment suggestions.

Less Money:
The payment scheme based on the Sponsorship Model would allow for the viewing of commercial messages by the instructor such as a movie trailer, which could be exchanged with content availability (Downes

2007). The Sponsorship Model could also be targeted to the learner who could view a trailer, and subsequently be given access to create user-generated content.

Attention:
Under the Conversion Model, clients get some content for free and then convert the consumer to a paying customer (Sterne and Herring 2005).

Exposure:
The exposure of the story world via educational extensions adds value to the franchise.

To sum up: the website and the content need to be interoperable on all platforms; that is, standards need to be put into place to ensure that end. In terms of accessibility, the user needs to have the technical skills to access data and also must be able to navigate around the story world in a meaningful way. Copyright laws could regulate educational use cross-culturally.

4.9   *Pedagogy of the Oppressed*

Paulo Freire's ground-breaking book *Pedagogy of the Oppressed* (first published in Portuguese in 1968 and in English in 1970) grew out of his experiences teaching literacy to Latin America's rural poor. His pedagogical work was rooted in revolutionary ideas, but his ideas are not dependent on a revolutionary context, and, therefore, they are also important within the context of e-learning and TmSE. It is essential to take a look at Freire's pedagogy because it includes a critique of the traditional educational system, and, more importantly, he offers insight into the collaborative and reflective practices that are central to online learning environments of today.

Freire did not feel that teachers possess absolute knowledge and that students were merely empty recipients of that knowledge. He thought that teachers should collaborate with students to solve problems. Freire opposed what he identified as 'banking education', in which the teacher 'fills' the students with knowledge because the teacher is said to have absolute authority. In this framework, education is merchandise that is packaged and delivered to the student. Under the banking model, students are excluded from gaining first-hand knowledge through inquiry and participation. This prescribed version of the world does not encourage any form of inquiry; what it does do is support the conventions and norms of society. Today, communication is multidirectional, which is antagonistic to the traditional model of banking education that consists of one-directional dialogue. In banking education, the exceptional students repeat the narrative that has been told to them by the instructor who is considered the authority figure. Under the banking model, critical thinking is suppressed and compliance and social conformism are encouraged. Ironically, banking education is still favored in the West and is prominent in traditional forms of teaching around the world.

In contrast to banking education is what Freire defines as 'problem-posing' education. Freire asserts that problem-posing education fosters collaboration between the instructor and the learner. In this scenario, the instructor does not have absolute authority over the subject matter. Both the instructor and the student seek truth, and the truth of matter is that the teacher does not always have all the answers. Freire argued, 'Whereas banking education anesthetizes and inhibits creative power, problem-posing education involves a constant unveiling of reality. The former attempts to maintain the submersion of consciousness; the latter strives for the emergence of consciousness and critical intervention in reality' (Freire 1996: 68). That is to say, those who are committed to liberation should accept problem-posing education. He connects problem-posing education to the Greek word 'praxis', which is contextualized as the act of engaging, exercising, applying, realizing, or practicing ideas.

Furthermore, Freire (1996) states: 'Problem-posing education bases itself on creativity and stimulates true reflection and action upon reality, thereby responding to the vocation of persons as beings who are authentic only when engaged in inquiry and creative transformation' (p. 71). In problem-posing education, teacher and student are mutually responsible for their growth, which is synonymous with the new learning environments of today. Moreover, the practical application of learning by way of digital storytelling aligns with the concept of praxis. Before we delve into digital storytelling, it is important to look at the Freirean concept of dialogue in action:

> In order to understand the meaning of dialogical practice, we have to put aside the simplistic understanding of dialogue as mere technique...dialogue characterizes an epistemological relationship. Thus, in this sense, dialogue is a way of knowing and should never be viewed as a mere tactic to involve students in a particular task...dialogue presents itself as an indispensable component of the process of both learning and knowing. (Freire 2000: 17)

Freire believed that liberating dialogue should not be understood as a tactic used to befriend students because as such it would only be a technique for manipulating them, and not a dialogue that creates reflection and illumination. According to Freire and Shore (1987), 'dialogue is a moment where humans meet to reflect on their reality as they make and remake it' (p. 98).

To put this into context, digital storytelling takes into account what Freire called *dialogical action* (1996), which is a combination of *reflection* and *action*, and what Schön called *reflective practice* (1983), which focuses on how tacit knowledge can be made explicit, the object of reflection. However, it was Dewey (1933) who formulated the concept of 'reflective conversation with the situation' (see Schön 1992). With this in mind, the act of creating a digital artefact engages the digital storyteller in a reflective conversation with the process. This aligns with both Dewey (1933) and Schön (1983), who contend that there needs to be 'a reflective conversation with the materials of a situation', and this forms what Freire called praxis, or simply put, the product of intention. To reiterate, Freire believed strongly in *dialogical action*, which he explains further:

> Action without reflection leads to 'activism' and that is doing without thinking, reflection without action leads to 'verbalism' and that is talking without doing. Action and reflection combined lead to personal and societal transformation through real work, and that is considered theory and practice in dialogue with one another or 'Action + Reflection = word = work = praxis'. (Freire 1996: 68)

The Freirean approach created circumstances which were images of real-world situations relevant to the lives of his poor students, and which were intended to generate dialogue, much in the same way a story does. The facilitators valued what the students already knew and built on their knowledge in order to achieve what Freire called a *critical consciousness*. Consciousness-raising was articulated as a theory of transformative learning, and to this end, Freire's work has influenced the development of a critical perspective in adult learning. Freire states, 'Acquiring literacy does not involve memorizing sentences, words, or syllables – lifeless objects unconnected to an existential universe – but rather an attitude of creation and re-creation, a self transformation producing a stance of intervention in one's context' (p. 48). This coincides with the digital storytelling movement of today because his pedagogy, which can be considered an act of 'creation and re-creation' and 'self-transformation', parallels the process of storytelling in many ways. That is to say, story-telling does not only foster dialogue and knowledge, but it transforms an individual, both in the act of creation and as spectator.

The Freirean method parallels online environments, where the participants construct knowledge and are guided by a mentor. Freire's pedagogy underpins web-based, constructivist-learning environments, and therefore has informed the e-module case study. Arias (2000) coined the term 'electronic pedagogy of the oppressed', which refers to the creative possibilities made viable by distance-learning technology.

The Freirean concept of critical pedagogy remains crucial to empowering learners, and it has been embraced by the academic community. The critical pedagogue Henry Giroux describes the philosophy of transformational education as an 'educational movement, guided by passion and principle, to help students develop consciousness of freedom, recognize authoritarian tendencies, and connect knowledge to power and the ability to take constructive action' (Giroux 17 October 2010). Shor defines critical pedagogy as going beneath the surface of meaning 'to understand the deep meaning, root causes, social context, ideology, and personal consequences of any action, event, object, process, organization, experience, text, subject matter, policy, mass media, or discourse' (Shor 1992: 129). Critical pedagogy, therefore, is an approach that empowers students for social change and it aims to democratize educational practices (Darder et al. 2009). Additionally, both critical and transformative practices have similarities in their theoretical influences, evaluation and critique of education, as well as their desire for individual and social change. For social change to occur, however, there needs to be an awareness of power relations and disparities that are built into universities. To this extent, the main goal of critical pedagogy is to transform formal education and its institutions.

The goal may be achieved by incorporating a storytelling approach because the thread that underlies critical pedagogy and transformative learning also underlies TmSE. The TmSE approach empowers students, creates awareness, and values collaboration in much the same way critical and transformative practices do. It is a form of active inquiry that revolves around dialogical and creative action. The populace has shifted gears from the information age to the engagement age, and in this new age, educators need to consider suitable transformative practices such as TmSE.

4.10   Transformative learning through transmedia storytelling: a critical-creative pedagogy

The world, and in particular higher education, is in flux, and there are opportunities to seize the moment and bring about educational change. The transformative model aligns within a socioconstructivist paradigm, where individuals collaborate and construct knowledge (Candy 1991; Cranton 1994). The transformative model extends the notion of collaboration and takes into consideration the individual's social construction of meaning, which, ironically, brings us back to the individual's learning style.

In writing this book, I initially set out to investigate learning styles and a new model of education; however, I was enlightened when TmSE emerged as a new model of transformative learning. Mezirow (2003) defines transformative learning as education 'that transforms problematic frames of reference – sets of fixed assumptions and expectations (habits of mind, meaning, perspectives, mindsets) – to make them more inclusive, discriminating, open, reflective, and emotionally able to change' (p. 58). On the other hand, Bowers (2005) views transformative learning as the 'Trojan Horse' of Western globalization, and argues that 'transformative approaches to learning undermine other forms of knowledge and intergenerational renewal that are essential to resisting the spread of the anomic form of individualism that is dependent upon consumerism' (p. 4). Kostoulias believes that 'transformative learning is not a fait accommpli; it is an organic theory and stance of pedagogical learning within which transformative approaches to learning can foster and grow' (Kostoulias et al. 2011: 668). Viewing transmedia storytelling from a transformative perspective, I do not agree that it undermines other forms of knowledge; rather it opens up other frames of references and perspectives to create meaning. It extends knowledge, and it does so holistically through the ancient art of storytelling. This ancient art has always been a form of teaching and learning, and it is appropriate even in this century. Nelson explores:

> Contrary to today's concept of all education being career training, indigenous societies were aware of innate gifts in individuals and nurtured those gifts towards a place and time that would allow the individual to contribute more effectively to the group. Education was considered a community process. Using storytelling, as initially developed in indigenous societies, can return the community awareness

and a spiritual view of connectedness to nature back to education in a holistic manner. (2009: 208)

Storytelling nurtures learners' individual creativity and makes them aware of those 'innate gifts'.

Patrick Hogan, at the University of Connecticut, believes narrative is a powerful tool that can be used for persuasion (quoted in Hsu 2008). Psychologist Melanie Green co-authored a study in 2006 that demonstrated that 'labelling information as "fact" increased critical analysis, whereas labelling information as "fiction" had the opposite effect'. This suggests that 'people accept ideas more readily when their minds are in story mode as opposed to when they are in an analytical mind-set' (quoted in Hsu 2008: 6). But if the power of stories makes them an exceptional educational tool, in the wrong hands they can become dangerous weapons. Therefore, the use of stories must be guided by ethical and moral considerations and by an understanding of the working of the human mind.

Nelson (2009) calls storytelling 'an ancient human technology', and likens it to computers: stories contain metaphors and symbols, just as computers contain machine codes. Nelson (1998b) believes that 'metaphors and symbols are in the realm of the non rational unconscious mind and as such can enhance non rational learning' (cited in Nelson 2009: 215). Pribram (1981) believes the unconscious mind encompasses a substantial amount of the overall brain mass. Nelson (1998b, 2003) explores, 'if the unconscious can be accessed for learning, students' potentials will be much greater and teachers' jobs will be much easier since more mind potential is available for learning' (cited in Nelson 2009: 216). Nelson continues, 'Since metaphors are processed in the nonrational unconscious parts of the brain, using metaphors in stories allows a teacher, guide or facilitator to actually communicate "underneath" the limited frames of reference in the conscious mind, speeding transformational learning' (p. 217).

The very fact that stories are supported by a variety of disciplines makes them alluring as pedagogy. Aligning with cognitive and educational psychologists are media psychologists, such as Rutledge, and neuroscientists, such as Zull and Medina, who are fascinated by the fact that the human brain is wired to enjoy and remember stories. Iacoboni (2009) concurs, and Buckner and Rutledge (2011) highlight that to the brain a story appears to be a real experience, and that 'people remember messages in stories far longer and with greater accuracy than any other form of communication' (p. 2). A story will be remembered long after it is told. The benefit of story is that not only does it induce engagement; the experience tends to be remembered.

According to Giroux, transformative learning is based on critically evaluating the assumptions underlying media practices:

> Educators need a more expansive view of knowledge and pedagogy that provides the conditions for young people and adults to engage popular media and mass culture as serious objects of social analysis and to learn how to read them critically through specific strategies of understanding engagement and transformation. Informing this notion of knowledge and pedagogy is a view of literacy that is multiple and plural rather than singular and fixed. (Giroux 2004: 68)

Taking a step further, Giroux suggests that we come to understand engagement and transformation associated with popular media, which essentially, is what will come into fruition as TmSE evolves. TmSE aligns with the thoughts of transformative learning theorists and provides an effective space for discourse. For those who participate, there will be full access to information and equal opportunities to explain, challenge and defend, and assess and judge arguments, as well as to advance beliefs. Critical-creative pedagogy along with TmSE transforms the learning process and allows learners to be creative, critical, and reflective. It helps learners decipher the text to discover true meaning. '*Transmedia Storytelling Edutainment* engages learners to re-create, reflect, refract, reframe and retain' (Kalogeras 2013: 118). In addition, critical reflection of the story transforms frames of references and establishes new points of views.

Giroux acknowledges critical pedagogy 'as a cultural practice that must be accountable ethically and politically for the stories it produces, the claims it makes on social memories and the images of the future it deems legitimate' (2004: 69). Transmedia storytelling can either emerge ethically, or it can materialize as an economic force. At its core TmSE is about 'return on education' but along with this comes a 'return on investment'. 'Transformative learning lends an ethical dimension to TmSE and the people behind the practice, as much as the pedagogy itself. This includes an ethical dimension associated with both methods and intentions' (Kalogeras 2013: 117–118).

Kegan (1994) acknowledges that transformative learning occurs when someone changes 'not just the way he behaves, not just the way he feels, but the way he knows – not just what he knows but the *way* he knows' (p. 17). According to Kegan, transformation must include formational development of self, such as mind, heart, and spirit, as well as the actual reconstruction of that self and the way in which the self discerns the world. As stated in 'Making a World of Difference: A Dice Resource for Practitioners on Educational Theatre and Drama', 'Drama creates dramatic situations to be explored by the participants, inviting them to find out more about the process of how the situation comes into being, to shift perspectives in the here and now, identify and sometimes solve problems and deepen understanding of them' (Dice Consortium 2010). Ultimately, this changes what someone feels and knows and how they behave.

The Socratic method is an ancient form of discourse that was developed from Plato's *Socratic Dialogues* and founded on Socrates's belief that the lecture was not an effective practice of teaching all students. The fundamental principle of the Socratic method is that students learn by practicing critical thinking, reasoning, and logic, and finding holes in their own theories and questioning are essential. According to Copeland (2005), 'Socratic questioning is a systematic process for examining the ideas, questions, and answers that form the basis of human belief. It involves recognizing that all new understanding is linked to prior understanding, that thought itself is a continuous thread woven throughout lives rather than isolated sets of questions and answers' (pp. 7–8). TmSE aligns with the Socratic method through the practice of questioning. That is to say, the cross-questioning, cross-examination, and cross-communication of cross-media analysis can enhance cultural sensitivity. It can help people better understand differences in views, perceptions, as well as provide potential solutions. The Socratic method of teaching is a student-centered approach that engages students in analytical discussion and critical thinking. Socratic teaching engages students in collaborative discussions and the goal is to help students engage with the topics on a much deeper level – this is also the goal of *transformative learning through transmedia storytelling edutainment.*

Moving forward, for transformative learning to take place it will go beyond the classroom to bridge inequalities and form partnerships. What is more vital to transformative learning is the educators and administrators who refuse to give up old practices. Cranton explains how fear hinders transformative teaching practices:

> Most of us feel discomfort in giving up positions of power, for example, and we worry about the reactions of colleagues or program administrators to our unorthodox approach to teaching. To become a

truly equal participant in the group process is to feel vulnerable as an educator. Perhaps the roles evolve best with confidence in what one is doing and experience in doing it well. (1996: 31)

As an educator in practice, I have witnessed 'discomfort' by the students who were not flexible to new methods of instruction; therefore, students will need to be trained to accept new teaching practices. Moreover, it appears that students are accustomed to the traditional lecture, even though their attention spans are limited, and learning retention is minimal. Nonetheless, for transformative learning to be effective the role of the instructor is critical for classroom modification.

Transformative learning by way of storytelling edutainment is an instructional strategy for all learning styles because it offers various modes of communication. It presents learning material in an appealing format, and because it is a multiplatform strategy, there are more ways to reach learners even when there is economic inequality that may be associated with a digital divide. A danger of the approach would be making the learner dependent on all platforms. On the other hand, TmSE can transcend education by removing the barriers between people and social systems, and thereby can contribute to the liberation of both. Further, TmSE can improve education through its four central elements: *media*, which is multimodal, multiplatform and multicultural; *content*, which is more ethical and democratic; *process*, which is strategically planned and administered; and finally, *technology*, which supports a broader gamut of learning content.

As I have written in the *International Journal of Information and Communication Technology*: 'Transmedia Storytelling Edutainment is a transformative learning strategy and critical-creative pedagogy, which is holistic to the way humans learn and prefer to learn. It empowers learners to uncover layers of meaning which they can verify or disapprove' (Kalogeras 2013: 119). The goal of TmSE is to capture learners' attention, which is the first step to achieving retention. For transformative learning to take place, however, it requires innovative educators, mechanisms of support, and above all, learners who make their expectations explicit. Today, learners are expressing their needs through media-generated activities like digital storytelling. Our focus now turns to the representation of knowledge through fiction and my personal narrative.

5
Fiction: A Screenplay-to-Understanding

In this chapter, fiction is shown to be a relevant form of educating. While fiction is a different way of reporting, it provides a profound way to express truth. What is more, the mythology of my own life story is presented in the context of diasporic discourse, which is vividly explained in reference to the screenplay *The Goddess Within*. The narrative theories, reflective practice, and the transmedia storytelling framework are introduced and analyzed.

5.1 The representation of knowledge through fiction

There is common ground between fiction and non-fiction, and literature can be considered a form of knowledge representation. In Benjamin's (1989) view, all knowledge of reality is subjective and is mediated by the forms that represent and describe it, and diverse modes of representation convey diverse visions of the world. Yet, there is a basic divide between literature and the social sciences, as Czarniawska-Joerges points out:

> The first is that one is fiction and the other is non-fiction: the basis for telling the story is different. However, this is relative. There are many writers who use factual events for their novels and many social scientists who use fictitious reality to illustrate... The second is that social scientists are obligated to be systematic, that is, to demonstrate a method, which is also relative. Writers often have a very systematic mood. (1992: 218)

In a different manner of thought, historian White (1973) dismisses the distinction between literature and science, and argues that the social sciences use a perceived aesthetic value rather than presumed factual data, or even objective theory. White's historical work focuses on accounts of the 19th century and shows how these accounts are structurally similar to the structure of a realist novel, which depicts life and society as they are. White explains that persuasion comes from rhetorical strategies and that this is because all interpretation is basically rhetorical. He says the uncertainty as to how to describe a phenomenon in a historical context can lead to a figurative account rather than an objective means of persuasion. In science the ideal is to be observer-independent; however, historians are aware that their conclusions are dependent on observation. According to Dray:

> While certain historians have from time to time wished for 'scientific' objectivity – wished to tell the past 'as it really was' – most historians have acknowledged that the problem of *point of view* is something that is built into historical scholarship, and that it cannot be avoided. History, in contrast to science, is necessarily a perspectival form of inquiry. (1989: 54)

There are fine lines between literature, social science, and history. Therefore, one is left to have their own point of view on the topic; however, it is vital to recognize the nuances of each. Curti (1998) argues that 'the debate within history studies suggests that there is more than one history, and that official histories exist in parallel with hidden ones... [and therefore] fantasy becomes another way to connect with reality and history' (p. 27). She believes that 'fact and fiction are different but crucial aspects of the same reality' (ibid.).

According to Nock (1943), the most important principle of literary aesthetics was formulated by Aristotle, who believed that history 'represents things only as they are, while fiction represents them as they might be and ought to be' (p. 191).

Likewise, Foucault (1984) contends that text categorized as literary fiction was once accepted as the principal medium for expressing truths related to humans and their understanding of the world. This corresponds with how positivist scientific discourse was received in its day as authoritative pro forma. In *The Complete Works of St. Thomas More*, More professed his fervent desire to pen his political piece *Utopia* (1516) as 'a fiction whereby the truth, as it smeared by honey, might a little more pleasantly slip into men's minds' (More 1964: 251). It appears that the written word, as it comes to us from novelists, playwrights, poets, and even screenwriters, is an alternative way to represent knowledge. It is not unusual for some works of literary fiction to be considered better than most scholarly writing, and this is because fiction can influence large bodies of people with its wide reach.

In 2007 the film version of Khaled Hosseni's popular novel *The Kite Runner* was released and nominated for a Golden Globe award in the best foreign-language film category. The book and film informed readers and viewers alike about life in Afghanistan. Based on the numbers, it is likely that more people saw the film worldwide ($73,276,047) (Boxoffice mojo n.d.) than read the book, which sold 10 million copies (Wark 11 April 2008). *The Kite Runner* was entertaining and informative, and perhaps made a greater contribution to public understanding of life in Afghanistan than many research projects could have. And Shrilal Shukla treated his award-winning novel, *Raag Darbari*, as a sort of research project, as he drew on personal experience to write about corruption in India. According to Lewis et al. (2008), '*Raag Darbari* arguably constitutes an example of literary fiction that can be considered "better" than much of the academic or policy-oriented research from this period as a result of its nuanced understanding and detailed depiction' (p. 6).

The Goddess Within screenplay holds a complex collection of creative, professional, and personal motives. The story, when presented in screentext form for use in the e-module, provides more subject matter knowledge because of the hyperlinks, and so the story itself has achieved insight into social adaptation and perception. Literature conveys complex ideas, and images can make those ideas come to life. The way stories are framed is critical to understanding dominant public ideas. Lewis et al. (2008) contend that 'having a good story is essential if one wants to make a difference in the world', and they argue that 'when one story is a more compelling means of articulating a situation than another, then development scholars and practitioners ought to perhaps think more positively about it, be it a novel, a poem, or a play rather than an academic monograph or policy report' (p. 11).

Such learning theorists as Knowles (1975, 1984) and Keller (1987) believe adult learners must see the relevance of something in order to be persuaded to learn about it. Concepts that are explained in the context of a story which learners can relate to are crucial to the learning process, while the realism of the story makes information easier to remember. Ausubel and Robinson (1969), Donald A. Norman (1994), and Stein and Trabasso (1982) believe that through the storytelling process learners can integrate knowledge into their mental models in meaningful and compelling ways. It seems that stories capture the big picture and movies make sense to the brain.

In his book *Things That Make Us Smart*, Norman (1994) aligns stories with cognitive events for the reason that stories encapsulate context, knowledge, information, and emotion. It appears to be much easier to remember lessons by way of stories than by way of lists of facts.

> The powers of cognition come from abstraction and representation: the ability to represent perceptions, experiences, and thoughts in some medium other than that in which they have occurred, abstracted away from irrelevant details. This is the essence of intelligence, for if the representation and the processes are just right, then new experiences, insights, and creations can emerge. (Norman 1994: 3)

Norman highlights a fundamental point which is that humans can produce symbols 'to represent something else and then do reasoning by using those marks'. People do this naturally, he says, it is not an 'abstract, academic exercise' (p. 3). It is the use of cognitive artifacts, in the form of symbols, or even characters, that substitute the unreal for the real. *The Goddess Within* uses the following artifacts: Athena, for myself; Kyriakos, for the ideal man; Peter, the non-ideal man; and Zeus, the strong father figure. There was also the silver heart pendant, which Athena fidgets with in an uncomfortable situation, and her comfort food of choice, chocolate. The story also draws on mythological symbols such as Athena's owl, Aphrodite's mirror, Hera's cow, and finally, the Golden Apple, which represents the 'fairest of them all' in both the modern and ancient story.

Putting the symbols of the Gods into context like this helps put things into perspective in the modern-day *Goddess* story. I begin with Athena and the owl. In folklore, myth, and pop culture, the owl is associated with wisdom. The patroness of the city of Athens, Athena, the goddess of wisdom and strategy, had several symbols, such as the owl and the olive tree; however, she was frequently described as '"grey-eyed" (*glaucopis*), which many believe refer not so much to her eye color as to the bright-eyed mental alertness that is her very essence' (Chrisler et al. 1998: ix). Aphrodite's mirror, in times both modern and ancient, is connected to beauty. Aphrodite, when gazing at her reflection in the mirror, takes pleasure in the sight of her beauty. Among the many symbols connected to Hera, I will focus on the cow which was used in *The Goddess* story. According to the website Greek-Gods.info, Hera was the goddess of marriage and motherhood. 'Her sacred animals were the peacock and the cow' and she was said to have cow eyes (Sosa 1998). She was known to disguise herself in various myths.

In the modern-day story of *The Goddess Within*, the symbols of the Gods take on a double meaning in that they are associated with their original source as well as adapted into a new context; thus they may be considered to be intertextual symbols. The owl is Athena's inner wisdom or the wisdom of the soul. In one of the paintings in the story, Aphrodite's mirror is resting near the apple when the glass animates, revealing Hera – the culprit behind the theft of the Golden Apple. Then there is the cow-eyed Hera, who disguises herself as a friend as she disguised herself as a cow in the Greek myths. *The Goddess Within* uses a number of symbols and representations to convey meaning. Norman (1994) believes 'a good representation captures the essential elements of the event, deliberately leaving out the rest', and he contends that 'representation is never the same as the thing being represented, else there would be no advantage to using one' (p. 4). However, he notes that getting the abstraction correct by representing the important versus the least important is essential. Representations can thus be either powerful or weak, and a powerful 'representation provides substantive power to enhance people's ability to reason and think' (ibid.).

Norman further explains that the 'ability to represent the representations of thoughts and concepts is the essence of reflection and of higher-order thought' and that 'once we have ideas represented by representations, the physical world is no longer relevant', because 'this is how we discover higher-order relationships, structures, and consistencies in the world or, if you will, in representations of the world' (1994: p. 5). The idea is to develop representations that 'capture the important, critical features of the represented world while ignoring the irrelevant'; that 'are appropriate for the person, enhancing the process of interpretation'; and finally, 'are appropriate for the task, enhancing the ability to make judgments, to discover relevant regularities and structures (ibid.).

The Goddess Within captures the relevant issues by staying true to the story world; for me personally, writing it was an important process which enhanced my understanding via ongoing reflection. Norman further explains that reflective artifacts have different roles from 'experiential' ones:

> Experiential artifacts provide ways to experience and act upon the world, whereas reflective artifacts provide ways to modify and act upon representations. Experiential artifacts allow us to experience

events as if we were there, even when we are not, and to get information about things that would be inaccessible, even if we were present. (1994: 5)

Experience and reflection, as they relate to writing a story, provide the distance that Norman discusses in relation to artifacts, which is the same distance required to create in-depth understanding. Nonetheless, experiencing actual events or through stories provide valuable information to act upon. Moreover, Lewis et al. (2008) contend that 'relevant fictional forms of representation can be valuable set alongside other forms of knowledge' and that stories or works of literature can sometimes 'do a "better" job in conveying complex understandings' (p. 11). Vargas Llosa (1996) notes that since 'men do not live by truth alone; they also need lies' (pp. 320–330); therefore, adding to the concept of needing lies by way of fiction, it may very well be that the presentation of facts can benefit from being presented in a fictional context.

The Goddess Within is a fictional story that connects yesterday's myths with today's in order to seek the truth. Humans need narrative because story helps put life into perspective, and no other discipline or text is able to do this better. And although fiction is usually read for entertainment, it has the potential to provide so much more. As the philosopher Arthur Danto (1997) contends, fiction provides a kind of metaphor for life which cannot be replaced by the social sciences, and fiction tends to be about the person who reads it in a very personal and immediate way. He believes that when you read fiction you recognize something deep within yourself, and you feel that the story is about you. Fiction is capable of giving you something that philosophy, psychology, and religion cannot because it broadens understanding. Philosophy cannot do what fiction does, Dante says, because it is too intellectual to reach people in profound ways. Fiction is ahead of psychology: art makes things vivid and mysterious, which psychology tries to remove. He believes Freudianism is formulaic and flattens the understanding of behavior rather than enhancing it, and says that he would visit a novelist for guidance before a psychologist any time. I am in alignment with Dante; however, rather than visit a novelist, I wrote my own vivid story and – by doing so – I was able to control the uncontrollable experiences of my personal journey through the journey of my protagonist. Moreover, I was able to put my thoughts into perspective, which my diasporic discourse embodied.

5.2   Realities of fiction: the identity and representation of a diasporic narrative and the mythology of my own life story

According to Cohen (1997) the word *diaspora*, in a traditional context, has meant the displacement of ethnic and religious groups from their original homelands, including that which results from the migration of guest workers and even refugees. Huttunen argues that 'the concept of diaspora refers to the migrations and movements, both forced and voluntary, that result from shifting global power structures' and contends that 'in recent theoretical debates, diaspora has been frequently connected with the constructed and transnational nature of identity formation' (Huttunen et al. 2008: xi). As a Greek-American, am I moving closer to my culture or further away by relocating to Greece? The answer, perhaps, is a state of in-betweeness. For me this state of in-betweeness is represented both in reality, as well as in fiction. Writers of diasporic narrative experiences are 'living in a state of in-betweeness [which reveals] a tendency to negotiate new kinds of identities, which cross boundaries of nation, gender and ethnicity. In so doing, they depict diasporic identity in an ongoing process of change and oscillation' (p. 225).

The Goddess Within, which can be classified as a diasporic narrative, flows between real life and imagination, and it links both of these worlds. I like to call it an autobiographical myth because the narrative structure intersects fantasy and autobiography with the person the writer is and the person the writer wishes to become. It is a path between one woman and another, between one and the same. A disaporic woman, which I am and which the character Athena is, as observer and speaker, is not a passive object or bystander. According to Curti (1998) 'fables and myth have always had a relation to gender' (p. viii), and this is true with my story as it has a relation to my narrative function, which is my own feminine voice. As second-generation Greek-Americans, both writer and character seek out their roots even as they share the same fears and desires. The writer and character are in between worlds that are both real and fantasy, and not only do they unite the past with the present, they, at the same time, underline and deny the similarity. It is both a subjective and an objective account between internal and external views. Above all, the story seeks the self by encountering the other self. The narrative is rooted in mythology reflecting the cultural background and identity of the writer/character. The main tension in the narrative is in the need to escape everyday life, the unresolved tension of today, of the here and now. This unresolved tension is one of the reasons the writing of the screenplay eludes any strict genre. It can be said that genres are guides which tell the reader what to expect from a story. Todorov (1990) believes that 'they function as "horizons of expectation" for readers and as "models of writing" for authors' (p.18). My model of writing was the genre of romantic comedy; however, the story is more accurately defined as a romantic dramedy with fantasy elements.

According to Ricoeur (1991), stories provide significant forms of knowledge about everyday living. They offer practical wisdom, in the form of what he calls 'thought experiments', which can solve problems that are imagined in mental spaces that are safe before they are tested in experience. He believes stories are dynamic because readers can infuse them with new meaning over time, and acknowledges that there are a range of stories that can be told based on one's lived experiences; moreover, the story one chooses to express is not arbitrary. *The Goddess Within* is not an arbitrary story because it is based on my lived experience or on experiences that I would like to live one day. The narrative is in many ways analogous to my life, either in reality or in the desire for that reality. For example, Athena, the protagonist, is a scholar with a doctorate degree, and while writing *The Goddess Within* I was seeking the same achievement. As a heterosexual woman, a romantic experience much like what is shown in the screenplay is engrained in my desire or even in my hope for unconditional and everlasting love. As Curti (1998) describes 'the heterosexual couple is a recurrent icon, a sort of linguistic constant of sentimental and domestic narrative, from novel to film and television' (p. 65). Likewise, Appadurai (1996) contends that in a globalized world, 'literary fantasies tell us something about displacement, disorientation and agency in the contemporary world' (p. 58). Creating a displaced fantasy world gave me a sense of agency to express my personal hopes, dreams, and concerns. The elements of my discourse are what I like to call 'realities of fiction' that take on therapeutic roles in the form of the characters and their experiences.

According to Curti:

> Fiction translates the overcoming of dichotomies – theory and politics, art and life, surface and depth, substance and appearance – into hybrid shapes and languages; its characters (sometimes monsters, sometimes shadows, sometimes ghosts) inhabit borders, intermediate spaces, and move in an indistinct zone at the intersection between

the human and the animal, the natural and the supernatural, the beautiful and the horrid, the self and many others. (1998: 29)

The Goddess Within 'translates the overcoming of dichotomies' and takes 'hybrid shapes'. There are two intersections worth noting: one is the 'natural and the supernatural' – Athena and the personification of Goddess Athena – and the other is between 'the human and the animal' – Goddess Athena shapeshifting into an owl, which alludes to the present day Athena. The natural female conflicted by the supernatural female travels between the human and the animal, a process celebrated by Deleuze and Guttari (1975) as an emblem of becoming another.

At the core of these intersections in *The Goddess Within*, both writer and character evolve; they come closer to the other rather than transform into another. It is the movement between the inside and outside, writer and character, fact and fiction, which tends to blur the line of narrative discourse. This movement between my self and my character, fact and fiction, subject and object, is a process in the realities of fiction, through which one can come closer to understanding her or his existence. McHale (1987) makes an observation about the world of fiction which he says is neither false nor true. He believes that fiction relates to the real and to other fictitious worlds and finds its place among the unreal, or nearly real, ontologies in a given culture. Aligning with McHale (1987) and the term *ontology* (which refers to the subject of existence) I believe what exists can be represented. I would add that what we think may exist can also be represented, as in the case of mythological deities and supernatural beings, which in *The Goddess Within* have been contextualized in a narrative that is neither false nor true, crossing the boundaries of fact and fiction. Van Riper (2011) argues that 'narrative films tell fictional stories, but set those stories against the backdrop of the real world rather than creating wholly new worlds' (p. 3).

The depiction of self by either telling real events or made-up ones can be contextualized as positioning oneself as a 'double outsider' looking in. By 'double outsider' I mean that the writer and character are exposed to cultural codes but reject them from the very core of their being. As a second-generation Greek living in Greece, the familiarity of the culture is both unsettling and surprising in the new context in which it is experienced. It is a contradiction of thoughts and feelings, swirling around in both the writer's and the character's heads. Torn and distressed by wanting to fit in, but unable to adapt to a code of living which is often harsh and unethical and fails to put anything into civilized order.

Greece, the country that created democracy, arts, literature, science, theater, and medicine is living on its past history and has no new story to tell. Digging for the answers, as Athena does at the archaeological site, represents the digging of her identity, the digging of my own identity and the digging of Greece's identity, which may be considered to be one and the same. The story symbolizes a strong past – and a strong future. This is represented by the discourse itself, which adapts an old story, 'The Judgment of Paris' in the *Iliad*, in an entirely new way. In order to progress, Greece, too, needs to create an entirely new story that contains intertextual elements of its past.

The diasporic discourse employed is both concrete and objective: I distanced the narrative from the self yet related it to my experiences in many ways. The story is fictional, but the theme is factual. It underscores my belief in truth and the message of finding truth. It is a personal journey to discover my roots, my culture, and my identity, set against a backdrop of desires and fears – experiences that I have lived and now relived in story form. The fictional story gave me a safe space in which to articulate my inner needs and desires; and more importantly, it was a way to refract a culture that felt both unfamiliar and deeply familiar and resonated against my American values. Ironically, while living in Greece over the years, I experienced itchy, skin disorders which I believe are a physical manifestation of my discontent with the behaviors and attitudes of the local Greek people, which were in all likelihood brought on by their own struggles and circumstances. My body experienced and resisted disagreeable foreign sounds and glances until my body surrendered, and the itchiness stopped. Likewise, the character Athena has the same restless dissatisfaction, and she expressed it by eating chocolate and fidgeting with her necklace. The refracting of cultural codes is in a sense an ongoing lesson that continually reevaluate and readjust one to metamorphoses. Huttunen argues that 'the metamorphoses of the narrator can be interpreted as symbols of unconscious desires and fears. Although they might seem internally motivated, one can also interpret them as reactions to the other world and its cultural codes and prohibitions' (Huttunen et al. 2008: 218). My American self resisted my Greek self in a constant battle for identity. This was true for Athena who was also challenged by her Greek-American self, the goddess personification as well as her modern-day conflicts. Perhaps the goddess symbolized the achieving of her true self (myself) and the goddess's and Athena's ultimate acceptance of 'ourselves'. As the story came to a close, the pieces eventually came together, united, identity-shaped and allowed the character to accept the Greek part of herself; although her sense of in-betweeness remains it is with a new sense of profound understanding. It is clear that Greek–American is quite different from a native Greek.

All the same, travel provides the opportunity to compare and observe cultures. I brought the character Athena to life to discover my own inner needs and desires, and to resolve the loneliness of feeling like a 'fish out of water' – together, we were both 'coming of age' in an all too familiar, yet unfamiliar, culture. Clifford (1997) analyzes the word 'theory' and suggests that the practices of both travel and observation are captured in the Greek word *theorein*:

> Theory is a product of displacement, comparison, a certain distance. A person was sent by the polis to another city to witness a religious ceremony, and in the process one compared and experienced displacement. To theorize, one leaves home. But like any act of travel, theory begins and ends somewhere. In the case of the Greek theorist, the beginning and ending are one, the home/polis. (p. 179)

In the case of *The Goddess Within*, or in the case of my own life, the body of citizenship, or the polis/city, lies in-between. This in-betweeness, or identification of the self, will always be in terms of the other. Writing then becomes the space where the identity dilemma is fictionally staged and where in-betweeness remains central. It is where realities of fiction can be safely expressed in the complexities of the person who is split between foreign and native, writer and character, truth and fiction. Similarly, introspection leads to a confrontation of one's own destiny.

Clifford (1997) characterizes travel as 'different modes of dwelling and displacement', of 'trajectories and identities', of 'storytelling and theorizing', a form of exploration and even discipline, and – above all – as a means to locate oneself, or find a home. Additionally, in their travel, both the writer and the character have come full circle via their lived experiences, and they have come to accept their in-betweeness. It is in this living through self and through the character that deep meaning or a sense of understanding can be achieved. As a second-generation Greek-American, I had an everlasting obsession that needed to be reconciled with my self and my roots. The obsession is all the more intense when it is faced head on, in both the real and fantasy world. In fact, the problem Americans of Greek descent may have is their search for their origins, for the old country, where their parents and most of their ancestors were born, and this is linked to the geographic identification of Greece as a territory of reference. Yet, beyond heritage, the question longs for an answer, for an identity, which is buried under the other self. The conflict which arises from having two nations, two nationalities, two languages, and two codes of living, that is, in the state known as in-betweeness, will always exist in my life; however, it is this very conflict of being in-between which makes for appealing narratives, and conflict is widely known as the driving force of engaging narratives.

Braidotti claims that within each woman 'there is a multiplicity in herself...a network of levels of experience...a living memory and embodied genealogy...[and] not one conscious subject, but also the subject of her unconscious: identity as identifications' (1994: 165). The experience of becoming another (woman), in fact, comes close to the Deleuzian notion of becoming nomadic: 'The process of becoming nomadic in the rhizomic mode favoured by Deleuze is not merely anti-essentialistic, but a-subjective, beyond received notions of individuality. It is a transpersonal mode, ultimately collective' (Deleuze and Guttari 1975: 13). It is, however, possible to be rooted and nomadic, individual and collective, and therefore, all things that come together are 'ultimately collective'. Further, a rhizome has no beginning or end and neither does story, its appearance of a beginning and end is superficial, and 'until death do us part' history and culture influence humans, who are in the middle, between things, or in a state of in-betweeness, always seeking equilibrium, and for some individuals, like myself, there is a deeper degree of this state of in-betweeness.

Benjamin (1986) puts narrative into a female perspective. She believes what is existentially female is their desire for space. She explains that the strength to possess one's own desire comes from within the self, from allowing one's self to be alone in the presence of the other. When writing *The Goddess Within*, I felt exactly what Benjamin describes, a desire for a personal space while in the presence of my other and the others (the rest of the characters). I existed fully in a world that crossed reality and fantasy, and it was a genuine experience, like the message of discovery of the truth that underlies *The Goddess Within* narrative.

Narrative is constantly evolving: emerging and converging. It is a sociocultural process that draws on the texts and influence of others; therefore, staying true to one's original vision is a constant battle. Nonetheless, 'realities of fiction', or 'realities of myth', are simply a way to explain the meaning of meaning, to acknowledge truth, to accept the self, and to exude compassion toward and understanding of others, whether the other 'self' or other beings. Perhaps, within the mythology of entertainment and education, one can come closer to truth, as I did in the mythology of my life story. In the following section, the narrative theories, the transmedia storytelling framework, and reflective practice are introduced. These were respectively applied to the screenplay.

5.3 The screenplay

My approach to writing the *The Goddess Within* screenplay was inspired by the work done by Christopher Vogler, a Hollywood development executive and president of *Storytech Literary Consulting*. Vogler drew on Joseph Campbell's work on myth and archetype, in particular his description of the hero's journey made famous in his 1949 book *The Hero's with a Thousand Faces*, and applied it to screenplay development and writing (see www.thewritersjourney.com). My screentext is also based on a constructivist-learning approach. Bruner's constructivist theory (1960) asserts that learning is a process whereby learners construct new ideas or concepts based upon what they already know. Bruner believes that the role of the instructor is to package information in a way which is suitable to the learner's current state of comprehension. A story is universally understood and is a format that continually builds on what people already know through plot development, in the same manner that knowledge builds on what students already know via scaffolding (Wood et al. 1976).

In his 1996 book *Toward a Theory of Instruction*, Bruner states that instruction has four major facets: first, a tendency or attitude toward learning; second, structure, that is, the ways in which knowledge can be structured so that it can be readily grasped; third, sequencing, that is, the sequences in which information is presented; and fourth, the nature and pacing of both rewards and punishments. Thirty years later, in *The Culture of Education*, Bruner (1996) expanded his framework to include the social and cultural aspects of learning. Stories support Bruner's framework because they naturally follow his theory of instruction. In fact, I considered Bruner's theory of instruction when planning the screenplay as well as placing the screentext appropriately into the learning context. On the other hand, I disregarded Sweller's (1994) cognitive load theory and the concept of seductive details (Garner et al. 1989; Mayer 2009). This decision is explained later when I reflect on the e-module.

To put narrative inquiry into practice so as to create the screenplay, I became thoroughly engrossed and familiar with Vogler's approach to story development and structure, which is used by screenwriters all around the world. In particular, his adaptation of Campbell's archetypes (Vogler, 'Archetype', 2006) provided models of people, their behaviors, and personalities. Moreover, the twelve-stage structure (Vogler 'Hero's Journey' 2006) was comprehensive and appropriate for my work, which includes a fictional screenplay that could easily be produced as a 'classical' Hollywood film, also known as the 'classic paradigm' in academic terms.

To create an appealing screenplay I had to master the following: script format, character development, dialogue, scene makeup, and the use of the three-act structure. I had to learn the fundamental elements of a good story. My process involved interacting online with screenwriters around the world, becoming part in a lively participatory culture in which writers share their work and give and receive feedback from other writers. I found that these discussions were extremely helpful, both in informing my understanding of my own story and in teaching me about the screenwriter's art. Moustakas (1990) argues, 'an unshakable connection exists between what is out there, in its appearance and reality, and what is within me in reflective thought, feeling, and awareness' (p. 12). He emphasizes on 'sustained immersion' in the issue being researched and 'direct personal encounter' with the objects of research. The process of screenwriting has been for me both immersive and reflective.

Clandinin and Rosiek (2007) elaborate by stating that 'narrative inquiry' is a methodology that explores experience and the interplay among individual, cultural, social, and institutional contexts. The main difference between narrative inquiry and narrative practice is that narrative inquiry requires the investigation of another person's artifacts, such as their stories, journals, letters, photos, and so forth; whereas narrative practice focuses on the direct experience of the author and exemplifies the work set forth in the investigation. The screenplay, however, apart from being a narrative inquiry is also a narrative autoethnography, which is defined as:

> Autobiographical genre of writing and research...displays multiple layers of consciousness, connecting the personal to the cultural. Back and forth autoethnographers gaze, first through an ethnographic wide-angle lens, focusing outward on social and cultural aspects of the personal experience; then they look inward, exposing a vulnerable self that is moved by and may move through, refract and resist cultural interpretations. (Ellis and Bochner 2000: 739)

Autoethnographic writings utilize fiction and link the experiences of individuals to a larger cultural context. Autoethnography focuses on subjective beliefs gained by practice and experience, while ethnography uses observation and interviews to gain insight. Autoethnography links the experiences of individuals to much larger cultural and institutional contexts, attempting to bridge 'the micro and macro levels of analysis' (Leavy 2009). This was my aim in *The Goddess Within*. It bridges my individual experience and beliefs in a fictional setting, and the customs and beliefs of the characters that arise from the time and place of both ancient and modern-day Greece. As mentioned, I created the story as part of an online participatory culture; therefore, there is this 'link of experience' to a much wider cultural context.

Schön's (1983) model of reflective practice was used during the screenplay practicum. Schön believes that the central importance of practice-led research is 'knowing in practice', or the knowledge that comes out of practice. Experienced practitioners can be blocked by what Schön calls 'overlearning', which results in narrow and rigid practice. The solution is to use reflection – in and on – action. Schön contends that one should 'surface and criticize the tacit understandings that have grown up around the repetitive experiences of a specialised practice, and can make new sense of the situations of uncertainty or uniqueness which he may allow himself to experience' (Schön 1983: 61). In the end, reflective practice with its feedback loops offers practice-led researchers a coherent framework from which to develop methods and tools for understanding practice.

As a result, the screenplay was based on the transmedia storytelling framework, which came out of the practice-based research. In other words, when writing the screenplay I had a conscious desire to determine and incorporate a framework. Since my search for a transmedia storytelling framework proved inconclusive, I had to develop one specifically for this analysis. A transmedia storytelling framework is a guideline for writing narrative scripts, and it also provides guidelines for determining whether a particular story can be used in higher education. Because the screen-text contains hyperlinks to further sources of information, it can become an efficient learning tool. The framework also provides a basis for determining whether educational extensions could be produced. My objective in this investigation was to define the parameters of what makes a good transmedia story that can also be used in higher education. I determined that the Five F's of Transmedia Storytelling (defined below) should be considered when developing or analyzing cross-platform storytelling, and it has been stated that the transmedia storytelling framework came out of the practice-based research. This process exemplifies the Enquiry Circle, which I used as the information-gathering method (see the discussion of the methodology). Information was gathered via practice-led research which was not documented but instead was used as a planning method. Finally, the convergence of theory, practice, and implementation unite the research methods and provide the foundation for the transmedia storytelling framework.

Finally, Schön's (1983) model of reflective practice was applied. As noted earlier, its importance is well recognized in education, in the same way narrative theories and archetypes are important to screenwriting. Reflective practice was used during the screenplay practicum, where the instruction took place online via peer collaboration.

Now we turn to the theoretical applications of both the screenplay and reflection.

5.4   The twelve stages of the hero's journey

In this section, I present Vogler's twelve stages of the hero's journey (Vogler, 'Hero's Journey', 2006) and indicate how I applied them in writing *The Goddess Within* screenplay, which shows that the theory isn't rigid. Vogler's text appears in italics; my text is in roman.

1. The Ordinary World. The hero, uneasy, uncomfortable, or unaware is introduced sympathetically so the audience can identify with the situation or dilemma. The hero is shown against a background of environment, heredity, and personal history. Some kind of polarity in the hero's life is pulling in different directions and causing stress.

The Ordinary World (applied). The hero (Athena) is first seen at a wedding party in ancient Greece. She is strong-looking but uneasy with her sensuality. Next, Athena is seen in present day New York, lecturing to a group of college students. She explains the myth that they had just seen, which is projected onto a screen behind her. The polarity, unknown to her at the moment, is causing her stress. Later, it is discovered that she is being pulled in several different directions in her personal life. Her mother wants her to marry; her father wants her to follow in his footsteps; and she wants to do her own thing, which is to teach.

The Ordinary World (flexible use of the format). The screenplay opens with ancient Greece and then moves to modern-day New York on page 3. 'The ordinary world' of Athena is delayed until she is shown lecturing to college students in present day. The ancient characters seen in the story are also the same characters in present day.

2. The Call to Adventure. Something shakes up the situation, either from external pressures or from something rising up from deep within, so the hero must face the beginnings of change.

The Call to Adventure (applied). Athena's boss, an older male professor, asks her to consider visiting an archeological site in Greece. Athena is not pleased. She prefers following her own dream rather than her dad's legacy, which was to excavate at The Judgment of Paris archeological site that had recently been discovered in Greece. Nonetheless, Athena finds herself contemplating 'the call to adventure'.

The Call to Adventure (flexible use of the format). The 'call to adventure', which usually takes place on pages 15 and 16 of a 120-page script, happens on page 4. This was done to keep things interesting since the first few pages were used to setup the back-story.

3. Refusal of the Call. The hero feels the fear of the unknown and tries to turn away from the adventure. Alternately, another character may express the uncertainty and danger [that lies] ahead.

Refusal of the Call (applied). Athena tries to turn away from the adventure by making excuses, like preferring to do her own thing.

Refusal of the Call (flexible use of the format). The 'refusal of the call' takes place on page 4, which is also early according to narrative theory. Again, I made a conscious decision to engage the audience early on since ancient Greece and mythology (which happens on the first page) may not be appealing to all audiences. After the scene in ancient Greece, the audience need to engage with the modern-day story, although information about ancient Greece continues to be woven into the story. This is kept to a minimum to simplify the story. The mystery surrounding the theft of a Golden Apple is complex enough without adding more backstory.

4. Meeting with the Mentor. The hero comes across a seasoned traveler of the worlds who gives him or her training, equipment, or advice that will help on the journey. Or the hero reaches within [him/herself] to a source of courage and wisdom.

Meeting with the Mentor (applied). Athena meets the Goddess, who gives her advice, which helps her on her journey to seek truth. Athena must discover the person behind the theft of the Golden Apple in order to save her reputation as well as discover her fate/truth. Along the journey she discovers her own courage.

Meeting with the Mentor (flexible use of the format). When Athena 'meets with her mentor', the Goddess, a personification of her own self, she begins to discover things that lead her to her destiny. Thus, her mentor in a sense comes from within her rather than from another character, as is customary.

5. Crossing the Threshold. At the end of Act 1, the hero commits to leaving the Ordinary World and entering a new region or condition with unfamiliar rules and values.

Crossing the Threshold (applied). When Athena falls into the spring at the end of Act 1, she leaves her ordinary world and enters into a new consciousness, that of coming into contact with herself.

Crossing the Threshold (flexible use of the format). At the end of Act 1, it is customary for the hero to make a conscious decision to take action. In other words, Athena would knowingly step into the new world (Act 2). And upon seeing the Goddess in the spring would jump in. In this case, the Goddess pulls Athena into the spring; but because Athena is a personification of the Goddess, being pulled in can be viewed as being the same thing as jumping in.

6. Test, Allies and Enemies. The hero is tested and sorts out allegiances in the Special World.

Tests, Allies and Enemies (applied). Athena is tested and begins to discover her allies and enemies. Peter turns on her. Daphne, Peter's secretary, is jealous, and Kyriakos becomes more than an ally.

7. Approach. The hero and newfound allies prepare for the major challenge in the Special World.

Approach (applied). Athena and Kyriakos have the same goal, to solve the mystery of the Golden Apple. Their attraction to one another is evident, although each refuses to admit it.

8. The Ordeal. Near the middle of the story, the hero enters a central space in the Special World and confronts death or faces his or her greatest fear. Out of the moment of death comes a new life.

The Ordeal (applied). Near the middle of the story, the Golden Apple is stolen and Athena is suspected. She must prove her innocence.

9. The Reward. The hero takes possession of the treasure won by facing death. There may be celebration, but there is also danger of losing the treasure again.

The Reward (applied). After facing a difficult situation in Peter's house, Athena takes possession of the phone records hoping that they will give her clues, but they are useless.

10. The Road Back. About three-fourths of the way through the story, the hero is driven to complete the adventure, leaving the Special World to be sure the treasure is brought home. Often a chase scene signals the urgency and danger of the mission.

The Road Back (applied). Heading into Act 3, Athena is driven to complete the adventure, searching for clues to the mystery behind the theft if the Golden Apple. Athena learns that she must take control of the Golden Apple before the clock strikes midnight, or discord will be set loose.

11. The Resurrection. At the climax, the hero is severely tested once more on the threshold of home. He or she is purified by a last sacrifice, another moment of death and rebirth, but on a higher and more complete level. Through the hero's action, the polarities that were in conflict at the beginning are finally resolved.

The Resurrection (applied). At the climax, Athena is severely tested once more. It is her last sacrifice, another moment of death and rebirth, but on a higher and more complete level. Peter states, 'your deadline is over', and Athena actively takes part in the search for the missing artifact. The finale arrives. The past is put to rest. The truth is discovered. The thief is exposed and destiny prevails. Through Athena's active pursuit of her goal, the polarities that were in conflict at the beginning are finally resolved, and a new Athena has emerged. Athena is the fairest of them all, after all.

12. Return with the Elixir. The hero returns home or continues the journey, bearing some element of the treasure that has the power to transform the world, as the hero has been transformed.

Return with the Elixir (applied). Athena continues her journey home to stay in Greece where she belongs, bearing the treasure of finding truth, her own truth. She has not only saved the world but herself. Athena has been transformed. She has lived the 'true experience' as well as found the root of her desire – True Love.

Screenplays usually have three acts and in Figure 5.1 below are the stages as they relate to the three act breaks in Vogler's 'Hero's Journey' (2006). I have further adapted the hero's journey model and added the page numbers as they relate to the three-act structure found in *The Goddess Within*.

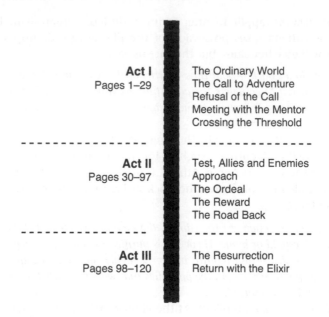

Figure 5.1   The Hero's Journey model: *The Goddess Within*
Source: (Vogler, 'Hero's Journey', 2006).

There are various versions of classical plot structures and they are called different things by different people, like the hero's journey model mentioned above, or the Three-Act Structure (Field 2005) or Act Design (Mckee 1997). To reiterate, in academia the term 'classic paradigm' was invented by scholars, and it defines the conventions used by popular film. Since this is an interdisciplinary study that combines Hollywood with academia, there are several terms from both fields that can be used to explain one thing. I have used the model and terminology that best represents my work.

It is also important to look at character types. According to Vogler (2006), archetypes reflect recurring patterns of human behavior. The term 'archetype' was used by Jung to indicate ancient patterns of personality and relationships found in myths, legends, folk tales, and modern-day stories and are part of our human collective unconscious. Each character in a story might be an archetype, or archetypes may be found in aspects of the protagonist. The archetype's role is to aid and teach or even show the dark side of the protagonist. In some cases, the protagonist may change archetypes for a specific situation. Archetypes are familiar to viewers because they provide a common framework within a story. According to Vogler (2006), there are eight archetypes that describe a character's function in a story, and they are outlined and applied to *The Goddess Within* below.

5.5 The archetypes

In writing the *The Goddess Within* screenplay, I also drew from Vogler's adaptations of Campbell's archetypes (Vogler, 'Archetype' 2006). As with the twelve stages above, Vogler's original text appears below in italics, followed by mine in roman.

Heroes. Central figures in stories. Everyone is the hero of his/her own myth.

Heroes (applied). Athena, Kyriakos, Peter, Daphne, and Zeta.

Shadows. Villains and enemies, perhaps the enemy within. The dark side of the force, the repressed possibilities of the hero, his or her potential for evil. Can be other kinds of repression, such as repressed grief, anger, frustration or creativity that is dangerous if it doesn't have an outlet.

Shadows (applied). Repressed grief and frustration, the Goddess, Peter, Daphne, and Zeta.

Mentors. The hero's guide or guiding principles. For example, Yoda, Merlin, a great coach or teacher.

Mentors (applied). Athena's strong moral character, the Goddess, and Dr. Efthimiou.

Heralds. One who brings the Call to Adventure. Could be a person or an event.

Heralds (applied). Howard, and The Judgment of Paris archeological find.

Threshold Guardians. The forces that stand in the way at important turning points, including jealous enemies, professional gatekeepers, or [the character's] own fears and doubts.

Threshold Guardians (applied). Peter, Daphne, Zeta, and Athena's lack of confidence.

Shapeshifters. In stories, creatures like vampires or werewolves who change shape. In life, the shapeshifter represents change. The way other people (or our perceptions of them) keep changing. The opposite sex, the way people can be two-faced.

Shapeshifters (applied). The Owl, Zeta, Peter.

Tricksters. Clowns and mischief-makers, Bugs Bunny and Daffy Duck, Richard Pryor and Eddie Murphy. Our own mischievous subconscious, urging us to change.

Tricksters (applied). The Goddess (Athena's subconscious).

Allies. Characters who help the hero through the change. Sidekicks, buddies, girlfriends who advise the hero through the transitions of life.

Allies (applied). Howard, the Goddess, Kyriakos, and Dr. Efthimiou.

Vogler's models as described in Sections 5.4 and 5.5 are a widely accepted and valued as being solid framework for executing high-calibre screenplays. The narrative models were applied to the screenplay because the formula is valued and often used in Hollywood films.

The above models, which underlie the structure of the screenplay, can also inform transformative learning environments because each stage of the story (twelve stages of the hero's journey) provides insight or lessons to be learned. People identify and connect with the archetypes found in stories because, as Jung noted, they are part of our collective unconscious; they are intrinsic to and reveal the nature of human experience. Nelson believes that 'by identifying with an archetype, the conscious mind can focus on the energy of the archetype to open the unconscious mind. This clears an opening between the conscious and unconscious mind to receive insight' (Nelson 2009: 217). Therefore, a story that develops a character's archetypal qualities and places the character on a adventure (journey) can cause a change in the self (transformational) when the self is open to the adventure. In this respect, the transmedia narrative of *The Goddess Within* is an archetypical journey. Athena experiences uncertain events that stall her progress, and eventually she reconnects with herself and her cultural identity. Moreover, Nelson states that 'by identifying with archetypes in stories and consciously evoking those archetypes in their lives, listeners can access more connection with their wisdom faculties' (ibid., p. 221).

The models alone (the twelve stages of the hero's journey and the archetypes) do not provide guidelines for the actual creation of transmedia storytelling projects. Transmedia storytelling is a strategic process where the 'scale and scope are a whole lot more than the sum of all its parts' (Norrington 2011). I therefore decided that the creation of guidelines would benefit the storytelling process. Below is the transmedia storytelling framework created for the *The Goddess Within* screenplay, together with a description of its applications.

5.6   Transmedia storytelling framework: the five *Fs*.

1. *Formula*. A proven script formula should be adapted to a screenplay which can be translated to any contemporary genre.

Campbell's hero's journey as interpreted by Vogler (2006) was applied to the screenplay of *The Goddess Within* to create a modern-day myth. This is a flexible formula which permitted the personification of Greek Gods in modern-day characters. *The Goddess Within* is an example of how a script formula can be structured around adaptable parameters.

2. *Format*. The script format should be rearrangeable without sacrificing creativity. The structure should allow for creative flexibility; therefore, the format should not be rigid. *Pulp Fiction* (1994) is a good example because of its non-linear structure. Creative variation is also important in order to keep content fresh; however, conventional storytelling elements are expected.

The Goddess Within extends 'The Judgment of Paris' from the *Iliad* and evolves into a new story. Thus it is an *original adaptation* as well as an *extension*. It exemplifies how 'extensions' can be part of transmedia practice, and it is a good example of format not being too rigid. *It is important to note that format here is discussed in reference to the story parts and should not be confused with the standard script writing format that deals with how the text should look on the page.*

3. *Form*. The story is shaped by a distinctive style (the writer's voice) and by its category of literary composition, which includes genre (comedy, drama, action, etc.) as well as type (linear, interactive, hypermedia, etc.).

The Goddess Within was based on the structure found in the romantic comedy genre, although it is more appropriately a dramedy. The story makes use of details, symbols, and metaphors to provide a unique style. All these elements support its form.

4. *Function*. The deployment of story on multiple media platforms (film, TV, Internet, mobile, etc.) and the benefit received (entertainment, education, edutainment).

The Goddess Within is intended for the film medium (to provide entertainment); however, the screentext is intended to be read online (to provide edutainment).

5. *Fit*. The value of the story depends on how well the story 'fits' the needs of the audience and the benefits received. Issues and themes such as the coming of age, 'fish out of water', relationships, romance, and morals and values can all provide a sense of value, individually or in combination. In TmSE, 'fit' relates to how well the story can be used in an educational discipline.

The Goddess Within has an 'educational fit' because it allows learners to immerse themselves in the subject matter via the hyperlinks. In addition, the text of *The Goddess Within* referenced the text of 'The Judgment of Paris', and meaning was derived via intertextuality. The story contained information on various deities, as well as the event that is believed to have led to the Trojan War. Simply stated, the screenplay was engaging and informative, which makes it appropriate as a learning tool. For instructors who are using a screenplay-to-understanding, it is important to consider suitable learning goals and objectives. The focus of the screentext was on the cognitive domain of knowledge, comprehension, analysis, synthesis, and evaluation. The learners were able to argue key points relating to the events that led to the Trojan War and to learn more about and discuss the Trojan War itself. Learners were able to sequence events in a logical and chronological order (from simple to complex and from known to unknown), and they were able to create story extensions (digital stories) from the core story.

Moreover, I have devised the following six 'fit' questions to help determine whether any other narrative work is suitable for use in an educational setting:

1. Can the story be integrated into an existing curriculum?
2. Is the story engaging, and can it help make learning more effective?
3. Does the story contain subject matter that is relevant to the module?
4. Do the hyperlinks found in the story provide valuable information in keeping with the learning objectives and outcomes?
5. Can additional learning extensions be created by subject-matter experts/producers?
6. Can the students create story extensions via digital stories to provide educational value?

The Goddess Within was appropriate for the educational mission because it successfully addressed the fit questions. Adapting the Five *F*s provides a valuable framework that can support transmedia storytelling. Next, the focus turns to reflection of *The Goddess Within* practicum. Reflection provides insight and is invaluable as a practice.

5.7   Schön's model of reflective practice

Schön (1983) defines reflection in practice as the capability of professionals to actively consider what they are doing while they are actually doing it. He believes the only way to manage professional practice is by applying previous experience to new situations.

The Reflective Practicum or the educational setting/environment: Schön (1983) argues, 'A practicum is a setting designed for the task of learning a practice' (p. 37). That is to say, students learn by doing something with the assistance of a mentor or coach. Learning-by-doing was discussed earlier as a method of knowledge construction; here, I considered it from my own perspective of *practice-by-doing*. Schön argues that a practicum is 'reflective' by virtue of helping students to become proficient and, in an ideal space, it involves dialogue between coach and student that takes the form of joint reflection-in-action.

The Goddess Within Practicum: The educational setting was the website Trigger Street Labs. The process involved peer collaboration and dialogue among members via e-mails and forum discussions. This shared dialogue and feedback was a form of reciprocal reflection-in-action. However, since the coaches were numerous and creative practice is subjective, experienced writers in the group were called on to decipher the feedback. In a one-to-one teacher student relationship, it may be easier to understand the feedback; however, it is also limited to the teacher's perspective.

Knowing-in-Action. Schön's concept of knowing-in-action refers to knowledge that can only be revealed in practice. The knowing is *in* the action. In *The Goddess Within*, I gained this kind of knowing-in-action by reading screenwriting books (self-teaching) and interacting with my online peers. Screenwriting is a form of learning-by-doing. It involves receiving input from mentors and then reflecting on the work. The process could be called 'action-feedback' because the practitioner receives feedback and then acts on it. In my case, peer comments were sometimes hard to decipher until I became more familiar with screenwriting terms. Additionally, the written word may not fully convey exact meanings. In my learning process self-teaching and action-feedback coexisted, which was time-consuming and complex. Screenwriting must be practiced for knowing-in-action to take place; there is no other way to learn the art of the narrative word without practice.

Reflection-in-Action. Reflection-in-action occurs while a problem is being addressed, in what Schön calls 'action-present'. He believes reflection-in-action is about challenging assumptions, whereas knowing-in-action forms the basis of assumption. Thus, reflection-in-action is about thinking about a problem in a new way. In *The Goddess Within*, the constant evaluation of feedback provided by peers and mentors led to reflection-in-action. Mentors were peers who became support systems to bounce ideas off, as well as people who helped clarify the notes of other peers who did not maintain open, ongoing communication. The notes involved comments in reference to: story structure, format, mechanics, act breaks, and pacing as well as the development of plot, characters, emotion, text, and subtext. Decisions had to be thoroughly considered before any rewriting was done because of the domino effect of revisions: changing one aspect of a story changes the other parts. However, a story can be told in many different ways, and even after a premise is locked in it can still be executed differently. Further, the story development process requires finding your own voice and conveying the theme and message. For instance, truth is very important to me, and this came through in the story. Moreover, solving a problem sometimes means doing nothing while the problem rests in the back of your mind; the answer comes not from action, but from silence in the form of intuition.

Reflection-on-Action. Schön believes that understanding arises from experience. Reflection-on-action is the reflection that we do after an event which was consciously undertaken and sometimes documented. Each new rewrite of *The Goddess Within* was a form of learning-by-doing, which I could then reflect on, gaining experience and understanding. This process is ongoing until the writer decides the story is complete, or, in a professional setting, when Hollywood executives are happy.

The Ladder of Reflection. Schön talks about a vertical dimension of analysis by using the analogy of a ladder to highlight the dialogue between the learner and the teacher. He contends that reflecting on activity is to move up the ladder, whereas moving from reflection to experimentation is to move down the ladder. It is also possible to reflect on the process of reflection. The idea behind this concept is to keep the learner active in order to help them with difficult learning situations. During story execution of *The Goddess Within*, there was both moving up and down the Ladder of Reflection. Moving up the ladder involved revisions and reflecting on them; moving down the ladder involved experimenting with new ideas, or new rewrites, which were numerous and complex. This process created movement and eventually helped me through some difficult situations.

The Convergence of Meaning. Schön believes, as it relates to the coach and the learner, that moving to another level may assist both to achieve what Schön refers to as 'convergence of meaning'. In *The Goddess Within* achieving a convergence of meaning with a mentor could be a difficult although, in the end, meaning could be determined. As is often the case with novice writers, my initial scripts of *The Goddess Within* were terrible.

But rather than move onto other scripts, like many writers do after writing their first screenplay, I stuck it out. In the entertainment business, they say it takes about ten scripts to become a decent screenwriter. I had way over that number with *The Goddess Within*. With each script, I moved from level to level in my attempt to reach the convergence of meaning. Much like writing this book, with each draft I came closer to understanding educational convergence and the value of narrative instruction. In the next chapter, we look at the e-module case study.

6
E-Module Case Study

The e-module was entitled 'The Practice of Digital HIStorytelling: Exploring the Trojan War', and it was taught at the University of Hull, as a practice of using transmedia content for the purpose of learning about storytelling engagement. It was a cross-mediated story-based approach for e-learning that used popular entertainment to engage learners. The e-module was designed primarily to teach digital storytelling, and secondarily, to teach history. Various modes and mediums of communication were also implemented. That being said, 'HIStorytelling' was the objective of the e-module as both a method of instruction and as an object of inquiry. History is comparable to story because both make use of narrative technique; yet, history is not the focus of the case study, the approach is, which can clearly be used in diverse disciplines.

There were five volunteers who participated in the study and they did not receive any incentives (other than learning), therefore, self motivation was key. The goal of the study was to discover if the TmSE approach was appropriate for e-learning, and more importantly, whether the module fostered engagement and retention. The course was administer to higher education students during the fall semester of 2011 and ran for 6 weeks.

6.1 Theoretical framework

As Garrison and Anderson (2003) argue, 'elearning has become the protagonist for change in higher education, but the plot needs a purpose' (p. 12). Teaching via 'a plot with a purpose', or more specifically, the use of narrative to 'edutain', is the basis for the e-module I developed to test TmSE in a practical setting. The digital storytelling module drew on a diverse set of research, models, theories, and frameworks. Several learning theories were considered; the following are those I found to be the most relevant to this project.

The Community of Inquiry Model (2000) developed by Garrison, Anderson, and Archer is a theoretical framework that elucidates the online learning environment in terms of three presences: social, cognitive, and teaching. 'Social presence' is the basis for collaborative and meaningful learning. 'Cognitive presence' is the extent to which learners are able to form meaning through discourse and reflective practice. The Community of Inquiry Model was taken into consideration during e-module design and instruction. According to Wang and Kang (2006), students present themselves cognitively, socially, and emotively, and they also learn better when these dimensions suffuse the learning process. Emotional engagement, which tends not to be a focus of most modules, was a key aspect of the HIStorytelling e-module. The pedagogical strategy is supported by Boud et al. (1993), who argue that the job of a teacher is to make learning engaging as well as meet the needs of the learners.

The following theories, models, and frameworks informed the e-module: Cognitivism (Bruner 1960; Schank 1975), Constructivism (Bruner 1960; Vygotsky 1978), Cognitive Theory of Multimedia Learning (Mayer 2009), Multiple Intelligence Theory (Gardner 1993), Communities of Practice (Lave and Wenger 1991), Social Development (Vygotsky 1978), Instructional Scaffolding (Sawyer, 2006); and Laurillard's Conversational Framework (1993), Kolb's Learning Cycle (1984); and the Cone of Emotion (Zull 2002). The teaching–learning approach that was implemented was Salmon's Five-Stage Model (2000). Besides putting multimedia learning at the core of the e-module design, I align with the sociocultural constructivist framework, which simply means that students collaborate to construct knowledge.

The two main learning theories for the educational practice that underlie the e-module are as below:

The first, is *cognitivism*, defined as follows:

> The cognitivist paradigm essentially argues that the 'black box' of the mind should be opened and understood. The learner is viewed as an information processor (like a computer). Originators and important contributors: Merrill -Component Display Theory (CDT), Reigeluth (Elaboration Theory), Gagné, Briggs, Wager, Bruner (moving toward cognitive constructivism), Schank (scripts), Scandura (structural learning). (Learning Theories Knowledge Base n.d.)

The focal point of Schank's script theory is the way knowledge is structured, and this is especially significant in the context of language understanding. Schank (1975) outlined his contextual dependency theory, which discusses the representation of meaning in sentences. Building upon this work, Schank and Abelson (1977) introduced the notions of scripts to contextualize story-level understanding. Schank (1991) applies his theoretical framework to storytelling, which supports story-based practices in education.

The second is *constructivism*, defined as follows:

> Constructivism as a paradigm or worldview posits that learning is an active, constructive process. The learner is an information constructor. People actively construct or create their own subjective representations of objective reality. New information is linked to prior knowledge, thus mental representations are subjective. Originators and important contributors: Vygotsky, Piaget, Dewey, Vico, Rorty, Bruner. (Learning Theories Knowledge Base n.d.)

The Internet and particularly the virtual learning platform align with the constructivism, where knowledge is constructed around a sociocultural perspective. In a constructivist-learning environment, it is important to manage educational resources and to create interesting learning activities. Good pedagogical design and consistency among curriculums, teaching methods, and assessments are crucial. Biggs (1987) uses the phrase 'constructive alignment' to describe this form of 'design and consistency'. The philosophy of learning-by-doing was also incorporated, and a student-centered or interest-based approach was encouraged during the e-module when activities were intended to achieve learning outcomes.

As for my teaching perspective and learning requirements, I reside under the social and situational theories, which are firmly positioned in the sociocultural constructivist framework following Vygotsky (1978); however, these theories, which involve the collaboration and construction of knowledge, do not completely represent my teaching philosophy, or my learning style for that matter. As Markham (2004) states, 'The general assumptions gained from the literature is that learning style research has, over the 40 or so years people have been looking at it, produced no substantive data that establishes that learning styles influence learning performance. What appears to be the case is that teachers would like learning styles to work and they continue to hope substantial data will be found' (p. 6). I find this view extremely disturbing, and therefore stress the importance of engagement through storytelling over learning styles. The practical framework used in the design of the e-module was Laurillard's (1993) Conversational Framework. This framework has also been considered a learning theory. The framework ascertains that there are four main dimensions of teaching–learning; I have categorized them into two groups: teacher's concepts and teacher's constructed learning environment, and student's concepts and student's specific actions, which are related to learning tasks as well as the educational media which can be implemented and analyzed in terms of these dimensions (Laurillard 14 May 2007). Moreover, Laurillard (1993) states that the Conversational Framework model needs to consider both communication and activities as part of its pedagogic strategy. The model takes into consideration both interaction and discussion between the teacher and the learner, whereby the learner's actions are adapted to the teacher's constructed environment; and finally, reflection of the learner's performance by both the teacher and the learner.

Laurillard (1993) further contends that teaching is to be done mainly via technology; I would add that narrative via media-rich environments is also appropriate. Additionally, learning in higher education is about what Laurillard calls 'second-order' experiences of the world. Laurillard talks about her Conversational Model on the School of Mathematics and Computer Sciences website, and states that experiencing and observing the world is not enough: you must examine the models and arguments of other people. Along those lines, I adapted Lave and Wenger's (1991) social learning theory into the e-module by incorporating different media forms and story worlds, allowing for student–student and student–teacher interactions through what Wenger calls communities of practice, which have the ability to provide second-order experiences (Laurillard 1993). A community of practice requires shared interests and regular interactions among learners so that each is an 'legitimate participant of the community' (Wenger 2006). The e-module unites a creative constructivist approach and Laurillard's framework.

Laurillard believes that different media forms possess different affordances for various kinds of learning experiences. She pinpoints five types: communicative, narrative, interactive, adaptive, and productive (Laurillard 14 May 2007). Conole and Fill (2005) elucidate Laurillard's approach: Communicative media make an exchange possible between people (e.g. e-mail). Narrative media show or tell a learner something (e.g. text images). Interactive media is responsive to what the learner does (e.g. search engines). Adaptive media change according to things the learner does (e.g. virtual worlds). Productive media permit the learner to produce some form of content (e.g. digital stories). The e-module incorporated only four of these five media forms because within the parameters of the study it was impossible to create an adaptive medium, such as an emerging story, due to the production costs involved. Based on those four forms, implementing, Conole and Fill's framework into cross-media storytelling edutainment looked something like this: communicative media (multimediated, multimodal, and transmedial), narrative media (text and image), interactive media (hypertext and hypermedia), and productive media (digital story).

What is more, theories of multimodality (Kress and Van Leeuwen 2001; Mayer 2001; Mayer and Moreno 2003) encouraged me to investigate how different modes of communication and representation contribute to the learner's meaning-making potential. Multimodality combined with various media technology offer a plethora of semiotic resources that educational designers can use. A central component of the TmSE instructional design is deciding which media channels and which communications will be used and how they will be combined. The foundation of the TmSE method is the creative presentation of material. The e-module centered on engagement, and students began their interactions with the content by viewing a digital story. This was used to entice the students to further inquiry of the subject matter. The educational design utilizes a multimodal approach to learning and incorporates transmedia storytelling as a pedagogy. This approach provides different perspectives through the use of narrative in different modes and mediums in order to gain deep knowledge of the topic. Students were required to interact with transmedia content relating to the Trojan War that was aggregated and assembled on a single platform. The screenplay *The Goddess Within* was used to in lieu of a textbook and was the only original content that was administered in the e-module. Hyperlinks were added to the screen-text, which students could click on to further investigate the topic.

For some students, the history/mythology subject matter was a barrier or challenge to engagement; however, drawing on a popular film, *Troy*, starring Brad Pitt which has worldwide appeal provides engagement through the emotional connection the story provides. Moreover, cross-media/transmedia means that the story world transverses onto other media platforms. Therefore, the e-module was created by aggregating cross-media educational material around a story world – 'The Trojan War'. The e-module was both multimedia and multimodal, and it was all accessible on the Internet. A blog was created to support the e-module. Likewise, this is where students gained access to the digital story as well as the screenplay. The popular film *Troy* and the documentary *National Geographic's Beyond the Movie: Troy* were uploaded onto a website and were accessible for download. In addition, a website created by the University of Cincinnati gave learners the opportunity to travel virtually around the city of Troy.

Students participated in online forums in which they discussed the effectiveness of narrative practice. To determine whether learning had been accomplished, a quiz was administered before and after the e-module.

The five students who participated in the module completed the following tasks:

* Digital Story: *Troy Story*
* Original Screenplay: *The Goddess Within*
* Film: *Troy* (2004), starring Brad Pitt
* Website: *Virtual Tour of Troy*
* Documentary: *National Geographic's Beyond the Movie: Troy*

Narrative instruction was the nexus of the e-module, and it was designed to encapsulate the ideas set forth in this book.

A main difference found between online pedagogy relative to traditional offline teaching practices had to do with the creation of tasks, which had to be thoroughly planned in advance because online learners with questions would not have any opportunity to receive any face-to-face clarifications. As stated by Tsang (n.d.), 'with good instructional design strategies and adequate technological resources, e-learning can provide a high level of learner-content interactivity that can motivate learners to engage in their learning. By engaging in e-learning, learners are actively involved in the process of creating, problem solving, reasoning and evaluation'. As educational convergence evolves, emotional engagement may bring to light what is lacking in education.

6.2   Reflection on the instructional theories, practice, and the screentext

The e-module was influenced by the sociocultural constructivist approach, which includes collaboration, knowledge construction, and learning-by-doing. The e-module abided by Salmon's (2000) Five-Stage Model, which is a model of teaching and learning for online environments. Advancing through the stages increases interactivity and therefore learning. During stage one, the learner must have technology experience and access to the virtual learning environment. During stage two, learners establish their identities and online socialization takes place. During stage three, information and knowledge is exchanged, and in the final two stages, knowledge construction and development is obtained. As the learners progressed through the stages, I noticed that they became more collaborative and that a common understanding began to form. Furthermore, each stage required different types of e-tutoring skills, such as encouragement, support, and provision of sociocultural and learning bridges. The students who participated in the e-module were volunteers who received no external reward for completing the module; therefore, they were motivated to participate by reasons that were personal and individual. The multimedia content approach created one-on-one learner-content activity versus a communities of practice approach (Wenger 1998) which includes a high degree of interaction, where people engage in collective learning around a shared discipline (Wenger 1998). This may have been because the small group size, which meant that students engaged with the content more than with each other.

In the future, I would design shorter learner-content activities so that students can interact more frequently in the forums. Tsang (n.d.) states, 'Multimedia learning content can arouse learners' interest and motivation at the beginning of participation in e-learning. It also prevents learning from becoming boring because learners must stay alert and play an active role in their learning process' (no page). This aligns with my own observations during the e-module. The sequence in which the learning content is presented is also relevant. I now believe that if the e-module had begun with the feature film *Troy* rather than with the digital story, it may have provided a stronger emotional hook as my research has shown. Laurillard (2002), Mayer (2005), and Schank (1977) argue that knowledge structures can be activated by engagement. According to Schank (2005), engagement activates existing schema and this creates new schema, which makes it easier to absorb new information. Schema theory emphasizes the fact that what we keep in mind is influenced by what we already know, and this was demonstrated by the learners in the e-module. Likewise, what is remembered could translate to working and long-term memory.

Instructors must consider the learner's prior knowledge when designing a module, in a process known as 'scaffolding' to the learner's prior knowledge (Laurillard 2002; McLoughlin 2002; Sawyer 2006). The e-module was scaffolded to support students who lacked the basic skills of story development and digital-storytelling production. Likewise, learning and emotional engagement were created by way of Kolb's Learning Cycle (1984) and the Cone of Emotion (Zull 2002).

Sturdevant (1998) postulated that films can engage the majority of these intelligences: linguistic intelligence – dialogue; visual-spatial intelligence – pictures, colors, and symbols; musical intelligence – sound; kinesthetic intelligence – movement; logical intelligence – plot; intrapsychic intelligence – self-reflection (pp. 27–32). For these reasons, the film *Troy* was incorporated into the e-module. Moreover, these intelligences divide along linguistic and visual channels, which appears to alleviate cognitive load. Sweller (1999) argued that working memory increases when auditory and visual information are necessary but not redundant. I found this to be accurate for the e-module. Alternatively, cognitive load theorists (Chandler and Sweller 1991; Kester et al. 2006; Van Gerven et al. 2006) elucidate the latent impact of learning content on performance. The premise of cognitive load theory is that a person wants to optimize the germane cognitive load and minimize any extraneous cognitive load. Simply put, learners prefer to engage in processes that help solve problems rather than processes that do not benefit learning. I disagree with cognitive load theory and the notion that added seductive details (Garner et al. 1989; Mayer 2009) are irrelevant and reduce text comprehension. I believe that these details, the extraneous information that is contextualized in a story, are what engages the learner, which is the objective of the screentext.

Salomon (1983) assesses the use of technology in constructivist-learning environments and notes the negative effects of learning in multimedia and hypermedia. He argues that the non-linear structure and visual appeal lure the learner into aimless wandering from one link to the next. Salomon and Almog (1998) distinguish this exploratory behavior from deeper search. They contend that the former is influenced by visual stimulation while the latter is metacognitively guided and goal-oriented. What Salomon has described may be true; however, exploratory behavior seems to be beneficial and should be encouraged for overall knowledge; but then again, it really depends on what is being explored. This sounds to me like a time-management issue more than an educational one. Nevertheless, new environments will lead to new practices. A possible way to eliminate exploratory behavior is to assign a task that is related to the multimedia/hypermedia environment; this would make it more 'metacognitively guided' for the student. It should be noted that this wandering behavior in cyberspace was not documented as a problem in the e-module, and therefore, I do not agree that 'non-linear structure and visual appeal' should be considered negatives for constructivist-learning environments.

When developing the screentext, it was essential to consider innovative pedagogical practices, proven learning theories, and suitable learning objectives. The e-resource, the screentext, focused on the cognitive domain, which is knowledge and comprehension, analysis and synthesis, and finally, evaluation. According to Lowe (2002), the narrative format organizes the information in a way that makes it easier for students to process and learn and thus engages them in the process. After reading the screentext, learners were able to argue key points related to the story, and they were able to sequence events in chronological and logical order. By interacting with different media, the learners displayed an increased aptitude in the subject matter. Upon completion of the e-model, the same quiz that was administered at the beginning of the module was readministered and this time all the learners achieved a 100%. Finally, drawing on a variety of narrative perspectives, the students learned how to create a digital story about the Trojan War. It was proven that both the edutainment e-module and the hypermediated screentext have the potential to create engagement and knowledge acquisition.

The overall ideas in this book, along with media convergence theory, and the specific theories, models and frameworks of learning influenced the design of the e-module. Media convergence removes entry points between media, technology, and content. Bolter and Grusin (1999) suggest that people understand new media through a process of remediation, whereby new media borrow and appropriate concepts, terminology, and definitions from previous media in order to make sense of it. However, I do not believe that it is only about remediation; rather it is a recontextualization of content, and placing literary work in a multimedia context makes the learning experience much more profound. The creation of the e-module advanced the idea of educational convergence because it combined media and technology and created a culture of shared artifacts with shared meanings. The e-module emphasized the need for adaptability across platforms, a sign that technological convergence is affecting education. Likewise, media intersection changes the patterns of production and consumption, as was displayed by the digital storytelling aspect of the e-module. Furthermore, media convergence encourages and supports the transmedia storytelling focus of the e-module. Through convergence new ways of telling a story are emerging. The way the e-module was contextualized in theory and in practice advances the idea of educational convergence.

6.3   Student feedback

The feedback that follows flows in the manner that the online discussion took place in an e-learning forum that was based out of the University of Hull. This approach keeps the dialogue in context so that an accurate interpretation can be made. Students were initially asked what their thoughts were on the multimodal, edutainment pedagogy approach. Hobson felt that it was a good approach for online learning environments and stated: 'I particularly like the digital story aspect'. Kalagani liked 'the way the course mixes in pop culture with multimodal communication and the way it integrates the subject matter in creative ways'. However, she wondered how the approach would be applied in other disciplines and what edutainment content would be used in those courses, noting that 'it would be nice if there was a library of content for instructors to access that would be listed under subject matter'. Byros said: 'I like the edutainment approach. I think story can be used in any discipline. I've seen different uses of film in the classroom'. These responses reflect positively on both multimodal communication and on the use of edutainment in e-learning, or at the very least, mixing in some pop culture and/or narrative into the current curriculum. Although Kalagani raised a valid concern about using this approach in other disciplines; there are different narrative forms and story curriculums, and it is highly likely that some aspect of the learning experience can utilize narrative.

Subsequently, the students were asked if they thought the hypertext screenplay was anti-immersive and anti-engaging, and whether they preferred a hypertext screenplay or a screenplay without the links. Androulakis responded: 'I think that using a screenplay is a great way to learn. There is less text to read on the screen, which makes it ideal for online learning. I would also tie in more questions to the links to make students explore them'. Byros added: 'I enjoyed learning about story structure as well as the event that led to the Trojan War via a screenplay. It is much more interesting to read about 'The Judgment of Paris' from a screenplay than say a textbook. I also like having the option to discover more about the topic through the hyperlinks'. Hobson also liked the idea of using a screenplay with hypertext, noting that 'adding questions about the links will encourage people to use them'. He also favored using links to provide a better understanding of the text, using Shakespeare as an example, 'I've read a fair bit of Shakespeare and I got used to skimming over words that I didn't know, inferring some meaning from the context in which they were used but never really confirming the detail of what they actually meant'. I responded: 'These are interesting comments, but didn't you find a hypertext screenplay to take you out of the story world? Isn't it anti-immersive and anti-engaging'? Androulakis replied: 'Even when you read a book, there are distractions, like the phone ringing etc.'. He did not feel the links were a problem because they 'informed the topic'. Kalagani agreed: 'I do not find this to be a problem'. Initially, I also had a concern that the hyperlinks might be disturbing; however, it turned out to be unfounded. And while the evidence shows adding hyperlinks for further investigation to be appealing; the students preferred the hyperlinks to be tied into an exercise, such as having to find answers to questions in an assignment or to perform a task.

The next question was in reference to using a screenplay to replace a textbook. Androulakis provided his views: 'If you can find a way to convey your message (learning objective) in a story versus a textbook, it is definitely more engaging, and may even foster better retention'. Byros replied: 'Reading for example, Homer's *Iliad* provides complexity, whereas watching a movie or reading a screenplay provides engagement. Both provide information. There seems to be a movement away from this sort of deep learning to deep engagement'. Byros asked rhetorically, 'Which is better? I don't know. But the movement cannot be escaped, so combining the two methods is probably best'. Hobson responded by quoting Albert Einstein: 'Knowledge is experience – everything else is just information.'

Hobson commented that 'getting people to engage with, and there-fore *experience* the material is key to learning, however, the main goal is then to direct people towards some form of valid learning outcome'. He stated, 'if a screenplay can act as the center of a valid activity then by all means use it. However, I would always consider directing students toward a relevant textbook if they want an opportunity to reflect on the learning experience'. I responded: 'A practice of juxtaposition could be incorporated between the old and the new modes which invites critical comparison. For example, reading Homer's *Iliad* and watching the movie *Troy* (or reading a textbook and screenplay) provides an opportunity to access two different forms – one of deep complexity and one of deep engagement'. Kalagani responded to Hobson's quote on Albert Einstein with a quote from Anton Chekhov: 'Knowledge is of no value unless you put it into practice', and added:

> You may be knowledgeable about something, but unless you practice it, what is even the point in knowing it? After all, with practice you gain even more knowledge. I believe that it is easier for a screenplay to affect someone in order to get more involved with something, rather than a book. It provides more visual aids and there is more motivation by people to watch a movie than read a book.

I asked Kalagani if she thought the practice of digital storytelling would provide her with both storytelling techniques and a deeper under-standing of the Trojan War. She said that she was 'learning both' and that learning was also taking place 'offline through the engagement with various media'. She believes that if there was more time, students could bring more discussion and collaboration to the forums.

It is evident from the feedback that the students found the screentext to be more engaging than a textbook; however, they were still inclined toward the use of a textbook. This may be partly attributable to their previous conditioning, because the learners were not familiar with the new form or even certain that it was suitable for education. The practice of juxtaposition between old and new modes is recommended because it helps target different learning preferences, which can only be a benefit. Nonetheless, more research is needed to compare the old with the new methods. Overall, it appears that the students were more involved with the learning content and more engaged with the screentext, which collectively appears to foster retention. Additionally, the students enjoyed learning how to create a digital story via a story-based curriculum. Conversely, it would be of interest to see the results if the students had only learned through the screentext, and not the other modes of content-interaction (film, digital story, documentary, and website).

Finally, the students were asked to compare and contrast the film with the virtual website, and to describe their similarities and dissimilarities. Androulakis thought that both the film and the website were efficient forms for providing information, and that they also complemented one another: 'The website is more of an informative method of communication whereas the film is more engaging. The website allows you to dig deeper into the information, like for example; the timeline of the Trojan War which puts things into perspective'. Byros stated: 'I think different types of learners prefer different types of media. I prefer to "dig deeper" if the subject matter is of interest; however, since history/mythology is not my thing, the film worked better here.' I noted, 'different modes of communication have different affordances and they can certainly complement one another. Students today are definitely multitasking more, so it may be harder to focus on one thing for long periods of time, thus creating shorter reading assignments may be preferable. In addition, video and text together may help with retention.' Hobson explored:

> Both the film and the website are trying to give us a picture of what life in the ancient world was like. The film does this through a narrative of a war, from the perspective of main characters. We can engage with the motives of people more strongly through this medium and imagine ourselves in their shoes. The need to create a strong narrative requires us to be in a particular moment of time, and to follow the struggles of particular people. Troy as depicted in the website gives us

a good overview of how Troy developed as a city and culture. We get to see how life was for the average person, not simply for heroes and rulers. Following the links in our own order of preference allows us to build up a detailed picture of the city and its inhabitants.

Byros thought that this was an excellent comparison and asked whether 'anyone preferred the website to the film or vice versa'. 'Androulakis commented: 'Hollywood doesn't always give an accurate interpretation of historical events, but that goes for history books too" (Kalogeras 2013: 9). 'Different sources can help in this respect' (2011 e-learning forum). Kalagani thought that both the website and the film provided information and noted: 'the movie is more appealing and entertaining, whereas the site is more informative. I think that I would visit the website, after I would have watched the movie, just in case I wanted to get additional information about it. I see it as a more supportive tool'.

As been previously noted, it appears that the sequence of tasks is just as important as the mode of inquiry. The students in the e-module interacted with material in the following sequence: digital story, screenplay (screentext), film, website, and documentary. It is important to note that since the e-module was twofold: students learned how to create a digital story and they learned about the Trojan War. Moreover, the subject-matter information was provided via the screentext and the film as modes of engagement, and following that was the in-depth information which was provided via the website and documentary. The digital story, which was the initial learner-content interaction, provided both engagement and instruction; it showed the students what a digital story should look like. As mentioned earlier, in retrospect, I believe the film, *Troy* should have been the first item used for student interaction, to better engage and hook the learners so that the content could be easily grasped. This aligns more with Bruner (1966), who believes the right structure of information leads to a simplification of information, making it easier to understand. In addition, Gagné's Nine Events of Instruction (1985), the first being 'gain attention', and the view expressed by Beard et al. (2007), De Fossard (2008), and Robin (2010) that online learners require a 'hook' to hold their attention, support the idea of learner-movie interaction coming first.

It is apparent that different sources provide different information, giving learners a broader perspective on the subject matter. The benefit for students is that they can compare and contrast information from different sources when there are different modes. Different types of learners may prefer different types of media, but generally speaking stories engage audiences worldwide. With regard to edutainment practice, I agree with the feedback from the students.

6.4 Evaluation

Following is an evaluation rating done using the Learning Object Evaluation Method (LOEM): Kay and Knaack's (2008) evaluation method was used as a criterion for measuring the overall success of the learning object (LO), the screentext. A student-centered approach for evaluating LOs was based on three prominent themes: learning, quality, and engagement. Lin and Gregor (2006) indicate that engagement is a key factor when evaluating LOs.

The following are the average LOEM ratings received from the students (based on a scale of 1 to 10, with 10 being the highest:

1. Learning – 9
2. Quality – 9
3. Engagement (plot) – 9
   - Interactivity (hyperlinks) – 6
   - Design (screenplay format) – 10
   - Usability content (informative) – 8
   - Reusability (in other e-modules) – 7

The 10 score for the screentext indicates that it is a suitable format for the screen; the 9 score for engagement is also significant.

Students were also asked to evaluate the screentext using Bloom's Taxonomy, as revised by Anderson in the mid-nineties (Clark 1999):

Remembering:
The students took a quiz prior to and after reading the screentext. All students scored higher on the quiz after reading the screentext.

Formative Assessment:
A quiz was provided to the students in advance, and the results were used in developing the screentext and choosing the appropriate links.

Summative Assessment:
The same quiz was administered after the screentext was read.

Understanding:
Students were able to comprehend and paraphrase information more vividly after reading the screentext.

Applying:
Students' ability to illustrate and interpret ideas was better after reading the screentext. They were more dramatic and more descriptive.

Analyzing:
Students were able to distinguish, examine, question, and reference different sources (screentext and links) for a more complete examination.

Evaluating:
Students were able to assess and assemble a broad range of information sources as well as argue and defend key points.

Creating:
Students were able to construct and formulate new points of view via words and digital stories.

The taxonomy shows that the screentext was successful relative to understanding, applying, analyzing, evaluating, and creating. Recall was also enhanced. This may be due to the sequential nature of the screentext and the visual stimulation. That being said, four out of the five students whose scores were average on the initial quiz, received a 100% score upon completing the e-module, and one student did not complete the module. Moreover, the following was determined through a discussion with a student teacher who observed the e-module:

- There would be no need to teach story creation if students knew how to tell a digital story (e. g. like writing an essay) before coming to higher education.
- Shorter tasks (chunks of information) would bring students back to the forums quicker. Therefore, there is a need for pre-produced material for education purposes.
- Hypertext screenplay has a place in education and is valuable, especially when accessing links that are tied to tasks.
- Different modes (film, textbook, screenplay, etc.) complement one another and different perspectives are valuable.
- Multimedia and multimodal edutainment provide engagement, foster learning, and may even help with retention.
- If the topic is of interest, then learners value having the option to dig deeper into the subject matter; however, lack of interest may lead only to engagement with popular media.

Following are the weaknesses of the screentext as a learning tool:

- Edutainment and story are not universally considered a scholarly method, and traditional instructors may not accept it as a pedagogic strategy.
- Strong collaboration is needed between subject-matter experts, screenwriters and educational designers to create different narratives for different contexts.
- The narrative resource is time-consuming to create, although professional screenwriters might be more efficient.
- Copyright issues may arise with professional screenplay authors and media conglomerates.
- In terms of costs, it is too difficult to evaluate; at this stage there are still too many variables.
- Accessibility issues for the learning disabled may be an issue although, accommodations can be made; for example, the story could be voiced for people that are visually impaired.
- A particular story genre may not appeal to all.
- Interactivity requires planning (more links are needed and tied to tasks).
- Innovation may not be readily accepted (new forms of narrative, i.e. non-linear).
- Conveying all instructional information in story form may not be possible.
- A graphic organizer that functions like a table of contents is required to highlight the hyperlinks in online text.

It is evident that a screentext and story-based curriculums have their place in e-education; however, not all film genres engage all audiences. This goes for textbooks as well, since they are not all equally engaging. A strong argument can be made that a bad film is still better than a bad book because film is readily accessible and does not demand the same amount of effort from the student. It would be interesting to compare a poor screentext to a poor textbook to gain a better understanding of their relative strengths and weaknesses. Nevertheless, using the transmedia storytelling framework, along with the narrative theories suggested throughout, could help alleviate the amount of poor-quality work as it relates to the screenplay/screentext. In addition, a main concern when taking a story-based approach would be how to convey all information via story; however, since story comes in all shapes and forms, information can easily be expressed in some narrative form.

7
Interviews and Discussion

In this chapter, the theoretical sample provides answers to the questions proposed in this study. The comments provided by the scholars and professionals are listed in sequential order under each question.

7.1 Developing the questionnaire

A questionnaire was developed and administered to a theoretical sample of professionals in order to bring forth three different points of view from three different disciplines – entertainment, education, and enterprise – as they relate to transmedia storytelling in e-learning. This was a non-random, theoretical sample supplied to a selected unit of transmedia professionals. Currently, the number of experts in the field is limited, and therefore the sampling size was small; however, the input received is immensely significant.

Respondents received a one-page background summary of the research along with and easily comprehendible questions. Structured questions were used in order to limit any nuances that could come along with the human factor and affect the responses. The idea was to standardize the questions while encouraging different perspectives from the individuals. For this reason, the questions were 'all things to all people', which was an advantage because the questions were directed to three different disciplines, and respondents provided feedback based on their individual knowledge areas, which in turn benefited the whole. Since there is no intermediary involved in this process, this form of questioning is considered both highly structured and open-ended. A structured question with an open-ended response was highly desirable in this context for obtaining a common understanding. A self-completion questionnaire was used because it allowed respondents to elaborate on some of their answers.

The questionnaire was distributed to and returned by respondents via e-mail; the e-mail questionnaire format was preferred over an electronic survey because of the small number of respondents. According to Gunter et al., (2002) 'while electronic surveys require respondents to work through the questionnaire by themselves as with the standard self-completion paper instrument, the interactive element of the electronic survey meant that it also had something in common with face-to-face interviews in which respondents interact with the source of questions' (p. 234). Gunter elaborates that 'these new forms of questionnaire delivery should not be seen as directly equivalent to conventional, offline questionnaires' (p. 234). Other methods, such as face-to-face interviews or live focus groups, were considered but rejected because of the geographical distance between respondents. Recruiting people to be part of the sample was a challenge in itself. Telephone interviews were considered; however, as Deacon and Pickering (2007) argue, the drawback of this approach is that 'you cannot gauge a person's reaction through visual clues' (p. 67). Thus, it was determined that the non-face-to-face, e-mail questionnaire would be the most convenient, cost-effective, and comprehensive method for this study.

Respondents' answers were recorded as 'open'. There was no predetermined set of possible answers. Answers had to be thought through, which resulted in richer responses than would have been possible in a closed-response format. Although open questions demand more of the respondent's time and are traditionally harder to summarize, the small sample size alleviated this problem. However, it should be noted that having a small sample does not mean a limited and narrow response. On the contrary, the respondents are pioneers in their fields, and this method provided a basis for cross-interview aggregation. Closed-response questions, which can be answered, coded, and analyzed faster, were considered but rejected because they often bring about certain types of answers, and were also considered too simplistic for the group. To summarize, the highest-caliber professionals in both entertainment and education provided their input on TmSE. Their input was requested on the feasibility of a transmedia storytelling framework and of the exploration of multimodal educational components as they relate to TmSE in higher education.

The respondents are as follows:

• Laura Fleming, Library Media Specialist at River Edge School and Transmedia Consultant. Ms. Fleming focuses her practice on transmedia in education.

- Jeff Gomez, President and CEO of Starlight Runner Entertainment. Mr. Gomez is an expert in transmedia productions for Hollywood enterprises. He has worked on the following blockbuster universes: *Pirates of the Caribbean, Prince of Persia, Tron, Avatar,* and *Transformers,* just to name a few.
- Dr. Henry Jenkins, American Media Scholar and Provost Professor of Communication, Journalism and Cinematic Arts at the University of Southern California. Dr. Jenkins is the author of several books and his influential work includes convergence and transmedia storytelling.
- Aaron Smith, Digital Media Planning at the advertising agency Wieden and Kennedy. Previously, Mr. Smith worked as a multimedia specialist at Pennsylvania State University, where he taught workshops on transmedia storytelling. (Note that some of Smiths remarks that were part of my study were published in Revista GEMInIS – Trento and Smith 2011.)

7.2   Theoretical sample: professional feedback

The responses from the transmedia experts are given below in their entirety and grouped under the individual questions to allow for comparison of the different viewpoints. The first question asked was whether transmedia storytelling or the interplay of fiction and non-fiction could be used as a tool to assist in the teaching of academic disciplines in e-learning environments in higher education.

Jeff Gomez:

Many children today inhabit a deeply interconnected world, and any number of screens, media platforms and methods of communication surround them. For some it will quickly become second nature to interact with all of these naturally. For those who are less fortunate, it will be vital to teach them multimedia literacy in order to keep them competitive in the society of the near future. Transmedia techniques, when carefully created and implemented, will convey information, messages and narratives to children in the multimodal way that emulates how they are already dealing with the world. Yes, the interactive nature of transmedia storytelling will certainly help to stimulate the minds of students, making it easier for them to absorb and retain information. But perhaps more importantly, it will teach them to better express themselves, to pinpoint what information they are missing and to access it for themselves.

My research focus was on higher education because this is where e-learning has flourished and because it is an ideal environment for TmSE; however, it is evident that children could also benefit from TmSE. Additionally, closing the digital divide as well as teaching 'multimedia literacy' will, as Gomez says, be vital for TmSE.

Laura Fleming:

> All too often in [the] higher education level, we forget that we still must address learning styles and differentiate our instruction to meet the needs of diverse groups of learners. Transmedia storytelling speaks to learners in a way that they inherently understand, and when purposefully designed, it can be an effective tool for all age-groups and all learning environments. Careful implementation of these techniques will provide an immersive and authentic learning experience that all learners are sure to benefit greatly from.

The capacity for storytelling and play are inherent in human beings. When combined with a carefully planned multimodal, pedagogic strategy I believe TmSE will accommodate most learning styles.

Aaron Smith:

> There is an important difference between saying: 'I want to use TmSE in my course because it will engage my students' and 'I want to use TmSE in my class because it is the very best way to convey the course material and meet my pedagogical goals.' If we are to use TmSE in education, the instructional design must be flawlessly sound. It must incorporate and promote the same intellectual rigor and critical thinking skills as any traditional assignment. TmSE can be experimental, yes, but I've seen many projects fall flat because of the lack of clear expectations for participation and evaluation.

The key points made by these experts are in reference to instructional design, which everyone in the sample agreed, should be sound. TmSE provides an authentic learning environment and when aligned with learning outcomes it can provide 'intellectual rigor and critical thinking skills' as Smith has noted, and more importantly, it can be transformative as I have already stated. To reiterate, multimodal pedagogies and narrative instruction are more apt to reach different learning styles.

The second question inquired about reading a screenplay online (with or without hypertext links), and if this was more engaging and appropriate over a textbook in e-learning environments (if learning outcomes were met). Gomez contended:

Jeff Gomez:

> We must understand that reading of any kind will continue to progress to the digital format, and that book reading will become less and less common in the coming decade. So what we will have to consider more strongly is how to design reading experiences on tablets or screens so that they maximize engagement and take into consideration the non-linear nature of the young and thriving mind.

This book is in alignment with Gomez and addresses new forms of text for the screen in order to replace 'book reading'.

Laura Fleming:

> We are in a culture that is changing our relationship with text and shaping our future reading patterns. Innovations in digital reading will continue to enhance instruction ensuring that students will become more connected to, engaged with, and make meaning from the content they are reading.

Digital reading will continue to evolve and the connection and engagement factor is extremely relevant as Fleming mentions and this research supports.

Aaron Smith:

> Yeah, I think it's an interesting exercise to read well-written screenplays in a classroom setting, especially when compared with the textbook. Screenplays are by definition about writing for the screen and thus must be entirely visual in nature. A screenwriter would never say, 'Tom was feeling happy today;' they'd have to express that emotion visually. Maybe he'd be dancing down the street, greeting random strangers while jovial music plays in the background. This is a different form of communication, and some students might excel at this form of self-expression and information processing over other forms.

Dialogue and description in screenplays are written in the present tense. This keeps the story moving and more interesting. Moreover, it is undisputed that text is evolving into the digital form and will be read more and more often on screens. The screen offers different affordances, and thus, allows for innovation in digital reading. Innovation was explored here in screenplay form, which combined the linear and the non-linear (hyperlinks); however, more research is needed both on screenplays in general and on non-linear and interactive stories.

The third question inquired about the issues and/or implications of producing a transmedia storytelling moving image component for educational purposes.

Jeff Gomez:

> At Starlight Runner, we believe there is huge potential in leveraging Hollywood and international entertainment properties into the education space. We have seen successful implementations of curricula co-developed by the filmmakers and educators for 'The Chronicles of Narnia' and 'Avatar' exposing kids to literature and the sciences. Costs were absorbed by the studios in such cases. Perhaps even more important is the fact that we can learn from the entertainment industry, particularly the rich interactivity of videogames, to help us design and provide narratives for curricula of our own. By understanding the basic tenets of good storytelling and the fact that good interactivity happens when the student's choices actually impact the outcome of the narrative, we can develop compelling educational implementations at relatively low cost.

I also believe 'there is huge potential in leveraging Hollywood and international entertainment properties into the education space' which includes video games as mentioned by Gomez; however, I agree with Fleming that this should be done along with subject-matter experts.

Laura Fleming:

> I strongly believe that educators need to be a part of the process for developing quality educational materials around entertainment properties. In addition, teachers desire content that enhances their instruction and allows them to meet their learning objectives and outcomes. These are important factors that need to be considered at the implementation and planning stages of designing the narratives.

Educators will need to be part apart of the TmSE process, as producers create interactive story worlds for educational purposes. Next, there are many challenges ahead for TmSE.

Aaron Smith:

> There are numerous barriers and challenges to *TmSE*, including copyright concerns, varying levels of technological expertise, lack of a

grading rubric, lack of technical support, lack of educator comfort, lack of student motivation/time/energy, costs for equipment, and the lack of available resources. On the flip side, I believe there is tremendous potential for creative expression. Rather than having students robotically regurgitate dates, or rush through an essay for a single reader, we can ask students to dive deep into their topic, discover the most compelling narrative elements, strategize how their message can best be conveyed, and convincingly show a public audience why we should care. The methodology for this is not clear. Yet when *TmSE* really works, the students become more than the experts; they become the teachers.

The methodology for creating a strong narrative, like a screenplay, is clear when it aligns with a model like the *Hero's Journey*. Additionally, extending narrative practice into the educational environment may not be so difficult when pedagogues agree on its importance. For example, after a national tragedy, a comedy might become a blockbuster; whereas if it had been released under normal circumstances, it may have had an average performance. The challenges to implementing TmSE are numerous, but they can easily be overcome once entertainment conglomerates and educational institutions understand the potential of the business model.

The fourth question addressed whether a transmedia storytelling framework can be developed and applied to screenplays, and whether it would help determine if a screenplay would make for a good transmedia narrative project.

Jeff Gomez:

There are certain criteria that Starlight Runner applies to screenplays to determine how easily the work will lend itself to multi-platform extension. These include whether the story world contains multiple characters, a rich and varied milieu, detailed past and interesting potential future, and whether there are opportunities for some form of participatory engagement by some portion of the audience. There also must be a willingness on the part of the storytelling team and stakeholders to maintain some form of dialog with the fan base. Even if the core fan base is a small fraction of the overall audience, they are the most vocal and can impact the popular culture's overall impression of the property. Otherwise the transmedia storytelling framework provided to me is a strong start.

The transmedia storytelling framework that was sent to Gomez was a work in progress, and subsequently it was further developed and completed.

Laura Fleming:

> A transmedia storytelling framework can be developed and applied to screenplays to determine if a transmedia approach is suited for the project. This should be done at the incubation stages of the project, of course. To me, transmedia is anytime and anyplace – extending way beyond the classroom or the hours of the school day. I think that transmedia implementations need to consider their potential impact on learning and understand the implications of the story they are telling.

Indeed the transmedia storytelling framework, which I designed was created at the incubation stage of my project. It was also designed as a tool so that others could use it to evaluate and develop projects. Additionally, online education is asynchronous and can happen anytime and anyplace. Narratives also have moved into the mobile space in which e-learning can flourish; thus, all stories and all formats must consider the impact on learning.

Aaron Smith:

> Both entertainment and education can use transmedia stories, yes, but from a design perspective, I believe a framework needs to be tailored toward one or the other to be helpful. Otherwise it becomes so general that it no longer considers the different audiences, contexts, practicalities, and objectives which affect how a transmedia story is told.

I agree with Smith that specific models and frameworks need to be designed for the educational mission and this work intends to be the starting point for that endeavor. Story extensions for the educational mission need to be further investigated, designed, and tested. The six fit questions mentioned in Chapter 5 are a good starting point for determining whether a story is suitable for educational purposes. And, it is extremely important that story extensions consider learning objectives.

It would be useful here to reflect on the questions Henry Jenkins asked as a response to mine. 'So, the question is what new layers of media are being added to the project you are describing? In what senses is it deeply transmedia'? (e-mail to author, 12 July 2011). The layers of media which would be added to a transmedia project are the educational components that would be produced between professional producers and subject experts. For example, the e-module case study aggregated a screenplay, digital story, film, documentary, and website. In a transmedia production for education, all the components would be created specifically for an education purpose, except for the theatrical films, which target a wider audience. Shorter films based on an entertainment property could be produced for the education space.

Further, Jenkins asked whether my goal was 'to use transmedia to motivate student engagement; or is it to teach students skills in moving across media, collecting and appraising information, and choosing among modalities for expressing their own insights on the story of the Trojan War?' (e-mail to author, 12 July 2011). Story-based multimedia/modal learning provides an opportunity to reach the greatest number of students while effectively supporting students with different learning styles. The argument is to move toward story-based curriculums and learning-by-doing. The objective of transmedia is student engagement, critical thinking, knowledge construction, and finally recall through the emotional connection that story offers. Basically, the idea is for students in higher education to have already obtained the 'skills to move across media, collecting and appraising information, and choosing among modalities for expressing their own insights on the story'. TmSE can certainly teach students the above skills via interaction with entertainment; however, it is likely that in the future, learners will know how to produce digital stories before they enter higher education, just like they know how to write research papers. In the same vein, a university's writing and learning center could help polish students' digital storytelling skills, as they already do by developing their writing skills.

Jenkins expressed some concerns about the approach: 'In other words, is transmedia a means to an end or is it a set of research and literacy skills you want to foster in students'? (e-mail to author, 12 July 2011). TmSE is a means. It is not a means to an end. And narrative practice as a whole is a stronger means but still not a means to an end. An even stronger means is a combination of experience-based learning with narrative/ entertainment instruction. In addition, online education encourages learning-by-doing, and e-modules would benefit from this approach. It seems experiential learning combined with story-based curriculums can be a highly effective means for educating.

7.3 Remarks on the feedback

It is well-known in academia that different pedagogical strategies are needed to reach all students, and that is why there is a diverse set of learning theories. As we have seen, narrative touches on emotions, and this is a characteristic that all learners respond to. Narrative instruction is capable of superseding outdated theories and views because it appears to reach learners and to foster retention. Margolis (2009) stated, 'All scientists agree. Human memory is a narrative-driven process' (p. 10). We remember in narrative; therefore, we should teach in narrative form because it seems to be a more intrinsic process. Narrative is proven within this work to have a significant importance in education, and therefore, its value cannot be overlooked. Further, TmSE can promote cognitive-skill development and visual literacy, and can strengthen the learner's ability to interpret stories, messages, and visual symbols in an increasingly complex media-saturated society. Above all, it can provide subject matter knowledge. It is important to note that TmSE represents designing and expanding popular stories across media, whereas SE (storytelling education) has a much broader term that can incorporate such practicums as Schank's Story-Centered Curriculum and case-study methods that are centered around popular or non-popular narratives. TmSE includes SE strategies. According to Margolis (2009), 'Anthropologists contend that 70 percent of everything we learn is through stories' (p. xv). Therefore, story in education cannot be overlooked. Thus, learning-by-doing as a primary methodology, in conjunction with a Story-Centered Curriculum and/or TmSE seem to be beneficial strategies. To answer Dr. Jenkins question, *learning by doing* and *learning by story* (TmSE and SE) may be the means.

The responses from the experts to my sample and the additional questions provided by Jenkins (2011) are all pertinent to this research. Also, I strongly agree with Fleming (2011) and Smith (2011) who say the learning objectives and pedagogic goals should be education's number one concern. The design of TmSE extensions and curriculums, or simply the use of transmedia storytelling as a tool to teach a topic, must meet rigorous academic standards. And module design must focus on the medium (online or offline). Any new pedagogic strategy in any form of classroom must first serve a learning objective. The success of the e-module will depend on the level of the learner's knowledge of technology and storytelling principles. These skills need to be obtained by an introductory digital storytelling module. A benefit of TmSE is that it enables learners to evaluate different stories (popular and non-popular) and to produce content from a range of media sources and then amalgamate them into coherent and meaningful components. It is about learning the skills needed to convey a story in a different manner. It is not about reworking written work to fit the visual medium; it is about creating work for the visual medium. It requires different skills from those needed to write an essay. There will be a slight learning curve for both teacher and learner, but this can easily be achieved once the value of the story-based methodology is agreed upon.

It is well-known that transmedia producers negotiate between existing media cultures to create transmedia projects. In the same way, transmedia theorists and/or practice-based researchers can negotiate existing research cultures and practices to create a new body of work. Research questions that arise out of practice are identified and formed by the needs of the practitioner, and the specific methods of inquiry, which are more in tune with the object of inquiry, are familiar to the practitioner. The investigation was multi-method and multidisciplinary. The phenomenon under investigation could have been studied within a specific discipline; however, the research questions would have been based on certain assumptions within the individual fields, and this would have been limiting in scope. Thus, the book drew on a broad set of literature from different disciplines, and targeted research questions within the field of transmedia in order to encapsulate three perspectives: entertainment, education, and enterprise.

More specifically, it has demonstrated that transmedia storytelling and the interplay of fiction and non-fiction have a place in e-education. It appears as though a hypermediated screenplay-to-understanding is a good alternative to a traditional textbook, or it can be used to supplement other readings. The transmedia storytelling framework has shown that it is in fact possible establish a framework for determining whether a screenplay would make a good transmedia narrative. In sum, the feedback from the theoretical sample is for the most part in sync with and supports the themes of the research.

8
Conclusion

This book has been a scholarly exploration that combined theory and practice and traditional forms of qualitative research in order to see how one can inform the other. It addressed the need for storytelling in higher e-education. Specifically, the aim of my research was to discover a style of teaching and learning that would be appropriate to the digital age. What emerged was a transformative learning and critical-creative pedagogy showing that edutainment via the practice of storytelling can be an effective teaching tool. To recap the key ideas:

In Chapter 1, I discussed the route to discover and provided an overview of media convergence theory and the media and educational landscape. Also discussed were the importance of narrative as a teaching aid and the concept of cross-media storytelling in education.

My research took the form of a screenplay created in order to develop a transmedia storytelling framework. It was designed to assist in the development of multiplatform stories that could be used for both entertainment and edutainment. The screenplay was later transformed into a screentext (online textbook) and hyperlinks were added, and it was used in an e-module to illustrate the TmSE pedagogic approach.

Chapter 2, 'Media Convergence Impact on Storytelling, Marketing, and Production', moved from the ancient art of storytelling around a campfire to transmedia and digital storytelling that are empowered by the Internet. Transmedia storytelling, having gone beyond marketing into the corporate strategy of entertainment conglomerates, has strategically positioned itself to include the new behaviors and new sociocultural practices of the 'viewser': sharing, interacting, networking, file sharing and so on, all aspects of the digital culture and associated with the creative expansion of digital artifacts and electronic education.

Traditional production models are giving way to a participatory production process in which non-professionals are producing and using knowledge. This new form of knowledge production through collaboration is made possible by peer-to-peer file sharing and Internet technologies, which are also reshaping higher education. Learning communities or communities of practice are becoming prominent sites of sharing, working, and learning. Members of these communities share experiences and resources to address problems. Social media, digital storytelling, and communities of practice are defining a critical-creative pedagogy linked to TmSE. Further, while writing *The Goddess Within* I was involved in a year-long, peer-based learning exercise that involved participation, collaboration and self-directed learning, supplemented by offline study. *The Goddess Within* was the empirical research and one of the practice-based projects; the other was the e-module case study.

Today, minority groups have a better chance of being heard because they can share their life stories more freely and openly via social media platforms. This is a form of democratic education crucial to critical-creative pedagogy and transformative learning. Fan fiction has recently gained visibility in academia and is an integral part of the new media landscape. Fans are proactive consumers and producers of fiction. They engage with media text as both users and authors, and this type of interaction with media has spread into the educational environment. Transformative processes are creating a discourse of alternatives that educational institutions cannot ignore.

Chapter 3, 'Media Convergence's Impact on Education' examined the history of educational media, and revealed that the traditional academic view of literacy is outdated because learning today occurs across time, place, and media. New literacies are responsive to current sociocultural practices in which students are both consumers and producers of information, and where text is replaced by images. The new multimedia age is fostering an environment based on visual communication. Educators can no longer ignore popular-culture media. Play and education are merging on the Internet because the computer is the first medium that allows the user to do both. In a world in which communication is both digital and cross-cultural, academics understand the need for students to be experienced in consuming texts that employ multiple modalities that will allow them to participate in a global democratic community.

There has been a shift in the cognitive styles of Digital Natives from focused attention to short attention spans, as a result of their growing up in media-rich environments. Research (LeDoux 1996; Zull 2006; Medina 2008) has shown that when learners form an emotional tie, whether with content or other people, learning is improved. Narratives in higher education are evolving, and the common theme of the new pedagogical models is *engagement through stories*.

Chapter 4, 'Challenges, Concerns and Critiques of Transmedia Storytelling Edutainment' addressed some of the challenges facing TmSE, particularly with respect to learning disabilities, cultural representations, minority representations, and technology-supported pedagogy. Media companies have expanded their services and are producing learning material for the education market. Multiplatform productions extend the shelf life of television and film products. These media assets can be reused and redistributed for educational purposes. The entertainment world, however, still has much to learn about instructional design, and this is where collaboration with subject-matter experts is essential. Although educators may understand the potential of moving images, they may not have the know-how to integrate media into teaching. As media and learning continue to merge, increasingly, media content will be appropriately packaged and positioned for the educational market. This type of critical-creative pedagogy is liberating to the disadvantaged because it increases dialogue. This is not only an issue of social justice (Freire 1970/2000; Giroux 2004), however; it is also about alternative transformative experiences that open up the conversation to explore and understand both the messages and the motives. Transliteracy and trans-engagement can be achieved through transmedia storytelling, and this can create social change as well as social action. In Freire's words (1976), education that focuses on critical consciousness (conscientization) is the process by which learners, 'as knowing subjects, achieve a deepening awareness of both the socio-cultural reality that shapes their lives and of their capacity to transform that reality' (p. 27). This is the ability to analyze, question, and affect the economic and sociopolitical and cultural realities in our lives. Transformative learning and critical-creative pedagogy inform TmSE, which is an innate and authentic way to learn.

In Chapter 5, 'Fiction: A Screenplay-to-Understanding' pedagogy and fiction were united to form understanding. Fiction was shown to have a solid place in education, and a mythology of my own life story was brought to light by the story process. The narrative models, *The Twelve Stages of the Hero's Journey* (1949, adapted by Vogler in 2006) and *The Archetypes* (1964, adapted by Vogler in 2006) were discussed and applied to the screenplay. The transmedia storytelling framework was discussed and it is much needed in order to facilitate the creation of transmedia projects.

Chapter 6, 'E-Module Case Study' introduced the module which was based on *The Practice of Digital HIStorytelling: Exploring the Trojan War.* The e-module was used to explore edutainment in practice, including e-tutoring and the use of the screentext. The hypermediated screenplay-to-understanding that was used in the e-module was favorably received by students, who affirmed its potential as a good alternative to the traditional textbook or as a supplement to other readings. Feedback from the students who took part in the e-module made it clear that transmedia storytelling and the interplay of fiction and non-fiction have a place as a critical-creative pedagogy in e-education.

Chapter 7, 'Interviews and Discussion', presented some conversations and questionnaire answers I received from the experts who were part of my theoretical sample. The overall response to the use of transmedia storytelling in education was positive, and these professionals and scholars provided valuable insights on the research questions.

8.1   Research contribution

This book contributes to research literature by proposing a transmedia storytelling pedagogy for higher e-education. It is the first research to address multiplatform education via narrative discourse. This is what Transmedia Storytelling Edutainment is:

- A form of transformative learning and critical-creative pedagogy for the digital age and beyond
- A form of activity – and inquiry-based learning
- A form of sociocultural practice that involves collaboration
- A form of metacognitive knowledge and experience

TmSE may evolve into its own pedagogic theory because it incorporates and extends existing learning theories and transformative ideas. The experimental results demonstrated that storytelling curriculums have a place in higher e-education:

- TmSE framework can be designed to create and evaluate screenplays that would supplement or replace textbooks in the educational setting.

- Hypertext screenplay is especially valuable when it links learners to additional sources of information that learners can consult to complete a specific assignment or task.
- Fiction can be used to educate.
- Narrative discourse is highly effective as a learning tool.
- The learner-centered approach versus the technology-centered approach to edutainment is a key factor for entertainment in education to progress.
- Different modes (film, textbook, screenplay, etc.) complement one another, and these different perspectives are valuable in educational settings.
- Multimedia and multimodal edutainment provides engagement, fosters learning, and appears to help with retention.
- The next generation learners appreciate alternative media and new digital formats (text and image) to replace or compliment a textbook.

This book took a media convergence perspective in order to draw attention to educational convergence. Jenkins has argued that new technologies offer a convergence of lifestyle, which will change how learners access and interact with content. He believes convergence occurs when individual consumers take media into their own hands as well as interact socially with others. Moreover, Jenkins contends that people have found ways to participate in knowledge cultures which are outside of educational settings. These are key aspects of both story convergence and educational convergence, and they are likely to transform education, because stories and education tend to adapt to social change. Moreover, when proactive learners begin to help shape their own learning experiences, educational convergence will be at its peak. For several hundreds years, fundamental educational curriculums have not changed all that much. Convergence is likely to bring about dramatic transformation of education for the first time in history.

8.2 Future research

The work presented here was a broad approach to Transmedia Storytelling Edutainment and the first in-depth look of an emerging field in a converging culture. Since this is a complex, interdisciplinary field, more research is needed. It would behoove researchers to look at story curriculums (transmedia, case studies, scenarios, simulations, games etc.) and see how they affect a diverse group of learners and whether instruction needs to be differentiated for learners under story-centered curriculums. It would be beneficial for subject-matter experts to consider transmedia storytelling from the perspective of their respective disciplines, so that special considerations can be determined, evaluated, and addressed. In addition, more research is needed to determine if every online or offline course can be delivered via a TmSE approach.

Future considerations should include stories that simulate real-life environments and interactions that engage students based on fictional story worlds. There are areas that can be contextualized like how edutainment materials are used in the classroom versus the home, hypermedia experiences on cognition, representations of cultures and of minorities in edutainment, and so forth. Another good research area is the platform-independent encounters envisioned for the future, where people tailor their own experiences. Research is needed to determine the amount of entertainment versus educational content in learning materials; what do multiplatform education and non-linear structures mean; and how technical logic may replace ethical, critical and political understanding. Also, it would warrant a look at how the extraneous and the engaging relate to cognitive load theory (Chandler and Sweller 1991; Kester et al. 2006; Van Gerven et al. 2006) and how seductive details (Garner et al. 1989; Mayer 2009) relate to stories and how this is perceived by learners. Into the bargain, there are political and economic factors to consider as well.

There is a need for more research on using entertainment properties to engage and educate learners and on combining the learning-by-doing and learning-through-story methodologies across diverse subjects More research is needed in the area of deculturalization or culturization in relation to edutainment content. Even more importantly, research should focus on transformative learning as a creative-critical pedagogy, and take into consideration popular-culture media, which goes beyond educational institutions. That being said, video games are important aspects of trans-media that warrant comprehensive research and a book of its own (or several books of its own). In view of that, any limitation of this research is due to the interdisciplinary aspects which cannot be contextualized in one body of work. The whole story cannot be presented or critically discussed in this book because edutainment is a comprehensive approach that involves a plethora of factors which are dependent on each other.

To reiterate, edutainment is not about fun, although if it is enjoyable, then all the better. Edutainment is about finding engaging methods that will interest learners. However, it also true that people are information consumers who often favor what's easy over what's hard, and that edutainment has the potential to compromise certain habits of the mind. Higher education should embrace technology but not as a given. Academics should not rush to adopt new technologies and edutainment practices without subjecting them to critical consideration.

To conclude, this documentation argues for and supports a new worldview on story-based education. And as Goffman (1959) stated in the introduction, it is important to understand the relation between narrative, experience, and meaning. This book helped put that relation into perspective by showing that narrative- and experience-based learning can create meaning. And so, while our prehistoric ancestors may not have called it edutainment when they were sitting around campfires interacting with stories, that is exactly what it was. Narrative was teaching them valuable lessons.

In alignment with the premise of education, it would behoove me to intertextualize my own story as a student. In hindsight, I did not set out to contribute research on transformative learning. What I set out to do was to 'like' education by finding a way to make it more engaging to me personally, as well as to discover how I actually learned. The process of writing this book was one of conflict. There was 'like' because I was able to inquire and create, and 'dislike' because of the oppressed way the institution of education views creativity. All the same, I wish to view education as a collaboration of ideas rather than a hierarchy of judgment – or, based on the theme of *The Goddess Within* screenplay – the Judgment of Stavroula. I wish to be an independent thinker rather than coursetaker and test-taker. And what I wish most, for all of us, is to unlearn, so that we can relearn. In spite of this, and within the restraints of scholarly work, my goal was to provide innovative and creative work, defined in academia as an original contribution to one's field. Transmedia storytelling edutainment crosses many fields; however, its main objective is to educate. I believe this body of work provides a strong argument that other researchers can build on.

As Montuori (2011) points out, the goal of creative inquiry is 'not to conclude the process by having the correct answer, but to encourage a more expansive, spacious approach to inquiry that actually generates more potential inquiry rather than stopping at the one "correct" answer, and illuminates the creation of knowledge' (p. 206). To expand on his words, a new educational story needs to be written for the benefit of edification. As stated by Jean-Luc Godard the French-Swiss film directory and screenwriter on the Internet Movie Database: *A story should have a beginning, a middle and an end...but not necessarily in that order.* It is my hope that this is...the beginning.

Appendix

This section provides a lesson plan for the e-module, 'The Practice of Digital HIStorytelling: Exploring the Trojan War', as well as screenshots of the e-module.

1. E-module lesson plan

The Practice of Digital HIStorytelling: Exploring the Trojan War

A pedagogical, cross-mediated edutainment approach for e-learning designed primarily to teach digital storytelling, and secondarily, to teach history.

Introduction

The practice of digital storytelling prepares learners to master skills they will need to excel in today's world. Digital natives respond positively to technology tools and video because they have a strong link to engagement. Today, visual communication is becoming the dominate mode of communication and stories are proven to be of great value in education. Stories connect people and they can be used to explain complex topics. Experts in any field tend to represent their knowledge in the form of narrative and it can be argued that to become knowledgeable in an area is to become familiar with its narrative as well as to construct new narratives (Zull 2002).

In this e-module you will learn how to create a digital story and, at the same time, learn about the Trojan War. The pedagogic strategy is a cross-media storytelling approach, which means through narrative instruction you will be informed. Not all topics, like the Trojan War, are appealing to everyone, but this is the idea; to engage learners using stories which have worldwide appeal.

Course Objectives

By the end of this module you should be able to:

- State what a digital story is
- Determine the similarities and dissimilarities of stories (e.g. digital and feature)

- Determine the internal components of story
- Map and storyboard a digital story
- Create a digital story with moving images or a slideshow

Unit Overview

Unit 1 – What is digital storytelling?
Unit 2 – What are the components of story?
Unit 3 – How do we create a digital story?

UNIT 1

What Is Digital Storytelling?

Objectives

By the end of this unit you will be able to:

- State what a digital story is
- Identify the components of digital storytelling
- Create a story map

Lesson 1

Digital storytelling refers to a short form digital movie which is approximately 2–10 minutes in length. This newer form of storytelling emerged with the advent of desktop publishing. One can think of digital storytelling as the modern extension of the ancient art of storytelling, now interwoven into the digital space. Digital stories are multimedia movies that combine video, photographs, animation, sound, music, text, and narrative voice. These stories can be any genre and either fiction or nonfiction. Storytellers manipulate the components of story such as the theme and message to reach their audiences. Once completed, these stories can easily be uploaded onto the Internet and made available to an international audience.

Task 1

Complete the following tasks in order to familiarize yourselves with digital storytelling:

- Read '7 things you should know about Digital Storytelling'. This can be found at http://net.educause.edu/ir/library/pdf/ELI7021.pdf.
- As an example, watch the digital story *Troy Story*. This can be found at http://www.screenplay-transmedia.blogspot.com/.

- Based on what you read and the digital story you saw, post your own definition of digital storytelling under the thread entitled, 'Digital Storytelling Definition'.
- Read the feature film screenplay entitled *The Goddess Within*. Please use the hyperlinks for deeper exploration. The screenplay can be found at http://www.screenplay-transmedia.blogspot.com/. Complete the survey on the blog by answering the questions.
- Read about the Three-Act Paradigm and apply it to *The Goddess Within*. The three- act structure can be found at http://www.cod.edu/people/faculty/pruter/film/threeact.htm.
- Contribute to the thread entitled *Three Act Structure*.
- Complete a story map (see below) for *The Goddess Within*. A story map is a one-page diagram showing how the essential components of a story are incorporated into the overall flow of the narrative.
- Post your completed story maps to the thread entitled *The Goddess Within*.

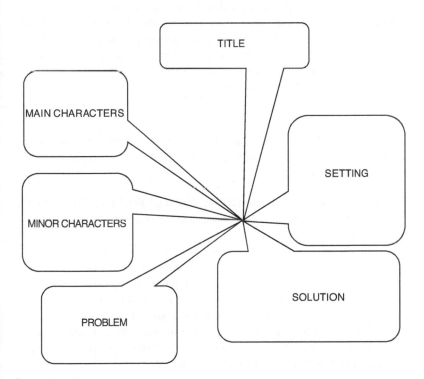

Figure A.1   Story map

Contribute to the *Hot Topic* discussions. This is where we discuss and evaluate the method of instruction for this module.

UNIT 2

What Are the Components of Story?

Objectives

By the end of this unit you will be able to:

- Identify the way modes (music, narration, images, text) of communication create emotion in storytelling
- Understand story structure
- Develop a storyboard around *Troy*, or some aspect of it

Lesson 2

Digital stories begin with an idea that turns into the script. The script is created from the story map which assists in the development of the story. By identifying the story plot, characters, setting, problem and solution, students are now ready to write the script. Once the script is completed, the storyteller pieces together the elements (image, music, narration, etc.) and edits the digital story, creating a short movie or slide show.

Task 2

Complete the following steps in order to learn about *Troy*, modes of communications, and the similarities and differences in representation between media platforms:

- Watch the feature film *Troy* (2004) that stars Brad Pitt. The links for the film will be emailed to you (uploaded onto rapidshare.com for download).
- Explore the virtual tour of *Troy*, which can be found at http://www.cerhas.uc.edu/troy/index.html. Here you will find information about the real *Troy* – one the archaeologists have been digging up for more than a hundred years. This site provides invaluable information that can be useful as you begin to think about story ideas.
- Identify the modes of communication in the film *Troy* and explain how they are used to create emotion. Contribute to the discussion threads entitled 'Modes of Communication'.

- Identify similarities and/or differences in relation to the film *Troy* versus the website and contribute to the thread.
- Complete the storyboard, which is below. This will assist you with completing your digital story.
- Post your creative story concepts (1 or 2 pages) based on your knowledge of *Troy* under the thread entitled 'Storyboard Concepts'.

Contribute to the *Hot Topic* discussions. This is where we discuss and evaluate the method of instruction for this module.

Image	Script

Figure A.2 Storyboard

UNIT 3

How Do We Create a Digital Story?

Objectives

By the end of this unit you will be able to via your group collaboration:

- Expand a creative concept into a digital story
- Create a storyboard and map of the concept
- Create a digital story presentation

Lesson 3

Engaging on your creative, technical, and problems solving skills you will work as a group to assign tasks and deadlines for the creation of your digital story. I suggest you divide the tasks based on your individual strengths. For example, a person who is proficient with PowerPoint or editing could create the final slide presentation; and a person who is artistically creative may be responsible for visuals and so on. Identify your concept and begin with the writing. It will help if you visualize your story.

Task 3

For the collaboration project you will need to work together to define a plan of action for completing the digital story under the thread entitled 'Collaboration Project'. From the executed storyboards, the group will choose a concept to develop further.

- Post your completed digital story under the thread entitled 'Final Project: Digital Storytelling Presentation'. You can use PowerPoint or any free slideshow software, such as Kizoa, which can be found at: http://www.kizoa.com/.

Contribute to the *Hot Topic* discussions. This is where we discuss and evaluate the method of instruction for this module.

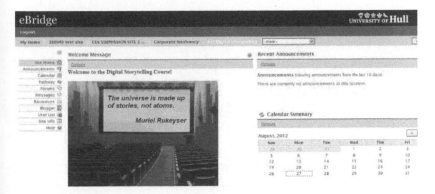

Figure A.3 University of Hull – The Practice of Digital HIStorytelling, screenshot from e-module (Image One)

Figure A.4 University of Hull – The Practice of Digital HIStorytelling, screenshot from e-module (Image Two)

The students were able to click on hyperlinks (boxes below) to get additional information.

```
EXT. COURTYARD ENTRANCE - SAME

Sinister ERIS has long dark, wavy hair that hits her knees.
Dressed in black and carrying a pouch, she sneaks by the
SLENDER HOSTESS, who talks to arriving guests.


EXT. COURTYARD - NIGHT

Eris enters.  She wears a menacing grin.

                       DR. ATHENA MALEAS (VO)
               Eris was the sinister offspring of
               Zeus and Hera...

Bearded ZEUS, carries a gold scepter with an eagle on top.
He shakes hands with the honored couple.  He is a mature,
sturdy figure.  HERA, a large-eyed stunning beauty, walks
along side him.  She wears a crown and holds a staff.

                       DR. ATHENA MALEAS (VO)
               ...And stepsister to Athena and
               Aphrodite.
```

Figure A.5   University of Hull – The Practice of Digital HIStorytelling, screenshot from screentext (Image Three)

About the Author

Dr. Stavroula Kalogeras is a television and film professional with experience in marketing communications, film licensing, programming and production. She holds a Bachelors of Arts in Communication, a Master of Business Administration in Telecommunications, a PhD in Media Culture and Society, and a Postgraduate Certificate in Research Training.

In the United States, Kalogeras has worked for leading entertainment conglomerates, such as E! Entertainment Television, Paramount Pictures, and DirecTV. In 2001, TBWA\Chiat\Day recruited her, and she relocated to Athens, Greece, to head up the company's television division. Kalogeras collaborated with two of the leading television networks in Greece – Mega Channel and Antenna TV – where she was responsible for creating their most successful branding campaigns.

In Greece, Kalogeras has taught communication and media courses at The American College of Greece – Deree, and with New York College Group in conjunction with the State University of New York. Currently, she teaches courses in marketing and communications with the Business College of Athens in conjunction with London Metropolitan University. In the USA, she teaches online graduate courses in the Department of Humanities at Tiffin University and the Knight School of Communication at Queens University of Charlotte.

Kalogeras's publications include 'Media-Education Convergence: Applying Transmedia Storytelling Edutainment to E-Learning Environments', 'Storytelling: An Ancient Human Technology and a Critical Creative Pedagogy for Transformative Learning'. Her award-winning screenplay, *The Goddess Within* has been highly praised in various screenplay contests. In addition, it earned the Orson Welles Award from the California Film Awards, the highest level of recognition.

Kalogeras is fascinated by storytelling and the use of narratives in education. She believes storytelling has the potential to revolutionize education. In addition to her teaching, research, and consulting, Kalogeras is enthralled by the exploration of how the mind reacts to and organizes persuasive information. As a mother, she is interested in how narratives bring about emotional engagement and influence the way we teach our children. Her aspiration is for every learner to be engaged in the learning process.

* * *

Transmedia Storytelling and the New Era of Media Convergence in Higher Education brings together a lifetime of experience in media and education – the first book of its kind to unite Hollywood and academia – which may very well be the new Ivy League.

If you would like to engage with the screenplay,
The Goddess Within
please visit our website at
http://www.palgrave.com/products/title.aspx?pid=716647
This will give you access to the original story without the hyperlinks.

Bibliography

Addie Model. *Learning Theories Knowledge Base*. Learning-theories.com. Available: http://www.learning-theories.com/addie-model.html.

Agence France-Presse (May 2006) 'Blast from the Past: Napster Tries Free Music, with a Twist'. Technology.inquirer.net. Available: http://technology.inquirer.net/infotech/infotech/view/20060505-1444/Blast_from_the_past%3A_Napster_tries_free_music,_with_a_twist.

American Association of University Professors (2006) *Policy Documents & Reports*, 10th ed. Washington, p. 143.

Anderson, L.W. (ed.), Krathwohl, D.R. (ed.), Airasian, P.W., Cruikshank, K.A., Mayer, R.E., Pintrich, P.R., Raths, J., & Wittrock, M.C. (2001) *A Taxonomy for Learning, Teaching, and Assessing: A Revision of Bloom's Taxonomy of Educational Objectives* (Complete edition). New York: Longman.

Anderson, C. (2006) *The Long Tail*. London: Random House.

Androulakis, D. (2011) 'Elearning Forum'. Digital Storytelling. UK: Hull University.

Appadurai, A. (1996) *Modernity at Large: Cultural Dimensions of Globalization*. Minneapolis and London: University of Minnesota Press.

Apple, M. W. (1991) 'The new technology: is it part of the solution or part of the problem in education?' *Computers in the Schools*, 8(1/2/3): 59–81.

Aragay, M. (2005) *Books in Motion: Adaptation, Intertextuality, Authorship*. Amsterdam-New York: Rodopi.

Arias, A. A. (2000) 'Agile learning, new media, and technological infusement at a new university: serving underrepresented students'. *JSRI Reasearch and Publications* (Occasional paper series No. 70).

Aroyo, L. & Dicheva, D. (2004) 'The new challenges for E-learning: the educational semantic web'. *Educational Technology & Society*, 7(4): 59–69.

Associated Press (20 April 2007) 'Going Hollywood: CDC Keeps Medical TV Real' on Msnbc.com. Available: http://www.msnbc.msn.com/id/18233164/.

Atkinson, R. D. (11 March 2011) 'The Failure of American Higher Ed'. Huffingtonpost.com. Available: http://www.huffingtonpost.com/robert-d-atkinson-phd/the-failure-of-american-h_b_626289.html.

Aufderheide, P. (1997) in Kubey, R. (ed.), *Media Literacy in the Information Age: Current Perspectives*. New Brunswick: Transaction Publishers.

Ausubel, D. P. & Robinson, F. G. (1969) *School Learning: An Introduction to Educational Psychology*. New York: Holt, Rinehart & Winston.

Aylett, R. (1999) 'Narrative in Virtual Environments – Towards Emergent Narrative', in *Proceedings of the AAAI Fall Symposium on Narrative Intelligence*. Cs.cmu.edu. Available: http://www.cs.cmu.edu/~michaelm/nidocs/Aylett.html.

Bakhtin, M. M. (1981) *The Dialogic Imagination: Four Essays*, Edited by M. Holquist. Austin: University of Texas Press.

Bandura, A. (1977) *Social Learning Theory*. New York: General Learning Press.

Banerjee, M. & Brinkerhoff, L. (June 2010) *Mining LD and ADHD Disability Documentation for Clues in Determining Eligibility for Specific Accommodations*.

Presentation at University of Connecticut Postsecondary Training Institute, Saratoga Springs, NY.

Baran, S. J. (2010) *Introduction to Mass Communication*, 6th ed. New York: McGraw-Hill International Edition.

Bareiss, R. & Singh, S. (25 September 2006) 'Welcome to Scenario-Based Curriculum Development'. Elc.fhda.edu. Available: http://elc.fhda.edu/dev_workshop/index.html.

Barrett, H. C. (2008) 'Multiple Purposes of Digital Stories and Podcasts in ePortfolios'. Research Associate Center for Advanced Technology in Education, School of Education, University of Oregon. Electronicportfolios.org. Available: http://electronicportfolios.org/portfolios/SITE2008DSpaper.pdf.

Barrett, H. C. (2006) 'Researching and Evaluating Digital Storytelling as a Deep Learning Tool', The REFLECTIVE Initiative. Electronicportfolios.com. Available: http://electronicportfolios.com/portfolios/SITEStorytelling2006.pdf.

Barthes, R. (1977) *Image-Music-Text*. London: Fontana.

Baskin, J. S. (2008) *Branding Only Works On Cattle*. New York: Business Plus.

Baudrillard, J. (2001) *The Uncollected*. Sage: London.

BBC. 'GCSE Bitesize'. Bbc.co.uk. Available at. http://www.bbc.co.uk/schools/gcsebitesize/art/.

Beard, C., Wilson, J. P. & McCarter, R. (2007) 'Towards a theory of e-learning: experiential e-learning'. *Journal of Hospitality, Leisure, Sport and Tourism Education*, 6(2). Heacademy.ac.uk. Available: http://www.heacademy.ac.uk/assets/hlst/documents/johlste/vol6n02/127_beard_vol 6no2.pdf.

Beck, V. (2004) 'Working With Daytime and Prime-Time Television Shows in the United States to Promote Health', in Singhal, A., Cody A., Rogers, M. J. & Sabido, E. M. (eds), *Entertainment-Education and Social Change*. New Jersey: Lawrence Erlbaum Associates, Inc.

Benjamin, J. (1986) 'A Desire of One's Own: Psychoanalytic Feminism and Intersubjective Space', in Teresa de Lauretis (ed.), *Feminist Studies/Critical Studies*. Bloomington: Indiana University Press.

Benjamin, W. (1989) 'On the Program of the Coming Philosophy', (trans. Ritter, M.) in Smith, G. (ed.), *Benjamin: Philosophy, Aesthetics, History*. Chicago: University of Chicago Press.

Benkler, Y. (2006) *The Wealth of Networks*. New Haven and London: Yale University Press.

Berens, B. (2008) 'Paramount's New Style Movie Marketing'. iMedia Connection. com. 24 September. Available: http://www.imediaconnection.com/content/20623.asp.

Bermejo, F. (2007) *The Internet Audience*. New York: Peter Lang Publishing, Inc.

Beveridge, W. I. B. (1950) *The Art of Scientific Investigation*. New York: Vintage Books.

Biggs, J. B. (1987) *Student Approaches to Learning and Studying*. Melbourne, Australia: Australian Council for Educational Research.

Biocca, F. & Harms, C. (2002) 'Defining and Measuring Social Presence: Contribution to the Networked Minds Theory and Measure'. Media Interface and Network Design Labs 14. Minlab.org. Available: http://www.mindlab.org/cgi-bin/labs.pl?id=1.

Blau, E. (22 January 1990) 'Can Thirtysomething Fans Accept a Bout with Cancer'? Newyorktimes.com. Available: http://www.nytimes.com/1990/01/22/arts/can-thirtysomething-fans-accept-a-bout-with-cancer.html?pagewanted=1.

Bloom, B. S. (1956) *Taxonomy of Educational Objectives, Handbook I: The Cognitive Domain*. New York: David McKay Co Inc.

Bluestone, G. (1957) *Novels into Film*. Berkley and Los Angeles, California: UP.

Board of Innovation (19 March 2009) 'How to Build any Business Model with Only 10 Blocks'. Board of innovation.com. Available: http://www.boardofinnovation. com/2009/03/19/how-to-build-any-business-model-with-only-10-blocks/.

Bolter, J. D. & Grusin R. (1999) *Remediation. Understanding New Media*. Cambridge Massachusetts: MIT Press.

Booker, C. (2006) *The Seven Basic Plots: Why We Tell Stories*. New York: Continuum.

Boud, D., Cohen, R. & Walker, D. (1993) *Using Experience for Learning*. Buckingham: The Society for Research into Higher Education and Open University Press.

Bowers, C. A. (2005) 'Is transformative learning the Trojan Horse of Western Globalization?' *Journal of Transformative Education*, 3(2): 116–125.

Box Office Mojo 'The Kite Runner'. BoxofficeMojo.com. Available: http://boxofficemojo.com/movies/?id=kiterunner.htm.

Braidotti, R. (1994) *Nomadic Subjects*. New York, Chichester: Columbia University Press.

Bransford, J., Brown, A. & Cocking, R. (2000) *How People Learn*. National Academy Press: Washington, DC.

Brown, S. (2009) *Play*. London: Penguin Books.

Brown, J. S. & Duguid, P. (2002) *The Social Life of Information*. Boston: Harvard Business School Press.

Bruner, J. (1960) *The Process of Education*. Cambridge, MA: Harvard University Press.

Bruner, J. (1966) *Toward a Theory of Instruction*. Cambridge, MA: Harvard University Press.

Bruner, J. (1986) *Actual Minds, Possible Worlds*. Cambridge, MA: Harvard University Press.

Bruner, J. (1990) *Acts of Meaning*. Cambridge, MA: Harvard University Press.

Bruner, J. (1996) *The Culture of Education*. Cambridge, MA: Harvard University Press.

Brunes, A. (2008) *Blogs, Wikipedia, Second Life and Beyond: From Production to Produsage*. New York: Peter Lang Publishing, Inc.

Buckingham, D. (1993) *Children Talking Television: The Making of Television Literacy*. London: The Falmer Press.

Buckner, B. & Rutledge P. (2011) 'Transmedia Storytelling for Marketing and Branding: It's not Entertainment, It's Survival'. KCommhtml.com. Available: http://www.kcommhtml.com/ima/2011_03/transmedia_storytelling.pdf.

Burn, A., Brindley, S., Durran, J., Kelsall, C., Sweetlove, J. & Tuohey, C. (2001) 'The rush of images: a research report into digital editing and the moving image'. *English in Education*, 35(2): 34–47.

Burnett, R. (2005) 'The Challenge of Change in Creating Learning Environments'. Learndev.org. Available: http://www.learndev.org/dl/VS3-00j-ChallChange.PDF

Butler, S. (trans.) (2010) Homer, *The Iliad*. United States by Madison Park: Pacific Publishing Studio.

Byros, E. (2011) 'Elearning Forum'. Digital Storytelling. UK: Hull University.

Calabrese, A. & Sparks, C. (2004) *Towards a Political Economy of Culture: Capitalism and Communication in the Twenty-first Century*. Lanham, MD: Rowman and Littlefield.

Calvert, S. L. (1999) *Children's Journey Through the Information Age*. Boston: McGraw-Hill.

Campbell, C. (2009) '10 Best Online Marketing Gimmicks'. Blog.spout.com. 21 April. Available: http://blog.spout.com/2009/04/21/10-best-online-marketing-gimmicks/.

Campbell, J. (1949) *The Hero with a Thousand Faces*. New Jersey: Pantheon Books.

Camus, A. 'Albert Camus Quotes'. Goodreads.com. Available: http://www.goodreads.com/author/quotes/957894.Albert_Camus.

Canclini N. G. (1997) 'Hybrid cultures and communicative strategies' in cultural boundaries: identity and communication in Latin America'. *Media Development, Journal of the World Association for Christian Communication*, 1(54): 22–29.

Candy, P. C. (1991) *Self-direction for Lifelong Learning: A Comprehensive Guide to Theory and Practice*. San Francisco: Jossey-Bass.

Carlson, K. S. & Zhao, G. X. A. (2004) 'Collaborative Learning: Some Issues and Recommendations'. Paper presented at The Centre for the Development of Technological Leadership Conference (CDTL) (National University Singapore, Singapore, 24–27 April, 2004). Available: http://www.cdtl.nus.edu.sg/brief/V7n4 /sec3.htm.

Castells, M. (1998) *End of Millennium*. Malden: Blackwell: Oxford.

Castells, M. (2006) *The Theory of The Network Society*. Great Britain: MPG Books Ltd, Bodmin, Cornwall.

Cattrysse, P. (1992a) 'Film (Adaptation) as Translation: Some Methodological Proposals', Target 4, 52–70 – (1992b) Pour une théorie de l'adaption filmique: le film noir américain. Bern: Peter Lang.

Centers for Disease Control and Prevention. 'A Broader Analysis of Three Years of Top Ten Prime Time Television Shows Indicates Nearly Six in Ten Episodes Featured a Health Storyline'. Cdc.gov. Available: http://www.cdc.gov/health-marketing/pdf/ThisJustIn/TJI_15_200912.pdf.

Center of Media Literacy 'Media Literacy: A Definition...and More'. Medialit.org. Available: http://www.medialit.org/reading_room/rr2def.php.

Center for the Study of Public History and Public Culture at George Washington University (2010) 'Teaching History through Film: Film Teaching Guides'. Mediapede.org. Available: http://mediapede.org/filmhistory/guides.php.

Chakravartty, P. & Zhao, Y. (2008) *Global Communication: Toward a Transcultural Political Economy*. Lanham, MD: Rowman and Littlefield.

Chandler, P. & Sweller, J. (1991) 'Cognitive load theory and the format of instruction'. *Cognition and Instruction*, 8(4): 293–332.

Channel 4 Learning (2010) 'Inspiring Teaching and Learning'. Channel4learning.com. Available: http://www.channel4learning.com/index.html.

Chatterjee P. (2010) '"Entertainment, Engagement & Education" – A Survey on E-Learning Approaches in Corporate Training (Respondents from USA, UK and India); Rights belong to TATA Interactive Systems'. Tatainteractive.com. Available: http://www.tatainteractive.com/pdf/Entertainment_in_elearning_whitepaper.pdf.

Chrisler, J. C., Quina, K. & Collins, L. H. (1998) *Career Strategies for Women in Academia: Arming Athena*. London. UK: Sage Publications.

Christ, W. G. & Potter, W. J. (1998) 'Media Literacy, Media Education, and the Academy'. *Journal of Communication*, winter (48): 5–15.

Cisco Systems Inc. (2008) 'Multimodel Learning Through Media: What the Research Says' (white paper). Cisco.com. Available: http://www.cisco.com/web/strategy/docs/education/Multimodal-Learning-Through-Media.pdf.

Clandinin, D. J. & Connelly, F. M. (2000) *Narrative Inquiry: Experience and Story in Qualitative Research*. San Francisco: Jossey-Bass.

Clandinin, D. J. & Rosiek, J. (2007) 'Mapping a Landscape of Narrative Inquiry: Borderland Spaces and Tensions', in Clandinin, D. J. (ed.), *Handbook of Narrative Inquiry*. London and New York: Sage, pp. 35–75.

Clark, D. (5 June 1999) 'Bloom's Taxonomy of Learning. Nwlink.com'. Available: http://www.nwlink.com/~donclark/hrd/learning/id/nine_step_id.html.

Clark, D. (1 October 2004) 'Robert Gagné's Nine Steps of Instruction'. Nwlink.com. Available: http://www.nwlink.com/~donclark/hrd/learning/id/nine_step_id.html.

Clifford, J. (1997) *Routes: Travel and Translation in the Late Twentieth Century*. Cambridge, MA: Harvard University Press.

Cody, M. J., Fernandes, S. & Wilkin, H. (2004) 'Entertainment-Education Programs of the BBC and BBC World Service Trust', in Singhal, A., Cody, M. J., Rogers, E. M. and Sabido, M. (eds), *Entertainment-Education and Social Change*. New Jersey: Lawrence Erlbaum Associates, Inc.

Cohen, R. (1997) *Global Diasporas: An Introduction*. Seattle: University of Washington Press.

Cole, H. P. (1997) 'Stories to live by: a narrative approach to health behavior research and injury prevention', in Gochman, D. S. (ed.), *Handbook of Health Behavior Research*. New York: Plenum Press, IV, pp. 325–349.

Conley, D. (2007) 'Toward a More Comprehensive Conception of College Readiness'. Eugene, OR: Educational Policy Improvement Center. S4S.org. Available: http://www.s4s.org/upload/Gates-college%20Readiness.pdf.

Conole, G. & Dyke, M. (2004) 'What are the affordances of Information and Communication Technologies?' 12(2): 113–124.

Conole, G. & Fill, K. (2005) 'A learning design toolkit to create pedagogically effective learning activities', in Tattersall, C. & Koper, R. (eds), *Journal of Interactive Media in Education* (Advances in Learning Design) Special Issue 2005/08.

Cooper, L. W. (2001) 'A comparison of online and traditional computer applications classes'. *Technological Horizons in Education*, 28(8): 52–58.

Copeland, M. (2005) *Socratic Circles: Fostering Critical and Creative Thinking*. Portland, MN: Stenhouse Publishers.

The Cosmonaut (19 June 2009) Cosmonaut.org. Available: http://www.thecosmonaut.org/

Cousins, N. (1950) 'The Free Ride', Part II, *The Saturday Review of Literature*, 33(4).

Cranton, P. (1994) *Understanding and Promoting Transformative Learning: A Guide for Educators and Adults*. San Francisco: Jossey-Bass.

Cranton, P. (1996) 'Types of group learning'. *New Directions for Adult and Continuing Education*, 71: 25–32.

Crawford, S. (2009) 'The Upside Down of New Media'. *Scott Crawford* (blog), 10 September. http://crawfordinsights.blogspot.com/2009/09/upside-down-world-of-new-media.html.

Cuban, L. (1986) *Teachers and Machines: The Classroom Use of Technology Since 1920*. New York: Teachers College Press.

Cuban, L. (2001) *Oversold and Understood: Computers in the Classroom*. Cambridge, MA: Harvard University Press.

Curti, L. (1998) *Female Stories Female Bodies*. London: Macmillan Press LTD.

Czarniawska-Joerges, B. (1992) *Exploring Complex Organizations: A Cultural Perspective*. Newbury Park: Sage Publications.

Damasio, A. (2010) *Self Come to Mind: Constructing the Conscious Brain*, New York: Pantheon Books: NY.

Danto (1997) 'Why we need fiction: an interview with Arthur C. Danto'. *The Henry James Review*, 18(3): 213–216. abuss.narod.ru. Available: http://abuss.narod.ru/Biblio/eng/danto_interview.htm.

Darder, A., Baltodano, M. & Torress R. (2009) *The Critical Pedagogy Reader*. New York/London: Routledge Falmer.

Davidson, D. et al. (16 January 2010) 'An Introduction to the Art of Creating Integrated Media Experiences'. Etc.cmu.edu. Available: http://www.etc.cmu.edu/etcpress/content/cross-media-communications.

Davies, M. A. (2000) 'Learning – the beat goes on'. *Childhood Education*, 76(3): 148.

Deacon, D. & Pickering, M. (2007) *Researching Communications: A Practical Guide to Methods in Media and Cultural Analysis*. Hodder Education: UK.

de Alva, J. K. (2000) 'Remaking the academy'. *Educause*, 32–40.

Debord, G. (1995) *Society of Spectacle*. Zone Books: New York.

De Fossard, E. (2008) *Using Edu-Tainment for Distance Education in Community Work*. New Delhi: Sage Publications.

Deleuze, G. & Guttari, F. (1975) *'Kafka: Toward a Minor Literature'. Theory and History of Literature*, Vol. 30 (trans. Polan, D.), Minnesota: University of Minnesota Press.

Dena, C. (2009) 'Transmedia Practice: Theorising the Practice of Expressing a Fictional World across Distinct Media and Environments'. *Ph.D. Thesis*, University of Sydney.

Desantis, N. (1 May 2012) 'Next Generation of Online-Learning Systems Faces Barriers to Adoption'. Chronical.com. Available: http://chronicle.com/blogs/wiredcampus/next-generation-of-online-learning-systems-faces-barriers-to-adoption-report-suggests/36226.

Deutsch, N. (6 February 2009) 'Engaging the Blended Classroom Learner'. Wiziq.com. Available: http://www.wiziq.com/online-class/85826-Engaging-the-blended-classroom-learner.

Dewey, J. (1933) *How We Think: A Restatement of the Relation of Reflective Thinking to the Educative Process*. Boston: D. C. Heath.

Dewey, J. (1963) *Experience and Education: The Kappa Delta Pi Lecture Series*. New York: Collier.

Dice Consortium (2010) 'Making a World of Difference: A Dice Resource for Practitioners on Educational Theatre and Drama'. Dramanetwork.eu. Available: http://www.dramanetwork.eu/file/Education%20Resource%20long.pdf.

Dillon, A. & Jobst, J. (2005) 'Multimedia Learning with Hypermedia', in Mayer, R. E. (ed.), *The Canbridge Handbook of Multimedia Learning*. New York: Cambridge University Press.

Dinehart, S. (15 September 2009) 'Creators of Transmedia Stories'. Narrativesesign.org. Available: http://narrativedesign.org/2009/09/creators-of-transmedia-stories-3-jeff-gomez/#more-118.

Doctorow, C. and McDonnell, T. (2010) 'Social TV in 2010: Conversation is Currency Monterosa'. 31 January. Monterosa.co.uk. Available: http://www.monterosa.co.uk/blog/conversationiscurrency?gclid=CILgwZeJn6ACFZlg4wod M2M2aw.

Dominguez, P. S. & Ridley R. (1999) 'Reassessing the assessment of distance education courses'. *THE Journal Technological Horizons in Education*, 27(2). Thejournal.com. Available: http://www.thejournal.com/magazine/vault/A2223.cfm.

Donaton, S. (2004) *Madison & Vine: Why the Entertainment and Advertising Industries Must Converge to Survive*. New York: McGraw Hill.

Downes, S. (2007) 'Models for sustainable open educational resources'. *Interdisciplinary Journal of Knowledge and Learning Objects*, 3: 29–44.

Downing, S. (2 August 2010) 'Teaching with Films'. Oncourseworkshop.com. Available: http://www.oncourseworkshop.com/Miscellaneous012.htm.

Dray, W. (1989) *On History and Philosophers of History*. Leiden: E. J. Brill.

Earthwit (2011) 'Top 10 Bollywood Movies Copied from Hollywood'. 3 February. Topyaps.com. Available: http://www.topyaps.com/top-10-bollywood-movies-copied-from-hollywood/.

Educause Learning Initiative (January 2007) '7 Things you Should Know About... Digital Storytelling'. Net.educause.edu. Available: http://net.educause.edu/ir/library/pdf/ELI7021.pdf.

Einav, G. (2004) 'College Students: The Rationale for Peer-to-Peer Video File Sharing', in Singhal, A., Cody, M. J., Rogers, E. M. & Sabido, M. (eds), *Entertainment-Education and Social Change*. New Jersey: Lawrence Erlbaum Associates, Inc.

El Cosmonauta (2010) 'Case Study'. 8 September. Creativecommons.Org. Available: http://wiki.creativecommons.org/Case_Studies/El_Cosmonauta.

Ellis, C. & Bochner, A. (2000) 'Autoethnography, Personal Narrative, Reflexivity: Researcher As Subject', in Norman K. Denzin & Yvonna S. Lincoln (eds), *Handbook of Qualitative Research*, 2nd ed. California: Sage, pp. 733–768.

Engebretsen, M. (2010) 'Making sense with multimedia'. *International Journal of Media, Technology and Lifelong Learning*, 6(2). Seminar.Net. Available: http://www.seminar.net/index.php?option=com_content&task=view&id=60&Itemid=1.

Egenfeldt-Nielsen, S. (2010) *Beyond Edutainment: Exploring the Educational Potential of Computer Games*. Publisher Lulu.com.

Everything Spacey. 'Kevin Spacey's Trigger Street'. Everything Spacey.com. Available: http://www.everythingspacey.com/triggerstreet.html.

Farkas, D. K. (2004) *'Hypertext and Hypermedia' Berkshire Encyclopedia of Human-Computer Interaction*, Massachusetts: Berkshire Publishing, pp. 332–336.

Federal Communications Commission (2003) 'Television Technology – A Short History'. Fcc.gov. Available: http//www.fcc.gov/omd/history/tv/.

Fernandez, M. E. (2006) 'ABC's Lost is easy to find, and not just on a TV screen'. *Los Angeles Times*, 3 January. Latimes.com.Available: http://articles.latimes.com/2006/jan/03/entertainment/et-lost3.

Ferren, B. (1997) 'Storytelling: The World's Oldest Profession'. Keynote address at the Siggraph 97 Conference, August 3. Siggraph.org. Available: http://www.siggraph.org/s97/conference/keynote/index.html.

Field, S. (2005) *Screenplay: The Foundations of Screenwriting*. New York: Bantam Dell.

Fisher, K. (13 March 2006) 'NBC Universal Chief Calls for Net-savvy TV Pitches'. Arstechnica.com.   Available: http://arstechnica.com/uncategorized/2006/03/6369-2/.

Fisher, R. W. (1987) *Human Communication as Narration: Toward a Philosophy of Reason, Value, and Action*. Columbia, SC: University of South Carolina Press.

Foucault, M. (1984) 'What Is an Author?' in Rabinow, P. (ed.), *The Foucault Reader*. New York: Pantheon.

Frankel, D. (2000) *The Revenge of Brand X*. United States of America: Rob Frankel.

Freepress (2011) 'Who Owns the Media'? Freepress.net. Available: http://www.freepress.net/ownership/chart/.

Freebody, P. & Luke, A. (1999) 'Further Notes on the Four Resource Model: Transcript of Online Conversation with the Authors'. International Reading Association Online Discussion Forum. Readingonline.org. Available: www.readingonline.org/research/lukefreebody.html#freeboduluke.

Freire, P. (1996) *Pedagogy of the Oppressed*. London: Penguin.

Freire, P. (1970/2000) *Pedagogy of the Oppressed*, 30th ed. (trans. Bergman-Ramos, M.). New York: Continuum.

Freire, P. (1976) 'A Few Notes on Conscientization', in Dale, R. (ed.), *Schooling and Capitalism*. London: Routledge.

Freire, P. & Shor, I. (1987) *A Pedagogy for Liberation: Dialogues on Transforming Education*. Massachusetts: Bergin and Garvey.

Fulford, R. (2001) *The Triumph of Narrative: Storytelling in the Age of Mass Culture*. New York: 1st Broadway Books.

Gagné, M. & Shepherd, M. (2001) 'Distance learning in accounting'. *T.H.E. Journal*, 28(9). The Journal.com. Available: http://www.thejournal.com/magazine/vault/A3433.cfm.

Gagné, R. (1985) *The Conditions of Learning and the Theory of Instruction*, 4th ed. New York: Holt, Rinehart, and Winston.

Gandz, J. (1997) 'The death of teaching: the rebirth of education', *Ivey Business Quarterly*, 62(1).

Gans (1975) 'The Entertainment Education Communication Strategy: Past Struggles, Present Status, Future Agenda', in Singhal, A. and Brown W. J. (eds) *Jurnal Komunicasi*, (12): 19–36. Ukm.my. Available: http://www.ukm.my/jkom/journal/pdf_files/1996/V12_2.pdf.

Gardner, H. (1993) *Frames of Mind: The Theory of Multiple Intelligences*. New York: Basic Books.

Garner, R., Gillingham, M. & White, C. (1989) 'Effects of seductive details on macroprocessing and microprocessing in adults and children'. *Cognition and Instruction*, 6: 41–57.

Garrison, D. R., Anderson, T. & Archer, W. (2000) 'Critical inquiry in a text-based environment: Computer conferencing in higher education'. *The Internet and Higher Education*, 2(2–3): 87–105.

Garrison, D. R. & Anderson, T. (2003) *E-Learning in the 21st Century: A Framework for Research and Practice*. New York: Routledge.

Gauntlett, D. (1995) *Moving Experiences, Understanding Television's Influences and Effects*. London: John Libbey.

Giddens, A. (1984) *The Constitution of Society: Outline of the Theory of Structuration*. Berkely: University of California Press.

Giovagnoli, M. (2011) 'Transmedia Storytelling: Imagery, Shapes and Techniques'. Thoughtmesh.net. 11 November. Available: http://thoughtmesh.net/publish/400.php#.

Giroux, H. A. (2004) 'Cultural studies, public pedagogy, and the responsibility of intellectuals'. *Communication & Critical/Cultural Studies* [serial online], 1(1): 59–79.

Giroux, H. A. (2007) *The University in Chains: Confronting the Military-Industrial-Academic Complex*. Boulder, CO: Paradigm.

Giroux, H. A. (2010) *Education and the Crisis of Public Values*. New York: Peter.

Giroux, H. A. (17 October 2010) 'Lessons From Paulo Freire'. *Chronicle of Higher Education*. Available: http://chronicle.com/article/Lessons-From-Paulo-Freire/124910/.

Glenn, M. (2008) 'The Future of Higher Education: How Technology Will Shape Learning'. NMC.org. Available: http://www.nmc.org/pdf/Future-of-Higher-Ed-(NMC).pdf.

Godard, J. 'Quote'. Thinkexist.com. Available: http://thinkexist.com/quotation/anyone_who_tries_to_make_a_distinction_between/152852.html.

Goffman, E. (1959) *The Presentation of Self in Everyday Life*. New York: Anchor.

Gokhale, A. (1995) 'Collaborative learning enhances critical thinking'. *Journal of Technology Education*, 7(1): 22–30. Scholar.lib. Available: http://scholar.lib.vt.edu/ejournals/JTE/jte-v7n1/gokhale.jte-v7n1.html.

Gomez, J. (2007) 'Panel discussion on *PGA NMC Blog*'. 2 October. Pganmc.blog-spot.com. Available: http://pganmc.blogspot.com/2007/10/pga-member-jeff-gomez-left-assembled.html.

Gray, C. (1996) ' Inquiry through Practice; Developing Appropriate Research Strategies'. 2rgu.ac.uk. Available: http://www2.rgu.ac.uk/criad/cgpapers/ngnm/ngnm.htm.

Greek-Gods Information. 'Olympian Gods, Hera the Goddess of Marriage'. Greek-Gods.info. Available: http://www.greek-gods.info/greek-gods/hera/.

Green, M. C. & Brock, T. C. (2000) 'The role of transportation in the persuasiveness of public narratives'. *Journal of Personality and Social Psychology*, 79: 701–721.

Greenberg, B. S., Salmon, C. T., Patel, D., Beck, V. & Cole, G. (2004) 'Evolution of an E-E Research Agenda', in Singhal, A., Cody, M. J., Rogers, E. M. & Sabido, M. (eds), *Entertainment-Education and Social Change*. New Jersey: Lawrence Erlbaum Associates, Inc.

Gregg, N., Hoy, C., Flaherty, D. A., Norris, P., Coleman, C., Davis, M. & Jordan, M. (2005) 'Decoding and spelling accommodations for postsecondary students with dyslexia – it's more than processing speed'. *Learning Disabilities: A Contemporary Journal*, 3(2): 1–17.

Gunter, B., Nicholas, D., Huntington, P. & Williams, P. (2002) 'Online versus offline research: implications for evaluating digital media'. *Aslib Proceedings*, 54(4): 229–39.

Hagerman, M. E. (ed.) (2006) *Babel*. Cologne: Taschen.

Hallahan, D. P. & Mercer, C. D. (2001). 'Learning Disabilities: Historical Perspectives'. Nrcld.org. Available: http://www.nrcld.org/resources/ldsummit/hallahan.html.

Harp, S. F. & Mayer, R. E. (1997) 'The role of interest in learning from scientific text and illustrations: on the distinction between emotional interests and cognitive interests'. *Journal of Educational Psychology*, 89(1): 92–102.

Hart, K. E. & Steven, K. K. (1995) 'The use and evaluation of video supplements in the teaching of introductory psychology'. *Journal of Instructional Psychology*, 22(2): 104–114.

Haven, K. F. (2007) *Story Proof: The Science behind the Startling Power of Story.* Westport, CT: Libraries Unlimited.

Hawkins, R. J. (1995) 'Lion King: An Industry in Itself,' *San Diego Union Tribune*, 2 March.

Hayles, N. K. (17 January 2008) 'Media Theory for the 21st Century.' Wordpress. com. Available: http://media08.wordpress.com/2008/01/17/my-article-on-hyper-and-deep-attention/.

Heiden, W. & Fassbender, E. (2010) 'An Edutainment Approach to Academic Teaching Based on Storytelling'. CSEDU 2010 Proceedings, Vol. 2, 2nd International Conference on Computer Supported Education, Valencia, Spain, 06–10 April 2010: 126–131.

Heisenberg, W. (1972) 'The Representation of Nature in Contemporary Physics', in Sears, S. & Lord, G. W. (eds), *The Discontinuous Universe*. New York: Basic Books.

Heron, J. (2001) *Helping the Client: A Creative Practical Guide*. London: Sage.

Hesse-Biber, S. N. & Leavy, P. (2008) *Handbook of Emergent Methods*. New York: The Guilford Press.

Higson, A. (2002) 'Talking film, talking identity: New Zealand expatriates reflect on national film'. *European Journal of Cultural Studies* (2009), 12 (1): 99–117.

Hinchey, P. (2003) 'Introduction: teaching media literacy: not if, but why and how'. *The Clearing House*, 76(6): 268–270.

Hobson, J. (2011) 'Elearning Forum'. Digital Storytelling. UK: Hull University.

Hoffenberg, H. & Handler, M. (2001) 'Digital video goes to school'. *Learning and Leading with Technology*, 29(2): 10–15.

Holt, J. (2004) *Instead of Education*. Boulder, CO: Sentient Publications, LLC.

The Holy Bible, English Standard Version. Copyright © 2001 by Crossway Bibles, a Division of Good News Publishers.

Howell, S. L., Saba, F., Lindsay, N. K. & Williams, P. B. (2004) 'Seven strategies for enabling faculty success in distance education'. *Internet and Higher Education*, 7(1): 33–49.

Hsu, J. (2008) 'The secrets of STORYTELLING: our love for telling tales reveals the workings of the mind'. *Scientific American Mind*, 19(4): 1–8.

Hull University (2010) The Practice of Digital HIStorytelling. 'Screenshot from E-Module: Image One', eBridge.hull. Available: https://ebridge.hull.ac.uk/portal/site/cmpst_00250/page/7e6f0117-3f08-435d-bb0d-62d04a1a6aa6.

Hull University (2010) The Practice of Digital HIStorytelling. 'Screenshot from E-Module: Image Two', eBridge.hull. Available: https://ebridge.hull.ac.uk/portal/site/cmpst_00250?panel=Main.

Hull University (2010) The Practice of Digital HIStorytelling. 'Screenshot from Screentext: Image Three', eBridge.hull. Available: https://ebridge.hull.ac.uk/access/content/group/cmpst_00250/FAIREST.pdf

Hull University (2010) The Practice of Digital HIStorytelling. 'Screenshot from Screentext: Image Four', Buzzle.com. Available: http://www.buzzle.com/articles/zeus-greek-god.html.

Huttunen, T., Ilmonen, K., Korkka, J. & Valovirta, E. (2008) *Seeking the Self – Ecountering the Other: Diasporic Narrative and the Ethics of Representation*. UK: Cambridge Scholar Publishing.

Iacoboni, M. (2009) *Mirroring People*. New York: Picador.

Iglesias, K (2005) *Writing for Emotional Impact*. Livermore, California: WingSpan Press.

Indiaonestop. 'The Film Industry in India: An IndiaOneStop Synopsis'. Indiaonesotp.com. Available: http://www.indiaonestop.com/film.htm.

Internet Movie Database, 'Alexander'. Imbd.com. Available: http://www.imdb.com/title/tt0346491/.

Internet Movie Database, 'Babel'. Imbd.com. Available: http://www.imdb.com/title/tt0449467/.

Internet Movie Database, 'Clash of the Titans'. Imbd.com. Available: http://www.imdb.com/title/tt0800320/.

Internet Movie Database, 'The Kite Runner'. Imbd.com. Available: http://www.imdb.com/title/tt0419887/.

Internet Movie Database, 'Slum Dog Millionaire'. Imbd.com. Available: http://www.imdb.com/title/tt1010048/.

Internet Movie Database, 'Troy'. Imbd.com. Available: http://www.imdb.com/title/tt0332452/.

Internet Movie Database, 'Jean-Luc'. Imbd.com. Available: http://www.imdb.com/name/nm0000419/bio.

Internet Movie Database, 'Pulp Fiction'. Imbd.com. Online. Available: http://www.imdb.com/title/tt0110912/?ref_=fn_al_tt_1.

Ito, M. (27 February 2010) 'New Media and Its Superpowers: Learning, Post Pokemon'. Itofisher.com. Available: http://www.itofisher.com/mito/publications/new_media_and_i_1.html.

Jenkins, H., Clinton, K., Purushotma, R., Robison, A. J. & Weigel. M. (2006) 'Confronting the Challenges of Participatory Culture: Media Education for the 21st Century'. 19 October. Digitallearning.macfound.org. Available: http://digitallearning.macfound.org/atf/cf/%7B7E45C7E0-A3E0-4B89-AC9C-E807E1B0AE4E%7D/JENKINS_WHITE_PAPER.PDF.

Jenkins, H. (1992) *Textual Poachers: Television Fans and Participatory Culture*. New York: Routledge.

Jenkins, H. (2001) 'Convergence. I Diverge'. Technology Review. Web.mit.edu. Available: http://web.mit.edu/cms/People/henry3/converge.pdf.

Jenkins, H. (2006a) *Convergence Culture*. New York and London: New York University Press.

Jenkins, H. (2006b) *Fans, Bloggers, and Gamers: Exploiting Participatory Culture*. New York: University Press, NY.

Jenkins, H. (2007) 'Transmedia Storytelling 101'. 22 March. Henryjenkins.org. Available: http://www.henryjenkins.org/2007/03/transmedia_storytelling_101.html.

Jenkins, H. (2011) 'Transmedia 202: Further Reflections'. 1 August. Henryjenkins. org. Available: http://henryjenkins.org/2011/08/defining_transmedia_further_re.html#sthash.YAwt0Edz.dpuf".

Jenkins, M. & Gravestock, P. (2009) in Jenkins, M. (7 November 2009) 'Digital Storytelling Synthesis'. Pbworks.com. Available: http://digitalstorytellingsynthesis.pbworks.com/Digital-storytelling-in-higher-education.

Jenkins, M. (2009) 'Storytelling and Teaching and Learning'. 17 November. Pbworks.com. Available: http://digitalstorytellingsynthesis.pbworks.com/Storytelling-and-teaching-and-learning.

Jenks, C. & Phillips, M. (1998) 'The Black-White Test Score Gap: Why it Persists and What Can Be Done'. Brookings.edu. Available: http://www.brookings.edu/articles/1998spring_education_jencks.aspx.

Johnson, R. T. & Johnson, D. W. (1986) 'Action research: cooperative learning in the science classroom'. *Science and Children*, 24 (2): 31–32.

Johnson, S. (2006) *Everything Bad Is Good For You*, New York: Penguin Group.

Jowett, B. (trans.) 'Laws, Plato'. mit.edu. Available: http://classics.mit.edu/Plato/laws.1.i.html

J. S. (2012) 'Stereotypes of Europe' Economist.com'. 30 May Available: http://www.economist.com/blogs/graphicdetail/2012/05/greeks-say-they-are-hardest-working-european-nation?fsrc=scn/gp/wl/bl/stereotypesofeurope.

Jung, C. G. (1964) *Man and His Symbols*. New York: Doubleday and Company.

Kadle, A. (2010) 'Story-based Learning'. 3 August. Upsidelearning.com. Available: http://www.upsidelearning.com/blog/index.php/2010/08/03/story-based-learning/.

Kalagani, M. (2011) 'Elearning Forum'. Digital Storytelling. UK: Hull University.

Kalogeras, S. (2011) 'The Goddess Within'. Screenplay. Transmedia.blogspot.com. Available: http://screenplay-transmedia.blogspot.com.

Kalogeras, S. (2013) 'Media-education convergence: applying transmedia storytelling edutainment in e-learning environments'. *International Journal of Information and Communication Technology Education*, 9(2): 1–11.

Kalogeras, S. (2013) 'Storytelling: an ancient human technology and a critical creative pedagogy for transformative learning'. *The International Journal of Information and Communication Technology*, 9(4): 113–122.

Kalogeras S., Voulakal@otenet.gr, 2011. Hi. [email] Message to A. Smith, (aaron.smith50@gmail.com), Sent 16 August 2011, 12:35. Received response: 16 August 2011.

Kalogeras S., Voulakal@otenet.gr, 2011. PhD Thesis – Transmedia. [email] Message to A. Smith, (aaron.smith50@gmail.com), Sent 10 August 2011, 3:18. Received response: 13 August 2011.

Kalogeras S., Voulakal@otenet.gr, 2011. PhD Thesis – Transmedia. [email] Message to H. Jenkins, hgjenkins3@gmail.com, Sent 8 March 2011, 10:38. Received response: 12 July 2011.

Kalogeras S., Voulakal@otenet.gr, 2011. PhD Thesis – Transmedia. [email] Message to J. Gomez, (Jeff@Starlightrunner.com), Sent 8 March 2011, 10:37. Received response: 13 March 2011.

Kalogeras S., Voulakal@otenet.gr, 2011. PhD Thesis – Transmedia. [email] Message to L. Fleming, (larfleming@yahoo.com), Sent 16 August 2011, 3:44. Received response: 16 August 2011.

Kalogeras S., Voulakal@otenet.gr, 2011. PhD Thesis – Transmedia. [email] Message to L. Fleming, (larfleming@yahoo.com), Sent 8 March 2011, 10:39. Received response: 14 March 2011.

Kalogeras S., Voulakal@otenet.gr, 2011. Research Student (Question). [email] Message to R. Mayer, (mayer@psych.ucsb.edu), 12 May 2011, 1:01. Received response: 13 May 2011.

Kalogeras, S. (2013) 'Storytelling: An Ancient Human Technology and a Critical Creative Pedagogy for Transformative Learning'. *International Journal of Information and Communication Technology*, 9(4): 113–122.

Karatzogianni, A. (2006) *The Politics of Cyberconflict*. London and New York: Routledge.

Karatzogianni, A. (2009) *Cyber Conflict and Global Politics*. London and New York: Routledge.

Karatzogianni, A. & Kuntsman A. (2012) *Digital Cultures and the Politics of Emotion*. Basingstoke: Palgrave Macmillan.

Katz, E., Blumler, J. G. & Gurevitz, M. (1974) 'Uses of Communication by the Individual', in Davidson, W. P. & Yu, F. T. C. (eds), *Mass Communication Research: Major Issues and Future Directions*. New York: Praeger, pp. 11–35.

Kay, R. H. & Knaack, L. (2008) 'A multi-component model for assessing learning objects: the learning object evaluation metric (LOEM)'. *Australasian Journal of Educational Technology*, 24(5): 574–591.

Kearney, M. D. & Schuck, S. R. (2004) 'Authentic learning through the use of digital video. research, reform, realise the potential?' in Au, W. & White, B. (eds), *ACEC2004*. Adelaide, Australia: Australian Council for Computers in Education, pp. 1–7.

Kearney, M. & Schuck, S. (2005) 'Students in the director's seat: teaching and learning with student-generated video', in Kommers, P. & Richards, G. (eds), *Proceedings of Ed-Media 2005 World Conference on Educational Multimedia, Hypermedia and Telecommunications*. Norfolk, VA: Association for the Advancement of Computers in Education.

Kegan, R. (1994) *In Over our Heads: The Mental Demands of Modern Life*. Cambridge, MA: Harvard University Press.

Keller, J. M. (1987) 'The systmeatic process of motivational design'. *Performance & Instruction*, 26(9–10): 1–8, November/December.

Keller, J. M. (1999) 'Motivation in Cyber learning environments'. *International Journal of Educational Technology*, 1(1): 7–30.

Kelly, J. W. (1985) 'Storytelling in High-tech Organizations: A Medium for Sharing Culture'. Paper presented at the Annual Meeting of the Western Speech Communication Association', Fresno, CA, February 16–19.

Kemmis, S. & McTaggart, R. (2003) 'Participatory action research', in Denzin, N. & Lincoln, Y. *Strategies of Qualitative Inquiry*, 2nd ed. Thousand Oaks: Sage: 336–396.

Kemp, S. (14 November 2012) 'Study: Global Online Ad Revenue to Hit $143 Billion by 2017'. Hollywoodreporter.com. Available: http://www.holly-woodreporter.com/news/study-global-online-ad-revenue-390377.

Kerr, C. (1982, October) 'Postscript 1982'. *Change*, 22–31.

Kerr, P. (2010) 'Babel's network narrative: packaging a globalized art cinema transnational cinemas'. *Transnational Cinemas*, 1(1): 37–51 Intellect Limited.

Kester, L., Lehnen, C., Van Gerven, P. W. M. & Kirschner, P. A. (2006) 'Just-in-time schematic supportive information presentation during cognitive skill acquisition'. *Computers in Human Behavior*, 22(1): 93–116.

Kintsch, W. (1980) 'Learning from text, levels of comprehension, or: why would anyone read a story anyway?' *Poetics*, 9: 87–98.

Klein, C. (2004) 'The Hollowing-Out of Hollywood'. 30 April. Yaleglobal.yale.ed. Available: http://yaleglobal.yale.edu/content/hollowing-out-hollywood.

Knill, O. (2005) 'First Lectures in College Teaching'. 13 September . Math.harvard. edu. Available: http://www.math.harvard.edu/~knill/pedagogy/first_lectures/index.html.

Knill, O. (March 2006–January 2010) 'Mathematics in the Movies'. Math.harvard. edu. Available: http://www.math.harvard.edu/~knill/mathmovies/.

Knowles, M. S. (1975) *Self-Directed Learning: A Guide for Learners and Teachers.* Englewood Cliffs: Prentice Hall/Cambridge.

Knowles, M. S. & Others (1984) *Andragogy in Action: Applying Modern Principles of Adult Education.* San Francisco: Jossey Bass.

Kolb, D. A. (1984) *Experiential Learning: Experience As the Source of Learning and Development.* New Jersey: Prentice-Hall.

Kopp, T. (1982) 'Designing the boredom out of instruction'. *NSPI Journal*, 23–27 and 29 May.

Koralek, D. 'The History of Storytelling'. Rif.org. Available: http://www.rif.org/educators/articles/storytelling.mspx.

Kostoulias, G., Hepper, L. & Argyropoulou, R. (2011) *Dialogic Pedagogy: The Road of Challenge in Higher Education.* 9th International Transformative Learning Conference, Athens 2011.

Kress, G., Jewitt, C., Ogborn, J. & Tsatsarelis, C. (2001) *Multimodal Teaching and Learning: The Rhetorics of the Science Classroom.* London and New York: Continuum

Kress, G. (2003) *Literacy in the New Media Age.* London and New York: Routledge.

Kress, G. & Van Leeuwen, T. (2001) *Multimodal Discourse. The Modes and Media of Contemporary Communication.* London, New York: Oxford University Press.

Kristeva, J. (1980) 'World, Dialogue and Novel', in Rudiez, L. S. (trans. Gora, T.) (eds), *Desire in Language: A Semiotic Approach to Literature and Art In.* New York: Columbia UP.

Kuntsman, A. (2004) 'Cyberethnography as home-work'. *Anthropology Matters Journal*, 6(2). Anghropologymatters.com. Available: http://www.anthropology-matters.com.

Kuyvenhoven, J. (2009) *In the Presence of Each Other: A Pedagogy of Storytelling.* Toronto, Buffalo, London: University of Toronto Press.

Landow, G. P. (2006) *Hypertext 3.0: Critical Theory and New Media in an Era of Globalization.* Maryland: John Hopkins University Press.

Lash, S. & Lury, C. (2007) *Global Culture Industry.* Cambridge, UK: Polity Press.

Laurillard Conversational Framework (14 May 2007) Edutechwiki.unige. Available: http://edutechwiki.unige.ch/en/Laurillard_conversational_framework.

Laurillard, D. M. (2002) *Rethinking University Teaching: A Conversational Framework for the Effective Use of Learning Technologies.* London: Routledge.

Laurillard, D. M. (1993) *Rethinking University Teaching: A Framework for the Effective Use of Educational Technology.* London: Routledge.

Lave, J. & Wenger, E. (1991) *Situated Learning: Legitimate Peripheral Participation.* Cambridge: Cambridge University Press.

Lea, H. C. (1902) 'The Eve of the Reformation', in Ward, A. W., Prothero, G. W. & Leathes S. (eds), *The Cambridge Modern History*, 1: 653–692. New York and London: The Macmillan Company.

Learning Theories Knowledge Base. Learning-theories.com. Available: http://www.learning-theories.com/.

Leavy, P. (2009) *Method Meets Art.* New York. The Guilford Press.

LeDoux, J. (1996) *The Emotional Brain.* New York: Simon and Schuster.

Leiblich, A., Tuval-Mashiach, Rivka & Zilber, Tamar (1998) *Narrative Research: Reading Analysis, and Interpretation,* Vol. 47. Thousand Oaks, CA: Sage Publications.

Leigh, F. (2007) Platonic dialogue, maieutic method and critical thinking. *Journal of Philosophy of Education*, 41(3): 309–323.

Leitch, T. (2003) 'Twelve fallacies in contemporary adaptation theory.' *Criticism*, 45(2): 149–71.

Lepionka, M. E. (1 September 2009) 'Textbook Authoring in the Digital Age-2'. Atlanticpathpublishing.com. Available: http://www.atlanticpathpublishing. com/blog/2009/09/textbook-authoring-in-digital-age-2.html.

Lessig, L. (2008) *Remix*. New York: The Penguin Press.

Levine, S. K. (2004) 'Art Based Research: A Philosophical Perspective'. Lesley.edu. Available: http://www.lesley.edu/journals/jppp/9/Levine.html.

Lévis-Strauss, C. (1995) *Myth and Meaning: Cracking the Code of Culture*. New York: Schocken.

Lévy, P. (2000) *Collective Intelligence, Mankind's Emerging World in Cyberspace*. New York: Perseus.

Lewis, D., Rodgers D. & Woolock, M. (2008) 'The Fiction of Development: Knowledge, Authority and Representation'. Bwpi.manchester.ac.uk. Available: http://www.bwpi.manchester.ac.uk/resources/Working-Papers/bwpi-wp-2008. pdf.

Lin, A. & Gregor, S. (2006) 'Designing websites for learning and enjoyment: a study of museum experiences'. *International Review of Research in Open and Distance Learning*, 7(3): 1–21.

Lindstrom, J. (2007) 'Determining appropriate accommodations for postsecondary students with reading and writing expression disorders.' *Learning Disabilities Research & Practice*, 22(4): 229–236.

Lodge, D. (1990) 'Narration with words', in Barlow, H., Blakemore, C. & Weston-Smith, M. (eds), *Images and Understandings*. Cambridge, UK: Cambridge University Press.

Long, G. (2007) 'Transmedia Storytelling: Business, Aesthetics and Production at the Jim Henson Company'. Ph.D Thesis, Massachusetts Institute of Technology.

Lotz, A. D. (2007) *The Television will be Revolutionized*. New York and London: New York University Press.

Lowe, K. (2002) *What's the Story: Making Meaning in Primary Classrooms*. ERIC Document No. ED468691.

Margolis, M. (2009) *Believe Me*. New York: Get Storied Press.

Market Research (2008) 'Digital Movie Marketing: A Convergence of Content, Devices and Services'. 1 September. Market Research.com. Available: http://www.marketresearch.com/product/display.asp?productid=1901241.

Markham, S. (2004) 'Learning Styles Measurement: A Cause for Concern'. Cerg.csse. monash.edu. Available: http://cerg.csse.monash.edu.au/techreps/learning_styles_review.pdf.

Massachusetts Institute of Technology, 'OpenCourseWare'. Ocw.mit.edu. Available: http://ocw.mit.edu/index.htm.

Massy, W. & Zemsky, R. (June 1995) 'Using Information Technology to Enhance Academic Productivity'. Educause.edu. Available: http://www.educause.edu/nlii/keydocs/massy.html.

Mavrogordatos, G. T. (24 May 2012) 'Styx and Stones'. Timeshighereducation.co. Available: http://www.timeshighereducation.co.uk/story.asp?sectioncode=26&storycode=420077.

Mayer, R. (1999) 'Designing instruction for constructivist learning in Instructional design theories and models', Vol. 2, Edited by C. Reigeluth. Mahwah, NJ: Erlbaum, pp. 141–159.

Mayer, R. E. (2001/2009) *Multimedia Learning*. New York: Cambridge University Press.

Mayer, R. E. & Moreno, R. (2003) 'Nine Ways to Reduce Cognitive Load in Multimedia Learning', in Bruning, R., Horn, C. A. & PytlikZillig, L. M. (eds), Web-Based Learning: What Do We Know? Where Do We Go? Information Age Publishing, Greenwich, CT, pp. 23–44.

Mayer, R. E. (2005) 'Introduction to Multimedia Learning', in Mayer, R. E. (ed.), *The Cambridge Handbook of Multimedia Learning*. New York: Cambridge University Press.

McClelland, G. & Markel, J. (2009) 'The New Media Value Chain – Emotional Connectivity'. Brandchannel.com. Available: http://www.brandchannel.com/images/papers/104_New_Media_Value_Chain.pdf.

McDrury, J. & Alterio, M. (2003) *Learning through Storytelling in Higher Education*. London and Sterling VA: Kogan Page.

McFarlane B. (1996) *Novel to Film: An Introduction to the Theory of Adaptation*. Oxford: Clarendon Press.

McKee, R. (1997) *Story: Substance, Structure, Style and the Principles of Screenwriting*. New York: HarperCollins.

McLoughlin, C. (2002) 'Learner support in distance and networked learning environments: ten dimensions for successful design'. *Distance Education*, 23(2). C31.uni-oldenburg.de. Available: http://www.c3l.uni oldenburg.de/cde/media/readings/mcloughlin.pdf.

McLuhan, M. 'MarshalMcLuhan'. En.wikipedia.org. Available: http://en.wikipedia.org/wiki/Marshall_McLuhan.

McLuhan, M. 'Quote'. Thinkexist.com. Available: http://thinkexist.com/quotation/anyone_who_tries_to_make_a_distinction_between/152852.html.

McLuhan, M. (1962) *The Gutenberg Galaxy: The Making of Typographic Man*. Canada: University of Toronto Press.

McLuhan, M. (1964) *Understanding Media: The Extensions of Man*. New York: McGraw Hill.

McHale, B. (1987) *Postmodernist Fiction*. New York and London: Methuen.

McKenzie, J. (2000) 'Beyond edutainment and technotainment' From Now On 10, 1.

McNiff, S. (2009) *Art-Based Research*. London. Jessica Kingsley Publishers.

McQuail, D. (2005) *McQuail's Mass Communication Theory*, 5th ed. London: Sage Publications.

Medina, J. (2008) *Brain Rules*. Seatle, WA: Pear Press.

Med 2010 (20 March 2007) 'Diagnosis Wenckebach'. Youtube.com. Available: http://www.youtube.com/watch?v=GVxJJ2DBPiQ.

Mendelsohn, H. (1966) *Mass Entertainment*. New Haven: College and University Press.

Mermiri, T. (8 December 2009) 'Beyond Experience: Culture, Consumer & Brand: The Transformation Economy'. Artsandbusiness.org. Available: http://www.artsandbusiness.org.uk/Media%20library/Files/Research/aandb_be_thetransformationeconomy.pdf.

Meyer, K. (6 January 2010) 'Transmedia Storytelling: Pioneers in the New Age of Narrative, Pt. III – Jeff Gomez of Starlight Runner Entertainment'.

Mezirow, J. (2003) 'Transformative learning as discourse'. *Journal of Transformative Education*, 1(1): 58–63.

Mierzejewska, Bozena I. (2011) *Managing Media Work*, Mark Deuze (ed.), London: Sage Publications.

Miller, C. (2002) *Can Sesame Street Bridge the Pacific Ocean?* Swarthmore College.

Miller, C. H. (2008) *Digital Storytelling: A Creator's Guide to Interactive Entertainment*, 2nd edn. Burlington, MA: Focal Press.

Montuori, A. (2011) 'Creativity in Transformative Education: An Exploration in Doctoral Education'. 9th International Transformative Learning Conference, Athens 2011.

More, T. (Sir) (1964) 'Letter to Peter Giles', in Surtz, E. and Hexter, J. H. (eds), *The Complete Works of St Thomas More*, Vol. 4. New Haven: Yale University Press.

More, T. ([1516] 2001) Utopia. New Haven and London: Yale University Press.

Morris, K. (2 November 2007) 'Learning Style of African American Children'. Faculty.tnstate.edu. Available: http://faculty.tnstate.edu/bchristian1/morrispres.ppt#256,1,Learning Styles of African American Children.

Mosco, V. & Schiller, D. (2001) *Continental Order? Integrating North America for Cybercapitalism*. Lanham, MD: Rowman and Littlefield.

Mosco, V. (2008) 'Current trends in the political economy of communication'. *Global Media Journal – Canadian Ed.*, 1(1): 45–63.

Mott, B. W., Callaway, C.B., Zettlemoyer, L. S., Lee, S. Y. & Lester, J. C. (1999) 'Towards Narrative-Centered Learning Environments', in *Working Notes of the 1999 AAAI Fall Symposium on Narrative Intelligence*. Cape Cod, Massachusetts, pp. 78–82.

Moustakas, C. (1990) *Heuristic Research Design, Methodology, and Applications*. California: Sage Publications.

Mumby, D. K. (1987) 'The political function of narrative in organizations'. *Communication Monographs*, 54: 113–127.

Murdock, G., Wasko, J. (2007) *Media in the age of marketization*. Creskill, NJ: Hampton Press.

National Council of Teachers of English (14 August 2008) 'Guidline on Teaching Storytelling'. Ncte.org. Available: http://www.ncte.org/positions/statements/teachingstorytelling.

National Geographic, 'Beyond the Movie: Troy'. Amazon.com. Available: http://www.amazon.com/National-Geographic-Beyond-Movie-Troy/dp/B0001J2K3K.

Nauert, R. (27 January 2010) 'Are Emotions Universal?' Psychcentral.com. Available: http://psychcentral.com/news/2010/01/27/are-emotions-universal/10999.html.

NDT, 'Teaching with the Constructivist Learning Theory' NDT-ed.org. Available: http://www.ndt ed.org/TeachingResources/ClassroomTips/Constructivist%20_Learning.htm.

Nelson, A. (1998b) *The Learning Wheel: Holistic and Multicultural Lesson Planning*. Tucson, Arizona: Zephyr Press and the WHEEL Council.

Nelson, A. (2003) 'Circle relationships of intelligence'. *International Journal of Learning*, 10: 693–712.

Nelson, A. (2009) 'Storytelling and Transformative Learning', in Fisher-Yoshida, B., Geller, K. D. & Schapiro S. (eds), *Learning Space, Cultural Diversity and the*

Performing Art: New Dimensions in Transformative Education. New York: Peter Lang.

Nichol, M. 'Narrative, Plot, and Story', Dailywritingtips.com. Available: http://www.dailywritingtips.com/narrative-point-of-view/.

Niekamp, R. (2008) *Audience Activity among Users of the World Wide Web.* Germany: VDM Verlag Dr. Muller Aktiengesellschaft and Co.

New World Encyclopedia 'Edutainment'. Newworldencyclopedia.org. Available: http://www.newworldencyclopedia.org/entry/Edutainment.

Nisbett, R. (2009) *Intelligence and How to Get It: Why Schools and Cultures Count.* New York: W. W. Norton & Company.

Nock, A. J. (1943) *Memoirs of a Superfluou.* New York: Harper & Brothers.

Norman, D. A. (1994) *Things that Make Us Smart: Defending Human Attributes in the Age of the Machine.* New York: Basic Books.

Norrington, A. (2011) 'Meet Alison Norrington, Conference Chair for StoryWorld Conference + EXP'. Digitalbookworld.com. Available: http://www.digitalbookworld.com/conference/alison-norrington-bio/.

Oblinger, D. & Oblinger, J. 'Is It Age or IT: First Steps Toward Understanding the Net Generation'. Educause.edu. Available: http://www.educause.edu/Resources/EducatingtheNetGeneration/IsItAgeorITFirstStepsTowardUnd/6058.

Ohio History Central Organization (1 July 2005) 'Radio'. ohiohistorycentral.org. Available: http://www.ohiohistorycentral.org/entry.php?rec=1536.

Oliver, S. (14 July 2000) 'In Filming History: Question, Disbelieve, Defy'. *The Chronicle of Higher Education*, 14 July: B9.

Ong, C.-S., Lai, J.-Y., & Wang, Y.-S. (2004). 'Factors affecting engineers' acceptance of asynchronous e-learning systems in high-tech companies', *Information & Management*, 41(6): 795–804.

Oppermann, M. & Coventry, M. (n.d) 'Digital Storytelling Multimedia Archive'. Digital commons.georgetown.edu. Available: https://digitalcommons.georgetown.edu/projects/digitalstories/. Accessed March 2010.

Orech, J. (2007) 'Tips for Digital Storytelling'. 1 November. Techlearning.com. Available: http://www.techlearning.com/article/8030.

Oxford Analytica (3 April 2006) 'Unbundled Media Content Poses a Challenge'. https://www.oxan.com/oxweb/logon.aspx?ReturnURL=%2Fdisplay%2Easpx%3FItemID%3DDB125174

Pagano, J. (1991) 'Moral Fictions: The Dilemma of Theory and Practice', in Witherell, C. & Noddings, N. (eds), *Stories Lives Tell: Narrative and Dialogue in Education.* New York: Teachers College Press.

Page, R. (2010) *New Perspectives on Narratives and Multimodality.* New York: Routledge.

Paulson, K. (2002) 'Reconfiguring faculty roles for virtual settings'. *The Journal of Higher Education*, 73(1): 123–140.

Pew Research Center (2010) 'Millennials'. Pewresearchorg. 24 February. Available: http://pewresearch.org/millennials/.

Gilmore, J. & Pine, J. (2009) *Using Art to Render Authenticity in Business.* Arts & Business.

Pool, I. D. (1983) *Technologies of Freedom: On Free Speech in an Electronic Age.* Boston MA: Harvard University Press.

Polkinghorne, D. (1988) *Narrative Knowing and the Human Sciences.* Albany: State University of New York Press.

Pollock, A. (20 June 2006) 'The Transformation Economy'. Typepad.com. Available: http://agentsofchange.typepad.com/weblog/2006/06/the_transformat.html.

Potter, J. (1998) *Media Literacy*. Thousand Oaks: Sage Publications.

Prensky, M. (2001) *Digital Game-Based Learning*. St. Paul: Paragon House.

Prensky, M. (2001) 'Digital Natives, Digital Immigrants'. Marckprensky.com. Available: http://www.marcprensky.com/writing/.

Prensky, M. (2001) 'Digital Natives, Digital Immigrants, Part II: Do They Really Think Differently?' Marckprensky.com. Available: http://www.marcprensky.com/writing/.

Pribram, K. H. (1981) *Language of the Brain: Experimental Paradoxes and Principles of Neuropsychology*. New York: Brandon House.

Prince, M. (2004) 'Does active learning work? a review'. *Journal of Engineering Education*, 93(3): 223–231.

Producers Guild of America (2010) 'PGA Board of Directors Approves Addition of Transmedia Producer to Guild's Producers Code of Credits'. 6 April. Producersguild.org. Available: http://www.producersguild.org/news/news.asp?id=39637&hhSearchTerms=TRANSMEDA

Public Broadcasting Organization. 'The World According to Sesame Street'. Pbs.org. Available: http://www.pbs.org/independentlens/worldaccordingtosesamestreet/film.html.

Quinn, C. N. (3 April 2006) 'Learning Solutions Online'. Quinnovation.com. Available: http://quinnovation.com:8000/eMotional-eLearning.pdf.

Raines, D. A. (2010) 'Digital Storytelling Brings a Human Connection to Online Education'. 9 August. Facultyfocus.com. Available: http://www.facultyfocus.com/articles/instructional-design/digital-storytelling-brings-a-human-connection-to-online-education/.

Ramanathan, S. (2008) 'International Forum on the Creative Economy. Bollywood behind the Scenes'. 24 January. Authorstream.com. Available: http://www.authorstream.com/Presentation/Matild-45433-Bollywood-Behind-scenes-11-International-Forum-Creative-Economy-whats-name-contd-Indian-Film-Industry-IFI-behin-Education-ppt-powerpoint/.

Reddy, R. (2010) 'Q & A with Jeff Gomez'. 26 January. Transmediatracker.com. http://www.transmediatracker.com/blog/ttqawithjeffgomez.

Reid, M., Burn, A. & Parker, D. (2002) *Evaluation Report of the Becta Digital Video Pilot Project*. Coventry, UK: Becta.

Rideout, V. J., Foehr, U. G. & Roberts D. F. (2010 January) 'Generation M2: Media in the Lives of 8- to 18-year-olds'. *A Kaiser Family Foundation Study*. Kff.org. Available: http://www.kff.org/entmedia/upload/8010.pdf.

Rice University, Connextions. Cnx.org. Available: http://cnx.org/.

Ricoeur, P. (1991) 'Life in Quest of Narrative', in Wood, D. (ed.), *On Paul Ricoeur: Narrative and Interpretation*. London: Routledge.

Roberson, T. J. & Klotz, J. (2002) 'How can instructors and administrators fill the missing link in online instruction'? *Online Journal of Distance Learning Administration*. Westga.edu. Available: http://www.westga.edu/~distance/ojdla/winter54/roberson54.htm.

Robin, B. (2010) University of Houston. 'The Educational Uses of Digital Storytelling'. Faculty.coe.uh.edu. Available: http://faculty.coe.uh.edu/brobin/homepage/Educational-Uses-DS.pdf.

Rockler-Gladen, N. (29 April 2008) 'Minority Media Representations'. Naomi-rockler-gladne.suite. Available: http://naomi-rockler-gladen.suite101.com/minority-media-representations-a52303.

Rosenbaum, S. (2008) 'Peer-to-Peer and User Generated Content: Flash in the Pan or the Arrival of a New Storytelling Paradigm'? in Noam, E. M. & Pupillo, L. M. (eds), *Peer-to-Peer Video. The Economics, Policy, and Culture of Today's New Mass Medium.* New York: Springer Science + Business Media, LLC.

Rubel, S. (2009) 'What to Watch in 2010'. *Forbes*, 30 November. Forbes.com. Available: http://www.forbes.com/2009/11/30/social-networking-tv-cmo-network-steve-rubel.html.

Ruggles, R. (1 August 1999) 'The Role of Stories in Knowledge Management', Storytelling Foundation.com. Available: http://www.storytellingfoundation.com/articles/business/stories-km.htm.

Ryan, R. C. (2000) 'Student assessment comparison of lecture and online construction equipment and methods classes'. *THE Journal*, 27(5). Thejournal.com. Available: http://www.thejournal.com/magazine/vault/A2596.cfm.

Ryan, S. (2002) 'Digital video: using technology to improve learner motivation'. *Modern English Teacher*, 11(2): 72–75.

Sabido, M. (2004) 'The Origins of Entertainment-Education', in Singhal, A., Cody, M. J., Rogers, E. M. & Sabido, M. (eds), *Entertainment-Education and Social Change.* New Jersey: Lawrence Erlbaum Associates, Inc.

Sachs, J. (trans.) (2001) *Aristotle's On the Soul and On Memory and Recollection.* New Mexico: Green Lion Press:

Saettler, P. (1968) *A History of Instructional Technology.* New York: McGraw-Hill.

Salomon, G. (1983) 'The differential investment of mental effort in learning from different sources'. *Educational Psychologist*, 18(1): 42–50.

Salomon, G. & Almog, T. (1998) 'Educational psychology and technology: a matter of reciprocal relations', *Teachers College Record*, 100(1): 222–241.

Sameshima, P. (2008). 'Seeing Red'. In *Authentic Dissertation, Alternative Ways of Knowing, Research, and Representation.* Edited by D. T. Jacobs New York: Routledge.

Salmon, G. (2000) *eModerating: The Key to Teaching and Learning Online.* London and New York: RoutlegeFalmer.

Sanders, J. (2009) 'Reflect 2.0: Using Digital Storytelling to Develop Reflective Learning by the Use of the Next Generation Technologies and Practices'. JISC. ac.uk. Available: http://www.jisc.ac.uk/publications/documents/reflectfinalreport.aspx.

Sarbin, T. R. (1986) 'The Narrative As a Root Metaphor in Psychology', in Sarbin, T. R. (ed.), *Narrative Psychology: The Storied Nature of Human Conduct.* New York: Aeger.

Sawyer, R. K. (2006) *The Cambridge Handbook of the Learning Sciences.* New York: Cambridge University Press.

Sensagent 'Edutainment'. Dictionary.sensagent.com. Available: http://dictionary.sensagent.com/edutainment/en-en/.

Scagnoli, N. I. (2001) 'Student orientations for online programs'. *Journal of Research on Technology in Education*, 34(1): 19–27.

Schaller, D. & Allison-Bunnell, S. (2003) 'Practicing What We Teach: How Learning Theory Can Guide Development of Online Educational Activities'. Paper presented at Museums and the Web 2003, Charlotte, NC, March. Archimuse.

com. Available: http://www.archimuse.com/mw2003/papers/schaller/schaller. html.

Schank, R. C. & Abelson, R. (1977) *Scripts, Plans, Goals, and Understanding.* Hillsdale, New Jersey: Earlbaum Association.

Schank, R. C. (1975) *Conceptual Information Processing.* New York: Elsevier.

Schank, R. C. & Abelson, R. (1977) *Scripts, Plans, Goals and Understanding.* Hillsdale, NJ: Lawrence Erlbaum Associates.

Schank, R. C. (1991) *Tell Me a Story: A New Look at Real and Artificial Intelligence.* New York: Simon & Schuster.

Schank, R. (2001) 'Educational Technology: The Promise and The Myth'. Available: http://www.socraticarts.com/docs/Educational_Technology_-_The_Promise_and_The_Myth.pdf.

Schank, R. (2007) 'Story-Centred Curriculum (SCC)'. Socrticarts.com. Available: http://www.socraticarts.com/about/scc.htm.

Schank, R. (2011) *Teaching Minds: How Cognitive Science Can Save Our Schools.* New York: Teachers College, Columbia University.

Scharmer, C. O. (20 October 2000) 'Presencing: Learning from the Future As It Emerges'. Dialogonleadership.org. Available: http://www.dialogonleadership. org/Presencing00.pdf.

Schatz, T. (1993) 'The New Hollywood', in Collins, J., Radner, H. & Preacher Collins, A. (eds), *Film Theory Goes to the Movies.* New York & London: Routledge/ BFI.

Schneider, M. (3 November 2008) 'Colleges as Failure Factories'. Insidehighered. com. Available: http://www.insidehighered.com/news/2008/11/03/failure.

Schoenmaker, J. & Stanchev, I. (2000) *Visualisation, Principles and Tools for Instructional Visualisation.* University of Twente: Andersen Consulting-ECC.

Scholastic, 'Pioneers in Our Field: John Dewey – Father of Pragmatism', *The Second Installment in Early Childhood Today's Series on the Roots of Early Childhood Education.* Scholastic.com. Available: http://www2.scholastic.com/browse/ article.jsp?id=3424.

Schön, D. A. (1983) *The Reflective Practitioner: How Professionals Think in Action.* New York: Basic Books.

Schön, D. A. (1991) *The Reflective Turn: Case Studies in and on Educational Practice.* New York: Teachers College Press.

Schön, D. A. (1992) 'Designing as reflective conversation with the materials of a design situation'. *Knowledge-Based Systems,* 5(1): 3–14.

School of Mathematics and Computer Sciences 'Laurillard's Conversational Model' Macs.hs.ac. Available: http://www.macs.hw.ac.uk/~rjr/dolweb/docs/ laurillardmoddoc.htm.

Scolari, C. (2008a) 'Online brands: branding, possible worlds and interactive grammars'. *Semiotica,* 169(1/4): 143–162, in Scolari, C. (2009) 'Transmedia storytelling: implicit consumers, narrative worlds, and branding in contemporary media production'. *International Journal of Communication,* 3: 586–606.

Scolari, C. (2008c) 'The Grammar of Hypertelevision: Character Multiplication and Narrative Complexity in Contemporary Television'. Paper presented at the 2008 ICA International Conference, Montreal, in Scolari, C. (2009) 'Transmedia storytelling: implicit consumers, narrative worlds, and branding in contemporary media production'. *International Journal of Communication,* 3: 586–606.

Scolari, C. (2009) 'Transmedia storytelling: implicit consumers, narrative worlds, and branding in contemporary media production'. *International Journal of Communication*, 3: 586–606.

Scott, S. (26 January 2010) 'UCL Study: Emotions are a Universal Lanuage'. Ucl. ac.uk. Available: http://www.ucl.ac.uk/news/news-articles/1001/10012601.

Seel, N. M. (2012) *Encyclopedia of the Science of Learning*. New York: Springer

Sharda, L. (22 April 2010) 'Using Digital Storytelling for Creative and Innovative e-Learning'. ELearning.Org. Available: http://elearnmag.acm.org/featured. cfm?aid=1773975.

Shaw, G. B. 'George Bernard Shaw Quote'. Thinkexist.com. Available: http:// thinkexist.com/search/searchquotation.asp?search=Words+are+only+postage+ stamps+delivering+the+object+for+you+to+unwrap.

Shea, P., Fredericksen, E., Pickett, A., Pelz, W. & Swan, K. (2001) 'Measures of Learning Effectiveness in the SUNY Learning Network', in Bourne, J. & Moore, J. C. (eds), *Online Education, Volume 2, Learning Effectiveness, Faculty Satisfaction, and Cost Effectiveness*. SLOAN-C Series 2001.

Shor, I. (1992) *Empowering Education*. University of Chicago Press: Chicago, IL.

Singhal, A., & Brown W. J. (1996) 'The entertainment education communication strategy: past struggles, present status, future agenda'. *Jurnal Komunicasi*, 12: 19–36. Ukm.my. Available: http://www.ukm.my/jkom/journal/pdf_files/1996/ V12_2.pdf.

Singhal, A., Cody, M. J., Rogers, E. M. & Sabido, M. (2004a) *Entertainment-Education and Social Change*. New Jersey: Lawrence Erlbaum Associates.

Singhal, A. & Rogers, E. M. (1999) *Entertainment-education: A Communication Strategy for Social Change*. Mahway, NJ: Lawrence Erlbaum.

Singhal, A., Sharma, D., Papa M. J. & Witte, K. (2004b) 'Air Cover and Ground Mobilization: Integrating Entertainment-Education Broadcasts with Community Listening and Service Delivery', in Singhal, A., Cody, M. J. & Rogers, E. M. (eds), *Entertainment-Education and Social Change*. New Jersey: Lawrence Erlbaum Associates, Inc.

Skinner, M. (2004) 'College students with learning disabilities speak out: what it takes to be successful in postsecondary education'. *Journal of Postsecondary Education and Disability*, 17(2): 91–104.

Smith, A. (2009) Transmedia Storytelling in Television 2.0. Bachelor of Arts thesis, Middlebury College.

Smith, G. M. (2003) *Film Structure and the Emotion System*. Cambridge University Press: Cambridge, UK.

Smoodin, E. (1993) *Animating Culture: Hollywood Cartoons from the Sound Era*. New Jersey: Rutgers University Press.

Socraticarts.com. Available: http://www.socraticarts.com/docs/Educational_ Technology_-_The_Promise_and_The_Myth.pdf.

Sosa, S. (1998) Hera, 'The First Greek Goddess'. Arthistory.sbc.edu. Arthistory.sbc. edu. Available: http://www.arthistory.sbc.edu/imageswomen/papers/sosahera/ hera.html.

Soul City Institute. 'Soul City Institute for Health and Development Communication'. Soulcity.org. Available: http://www.soulcity.org.za/.

Stam, R. (2000) 'Beyond Fidelity: The Diologics of Adaptation', in Naremore, J. (ed.), *Film Adaptation*. London: Athlone, pp. 54–76.

Standage, T. (1998) *The Victorian Internet*. New York: Walker and Company.

Sterne, P. & Herring, N. (30 December 2005) 'LinuxWorld: The Conversion Model'. De.sys-con.com. Available: http://de.sys-con.com/read/158863.htm.

Stein, N. L. & Trabasso, T. (1982) 'What's in a Story: An Approach to Comprehension and Instruction', in Glaser, R. (ed.), *Advances in Instructional Psychology*, 2: 213–267. Hillsdale, NJ: Erlbaum.

Stone, O. (14 July 2000) 'In Filming History: Question, Disbelieve, Defy'. Chronicle.com. Available: http://chronicle.com/article/In-Filming-History-Question/10740/.

Sturdevant, C. G. (1998) *The Laugh & Cry Movie Guide: Using Movies to Help Yourself through Life's Changes*. Larkspur, CA: Lightspheres.

Sweller, J. (1994) 'Cognitive load theory, learning difficulty, and instructional design'. *Learning and Instruction*, 4(4): 295–312.

Sweller, J. (1999) *Instructional Design in Technical Areas*. Camberwell, Victoria, Australia: Australian Council for Educational Research.

Tan, E. S. (1996) *Emotion and the Structure of Narrative Film: Film as an Emotion Machine*. Hillsdale, NJ: Erlbaum.

Transformative Learning Centre at the University of Toronto OISE – 'Ontario Institute Studies for Studies in Education'. Tlc.oise.utoronto.ca. Available: http://tlc.oise.utoronto.ca/index.htm.

The Cosmonaut (19 June 2009) Cosmonaut.org. Available: http://www.thecosmonaut.org/.

The Cosmonaut Organization. 'A film project by Riot Cinema Collective'. thecosmonaut.org. Available: http://www.thecosmonaut.org/.

Thomas, S., Joseph, C., Laccetti, J., Mason, B., Mills, S., Perril, S. & Pullinger, K. (3 December 2007) 'Transliteracy: Crossing Divides'. Uic.edu. Available: http://www.uic.edu/htbin/cgiwrap/bin/ojs/index.php/fm/article/view/2060/1908.

Thompson, V. (2009) 'The Power of Transmedia Storytelling'. 21 September. Smartplanet.com. Available: http://www.smartplanet.com/people/blog/puregenius/the-power-of-transmedia-storytelling/695/.

Todorov, T. (1990) *Genres in Discourse* (trans. Porter, C.) Cambridge: Cambridge University Press.

Trento, F. & Smith, A. (2011) 'The experience of story worlds across media: a conversation with Aaron Smith.' *Revista GEMInIS*, 2(2): 276–284.

Triggerstreet Labs. 'Labs'.triggerstret.com. 'Feedback. Exposure. Opportunity'. Available: http://labs.triggerstreet.com/.

Tsang, E. Y. M. 'Learner-Content Interactivity: Instructional Design Strategies for the Development of E-Learning Materials'. Ebooks.worldscient.com. Available: http://ebooks.worldscinet.com/ISBN/9789812799456/9789812799456_0016.html.

UniJapan (2009) 'The Guide to Japanese Film Industry & Co-Production'. UniJapan.org. Available: http://www.unijapan.org/project/information/co-production_guide.pdf.

University of Cincinnati. 'Troy'. Cerhas.uc.edu. Available: http://www.cerhas.uc.edu/troy/index.html.

University of the People. 'About Us'. Uopeople.org. Available: http://www.uopeople.org/groups/tuition-free-education.

Van Gerven, P. W. M., Paas, F. & Tabbers, H. K. (2006) 'Cognitive aging and computer-based instructional design: where do we go from here?' *Educational Psychology Review*, 18(2): 141–157.

Van Riper, A. B. (2011) *Learning from Mickey, Donald and Walt: Essays on Disney's Edutainment Films*. North Carolina, and London: McFarland & Company, Inc.

Vargas Llosa, M. (1996) 'The Truth of Lies', in *Making Waves: Essays* (trans. King, J.) London: Faber and Faber.

Vaughan, P. W., Regis, A. & St. Catherine, E. (4 December 2000) 'Effects of and Entertainment – Education Radio Soap Opera on Family Planning and HIV Prevention in St. Lucia'. Guttmacher.org. Available: http://www.guttmacher.org/pubs/journals/2614800.pdf.

Voeltz, R. A. (2010) 'Teaching American history through film: Hollywood blockbuster, PBS, history channel, or the postmodern?' *Emporia State Research Studies*, 46(1): 26–32. Emporia.edu. Available: http://www.emporia.edu/esrs/vol46/voeltz.pdf.

Vogler, C. (2006) The Archetype. 'The Hero's Journey Outline'. Thewritersjuorney.com. Available: http://www.thewritersjourney.com/.

Vogler, C. (2006) 'The Hero's Journey Outline'. Thewritersjuorney.com. Available: http://www.thewritersjourney.com/.

Voice of America (2009) 'Indian Entertainment Conglomerate to Finance Hollywood Films Online'. 17 July. VOAnews.com. Available: http://www.voanews.com/english/news/a-13-2009-07-17-voa16-68652542.html.

Vygotsky, L. S. (1978) *Mind in Society: The Development of Higher Psychological Processes*. Cambridge, Massachusetts, USA: Harvard University Press.

Wallace, C. (2000) 'Storytelling: Reclaiming an age-old wisdom for the composition classroom'. *Teaching English in the Two-Year College*, 27(4): 434–439.

Wallerstein, I. (2004) *The Uncertainties of Knowledge*. Philadelphia, PA: Temple University Press.

Wang, G. & Yeh, E. Y. (2005) 'Globalization and hybridization in cultural products: the cases of Mulan and Crouching Tiger, Hidden Dragon'. *International Journal of Cultural Studies*, 8(2): 175–193.

Wang, M. J. & Kang, J. (2006) 'Designing Online Courses that Effectively Engage Learners from Diverse Cultural Backgrounds'. Web.ebscohost.com. Available: http://web.ebscohost.com/ehost/pdfviewer/pdfviewer?vid=18&hid=101&sid=422abe44-4451-4cd8-a2ce-2dd630248985%40sessionmgr111.

Wankat, P. C. (2002) *The Effective, Efficient Professor: Teaching, Scholarship and Service*. Boston: Allyn and Bacon.

Wark, P. (11 April 2008) 'From Kabul to California: the incredible journey of Khaled Hosseini'. Thetimes.co.uk. Available: http://www.thetimes.co.uk/tto/news/.

Webster's Online Dictionay. 'Edutainment'. Websters-online-dictionary.org. Available: http://www.websters-online-dictionary.org/definitions/edutainment? cx=partner-pub-0939450753529744%3Av0qd01-tdlq&cof=FORID%3A9&ie=UTF-8&q=edutainment&sa=Search#906.

Wells, G. (1986) *The Meaning Makers: Children Learning Language and Using Language to Learn*. Portsmouth, NH: Heinemann.

Wenger, E. (1998) *Communities of Practice, Learning, Meaning, and Identity*. Cambridge: Cambridge University Press.

Wenger, E. (2006) 'Communities of Practice: A Brief Introduction'. Ewenger.com. Available: http://www.ewenger.com/theory/index.htm.

White, H. (1973) *Metahistory: The Historical Imagination in Nineteenth Century Europe*. Baltimore and London: John Hopkins University Press.

Williams, R. (1980) *Problems in Materialism and Culture*. London: Verso.

Woltz, B. (2005) *E-Motion Picture Magic: A Movie Lover's Guide to Healing and Transformation*. Colorado: Glenbridge Publishing, Ltd.

Wood, D., Bruner, J. S. & Ross, G. (1976) 'The role of tutoring in problem solving'. *Journal of Child Psychology & Psychiatry & Allied Disciplines*, 17(2): 89–100.

Wu, A. S., Farrell, R. & Singley, M. K. (2002) 'Scaffolding Group learning in a Collaborative Networked Environment'. *The International Conference on Computer-Supported Collaborative Learning*, Boulder, Colorado, USA.

Wu, H. & Chan, J. M. (2007) 'Globalizing Chinese martial arts cinema: the global-local alliance and the production of Crouching Tiger, Hidden Dragon'. *Media Culture & Society*, 29(2): 195–217.

Wyatt, J. (1994) *High Concept*. Austin: University of Texas Press.

Zettl, H. (1998) 'Contextual media aesthetics as the basis for media literacy'. *Journal of Communication*, winter, 81–95.

Zull, J. E. (2002) *The Art of Changing the Brain Enriching the Practice of Teaching by Exploring the Biology*. US: Stylus Publishing.

Zull, J. E. (2006) 'Key aspects of how the brain learns'. *New Directions for Adult and Continuing Education: The Neuroscience of Adult Learning*, 110: 3–9.

Index

Printed and bound in Great Britain by
CPI Group (UK) Ltd, Croydon, CR0 4YY